W9-BPM-787

Whitman in His Own Time

AN EXPANDED EDITION

WHITMAN IN HIS OWN TIME

A Biographical Chronicle of His Life,

Drawn from Recollections, Memoirs,

and Interviews by Friends and Associates

Edited by
Joel Myerson

University of Iowa Press   Iowa City

University of Iowa Press, Iowa City 52242
Copyright © 1991 by Omnigraphics, Inc.
All rights reserved
Printed in the United States of America
First University of Iowa Press edition, 2000

http://www.uiowa.edu/~uipress

The publication of this book was generously supported by
the University of Iowa Foundation.

Printed on acid-free paper

Library of Congress Cataloging-in-Publication Data
Whitman in his own time: a biographical chronicle of his life, drawn
from recollections, memoirs, and interviews by friends and associates /
edited by Joel Myerson–Expanded ed.
    p.   cm.
    Includes bibliographical references and index.
    ISBN 0-87745-728-X (pbk.)
    1. Whitman, Walt, 1819–1892. 2. Whitman, Walt, 1819–1892–
Friends and associates. 3. Poets, American–19th century–Biography.
I. Myerson, Joel.
PS3231.W47 2000
811'.3–dc21   00-057720

00 01 02 03 04 P 5 4 3 2 1

CONTENTS

CONTENTS

INTRODUCTION TO THE EXPANDED EDITION

. . . there is properly no history, only biography.
    –Ralph Waldo Emerson, "History"

Few American writers were as concerned about their public image as was Walt Whitman. To help readers recognize the value of his books, he praised them in unsigned reviews that he himself wrote. To help others "see" him properly, he included engravings or photographs of himself in various editions of his works (he once even tied a cardboard butterfly to his hand to obtain a "natural" picture). To safeguard his words, he published (and often helped set type for) his own books. To help those interested in his life, he assisted in the writing of two biographies of him,[1] and, from March 1888 until right before his death, he dictated his reminiscences to Horace Traubel on a daily basis.[2] The present volume contributes to Whitman's image by portraying him as others saw him.

Throughout his life Whitman personally and carefully saw to the creation of the author and public figure called "Walt Whitman." He did this in a number of ways: through a character named "Walt Whitman" or "I" in his poetry and prose; by controlling the photographic record of his life; by personally overseeing the production, distribution, and marketing of most of his books; and by making sure that the "right" image of Whitman was presented to the press.

Whitman's presence in his writings was obvious from the first. The initial poem of the first edition of *Leaves of Grass* in 1855 (later titled "Song of Myself") begins with "I celebrate myself," and later in the poem the author is identified as

Walt Whitman, an American, one of the roughs, a kosmos,
Disorderly fleshy and sensual . . . . eating drinking and breeding,
No sentimentalist . . . . no stander above men and women or apart from them
    . . . no more modest than immodest.

His later writings chronicle his own experiences in the Civil War, his views of language, and his comments on his times and the events and people that made them.

No other nineteenth-century American authors, with the possible exception of Mark Twain, were so much photographed and so controlled their own image in those pictures as did Whitman. Whitman was probably the first American author for whom the photographic record of his life was as compelling as the written one that was conveyed in his own letters and journals. Over 130 photographs of Whitman exist.[3] According to Ed Folsom, who has studied these pictures more than anyone else, built into the photographs that covered a lifetime were "fragmentation and change, and it was in reading that fragmented and shifting process of his life, that crowd of former selves, that Whitman finally prevented himself from resting in a simplistic summary of his identity." To Folsom, Whitman's "photographs helped turn the moments of his life into something of a democracy, a democracy of various versions of the self in time, each claiming equal status, each insisting on its own identity even while clearly merging into the overall process of the life."[4]

Whitman controlled the production and distribution of his books from the first edition of *Leaves of Grass* to the last version of it in 1891, as well as most of his works done in between those dates.[5] Too many people forget that Whitman published other books than *Leaves*: *Drum-Taps* (and its *Sequel*) (1865), *Democratic Vistas* (1870), *Passage to India* (1871), *After All, Not to Create Only* (1871), *As a Strong Bird, on Pinions Free* (1871), *Memoranda during the War* (1876), *Two Rivulets* (1876), *Specimen Days & Collect* (1882), *November Boughs* (1888), and *Good-Bye My Fancy* (1891). Four of these books were published by commercial firms, while the others were privately printed and distributed by Whitman and selected booksellers. Five of these books had pictures of Whitman in them. For *Leaves*, Whitman helped set type for at least two of the editions, oversaw the design or printing of all six of the American editions, and personally sold all printings of *Leaves* done between 1867 and 1876. He wrote advertisements for many of his books, some of them as posters.[6] Moreover, he inserted himself pictorially (as well as through his authorial character) in nearly every edition of *Leaves*: engravings or photographs of him appeared in at least one printing of the 1855, 1856, 1860, 1871, and 1881 editions.[7]

Whitman's self-promotion of his works is legendary. Throughout his life he wrote reviews of his own books, and for the 1860 edition of *Leaves of Grass* he edited *Leaves of Grass Imprints*, a type of early press kit.[8] This pamphlet reprinted many positive notices of the two earlier editions of

Leaves, as well as four positive reviews of the book written by the author himself.[9] After Ralph Waldo Emerson wrote him a letter praising the 1855 *Leaves*, Whitman published it, without Emerson's permission, as a broadside and in the 10 October 1855 *New-York Daily Tribune*; and then, again without Emerson's permission, Whitman goldstamped a phrase from the letter ("I Greet You at the Beginning of A Great Career") on the spine of the 1856 Leaves, and identified Emerson as its author.[10] In a sense, Whitman had the genius to invent the dust jacket blurb before there were dust jackets.

He regularly wrote to newspapers and journals about his books and his life; and these letters or articles were usually printed without being attributed to him: the *Philadelphia Press* contained such articles as "Walt Whitman's Birthday" (31 May 1884) and "A Poet's Prose: The Place Walt Whitman Thinks Gratitude Fills in a Fine Character" (27 November 1884); the *Camden Daily News* reported on the local Whitman Society (6 August 1887); the *Camden Daily Post* described "Walt Whitman Mending" (27 December 1888); the *New York Times* told its readers "Walt Whitman Ill" (6 April 1890); and Whitman assisted (uncredited, of course) John Habberton, the possible author of "Walt Whitman's Words" in the *New York Herald* (23 September 1888). Incorrigible to the last, he even wrote an advertisement for his own books in the *festschrift* published in his honor in 1889.[11]

Whitman also was shrewd about allowing personal access to himself. Some visitors viewed a relatively unscripted Whitman, but many others were rewarded with a staged performance. Indeed, Whitman once published under a pseudonym an extended account of a visit to himself.[12] Anne Gilchrist came all the way from England to meet Whitman because she had fallen in love with him through his writings.[13] A Whitman fellowship sprung up in Bolton, England, and some of them visited the master at his home in Camden.[14] Numerous articles and books were published by these visitors, male and female.[15] The various Whitmans that they saw are the subject of this book.

The interviews and recollections printed in *Whitman in His Own Time* offer the best firsthand accounts–published and unpublished, adulatory and critical–written both by now-forgotten and by famous contemporaries. Because these works are presented in chronological order of publication, we are able to gain insight into how Whitman's public persona evolved. Taken as a whole, the accounts provide wide-ranging descriptions of his life. Interviews allow the writer to speak directly to the reader; recollections by associates show the personal effect the writer had on others.

The interviews with and recollections of Whitman published here represent a wide spectrum of accounts. The people who made these contemporary comments and later reminiscences of Whitman include children; one-time, occasional, or regular visitors from America, England, and Germany; newspaper interviewers; his doctor and nurse during his final illness; his literary executors; his first biographers; a child from his early schoolteaching days; and such well-known authors as Amos Bronson Alcott, John Burroughs, Moncure Daniel Conway, Hamlin Garland, Franklin Benjamin Sanborn, and Henry David Thoreau. Surprisingly, Emerson made but few comments on Whitman in his letters, journals, and published works; fortunately, his oral comments to others (especially Sanborn) survive and are printed here. Whitman's own rambling comments, dictated to Traubel (and later published in *With Walt Whitman in Camden*) are also sampled.

These selections paint a well-rounded portrait of Walt Whitman, from his early days as a schoolteacher to the moment of his death. There are detailed descriptions of his life as a newspaper reporter, of his seeing the various editions of *Leaves of Grass* through the press, of his work in Washington ministering to wounded soldiers, and of his declining years of poor health in Camden. Of special note is the information about Whitman's revisions of *Leaves of Grass* as it grew from 95 pages in its first edition of 1855 to 438 pages in the final (or "Deathbed") printing of 1892. Also here are reports on Whitman's comments concerning American literature and publishing, on his poetic theories, on his own poetry, on his reading (including the Bible and Shakespeare), and on his literary contemporaries (including William Cullen Bryant, Thomas Carlyle, Charles Darwin, Charles Dickens, Emerson, Bret Harte, Nathaniel Hawthorne, Oliver Wendell Holmes, Henry Wadsworth Longfellow, James Russell Lowell, Edgar Allan Poe, A. C. Swinburne, Alfred Tennyson, Thoreau, Leo Tolstoy, and John Greenleaf Whittier).

The contributors to this volume have a wide range of attitudes toward their subject. On one hand, there are those who came to praise Whitman, the most embarrassingly eulogistic being George Johnston, who comments on "the world-renowned" Whitman, "the poet par excellence of the nineteenth century, the exponent of the millennial splendors and harmonies which greeted the prophetic vision of Holy John in the Patmian Isle." On the other hand, there are a few who are frankly skeptical, such as William Roscoe Thayer, who feels he recognizes in Whitman "a poseur of truly colossal proportions, one to whom playing a part had long before become so habitual that he had ceased to be conscious that he was doing it."

In these writings we discover things about Whitman ranging from the mundane to the surprising, such as his use of champagne as a laxative, his refusal to read his own works of poetry aloud, his genuine fondness for the common people, and his occasional withdrawal from groups whenever he was brought out for display as a "famous poet." And we hear over and over again about the incredible clutter of his rooms in Camden, which Jeannette Gilder describes in phrenological terminology as a place where anyone with "the bump of order even half developed would have been driven wild," and about which his nurse, Elizabeth Keller, says that the "tables stood like cows in a meadow with the grass up to their bodies." And through all this, Whitman himself holds center stage, and we see him as close-up as it is possible to do over a hundred years after his death.[16]

NOTES

1. The two biographies are John Burroughs, *Notes on Walt Whitman, as Poet and Person* (New York: American News Company, 1867; 2d ed., New York: J. S. Redfield, 1871), and Richard Maurice Bucke, *Walt Whitman* (Philadelphia: David McKay, 1883).

2. Traubel's Boswellesque recordings of Whitman's recollections and statements on contemporary matters are published in nine volumes under the general title of *With Walt Whitman in Camden*, with individual volumes covering the periods of 28 March–14 July 1888 (Boston: Small, Maynard, 1906), 16 July–31 October 1888 (New York: D. Appleton, 1908), 1 November 1888–20 January 1889 (New York: Mitchell Kennerley, 1914), 21 January–7 April 1889 (ed. Sculley Bradley; Philadelphia: University of Pennsylvania Press, 1953), 8 April–14 September 1889 (ed. Gertrude Traubel; Carbondale: Southern Illinois University Press, 1964), 15 September 1889–6 July 1890 (ed. Gertrude Traubel and William White; Carbondale: Southern Illinois University Press, 1982), 7 July 1890–10 February 1891 (ed. Jeanne Chapman and Robert MacIssac; Carbondale: Southern Illinois University Press, 1992), 11 February–30 September 1891 and 1 October 1891–3 April 1892 (both ed. Chapman and MacIsaac; Oregon House, Cal.: W. L. Bentley, 1996).

3. See Ed Folsom, "'This Heart's Geography's Map': The Photographs of Walt Whitman," *Walt Whitman Quarterly Review*, 4, nos. 2–3 (Fall/Winter 1986–1987): 1–76.

4. Ed Folsom, *Walt Whitman's Native Representations* (New York: Cambridge University Press, 1994), p. 172. See especially the chapters "Whitman and

Photography," pp. 99–126, and "Whitman and Photographs of the Self," pp. 127–177.

5. For more information on Whitman's bibliographic history, see Joel Myerson, *Walt Whitman: A Descriptive Bibliography* (Pittsburgh: University of Pittsburgh Press, 1993), and "Whitman: Bibliography as Biography," in *Walt Whitman: The Centennial Essays*, ed. Ed Folsom (Iowa City: University of Iowa Press, 1994), pp. 19–29.

6. See, for example, items F 9, F 23, and F 94 in Myerson, *Walt Whitman: A Descriptive Bibliography*.

7. Only the 1867 edition lacks a likeness of Whitman.

8. *Leaves of Grass Imprints* (Boston: Thayer and Eldridge, 1860).

9. Whitman had earlier collected three of these reviews into an advertising supplement bound into some copies of the 1855 edition of *Leaves of Grass*.

10. For Whitman's relations with Emerson, see Jerome Loving, *Emerson, Whitman, and the American Muse* (Chapel Hill: University of North Carolina Press, 1982).

11. *Camden's Compliment to Walt Whitman, May 31, 1889*, ed. Horace L. Traubel (Philadelphia: David McKay, 1889). Whitman's advertisement for his books is on p. 74.

12. "George Selwyn," "Authors at Home. VII. Walt Whitman at Camden," *Critic*, 6 (28 February 1885): 97–98; reprinted in *Authors at Home*, ed. J. L. and J. B. Gilder (New York: Cassell, 1888), pp. 335–342.

13. See Marion Walker Alcaro, *Walt Whitman's Mrs. G: A Biography of Anne Gilchrist* (Rutherford, N.J.: Fairleigh Dickinson University Press, 1991).

14. See Paul Salveson, "Loving Comrades: Lancashire's Links to Walt Whitman," and Joann P. Krieg, "Without Walt Whitman in Camden," *Walt Whitman Quarterly Review*, 14 (Fall 1996/Winter 1997): 57–84, 85–112.

15. The current interest in Whitman's homoeroticism often neglects the many women who were attracted to him; see Sherry Ceniza, *Walt Whitman and Nineteenth-Century Women Reformers* (Tuscaloosa: University of Alabama Press, 1998).

16. For additional information on Whitman and his contemporaries, and especially the people whose works are reprinted in this book, see the numerous biographies of Whitman, particularly Jerome Loving, *Walt Whitman: The Song of Himself* (Berkeley: University of California Press, 1999); Joann P. Krieg, *A Whitman Chronology* (Iowa City: University of Iowa Press, 1998); and *Walt Whitman: An Encyclopedia*, ed. J. R. LeMaster and Donald D. Kummings (New York: Garland, 1998).

CHRONOLOGY

1789   Walter Whitman, the poet's father, born

1795   Louisa Van Velsor, the poet's mother, born

1816   Walter Whitman and Louisa Van Velsor married

1818   A brother, Jesse Whitman, born

1819   Walter Whitman born in West Hills, Huntington, Long Island, on 31 May

1821   A sister, Mary Elizabeth Whitman, born

1823   A sister, Hannah Louisa Whitman, born
Moves to Brooklyn with his family

1825   Attends the public schools

1827   A brother, Andrew Jackson Whitman, born

1829   A brother, George Washington Whitman, born

1830   Leaves the public schools

1831   Joins the staff of *Long Island Patriot*

1834   A brother, Thomas Jefferson Whitman, born

1835   Moves to New York City

1836   Moves to Hempstead, Long Island, and begins teaching school

1838   Begins newspaper career by serving as publisher and editor of *Long Islander*

1839   Moves to Jamaica, Long Island
       Works on *Long Island Democrat*
       Resigns from the paper and returns to schoolteaching

1841   Returns to New York City and works for various newspapers

1842   *Franklin Evans*, a temperance novel, published
       Edits *New York Aurora* and *New York Evening Tattler*

1843   Edits *New York Statesman*

1844   Edits *New York Democrat*

1845   Edits *Long Island Star*
       Moves to Brooklyn

1846   Edits *Brooklyn Daily Eagle*

1848   Visits New Orleans and works on *New Orleans Daily Crescent*
       Edits *Brooklyn Daily Freeman*

1855   *Leaves of Grass* published by Fowler and Wells in New York
       Father dies on 11 July

1856   *Leaves of Grass* published by Fowler and Wells in New York

1857   Edits *Brooklyn Daily Times*

1859   Dismissed as editor of *Brooklyn Daily Times*

1860   *Leaves of Grass* published by Thayer and Eldridge in Boston

1862   Visits hospitals in Brooklyn to help Civil War wounded
       Goes to Washington to find his brother George, wounded in
            battle

1863   Secures an appointment as a copyist in the paymaster's office
       Begins visits to wounded soldiers in Washington hospitals

1864   Returns to Brooklyn

1865 *Drum-Taps* and *Democratic Vistas* published
Returns to Washington and works as clerk in Interior Department

1865 Fired by James Harland, new secretary of interior, but secures appointment in attorney general's office

1866 William Douglas O'Connor publishes *The Good Gray Poet: A Vindication* in defense of Whitman

1867 *Leaves of Grass* published by William Chapin in New York
John Burroughs publishes *Notes on Walt Whitman as Poet and Person*

1868 *Poems*, edited by William Michael Rossetti, published in England

1871 *Leaves of Grass* published by J. S. Redfield in New York
Passage to India and *After All, Not to Create Only* published

1872 *Leaves of Grass* pirated and published by John Camden Hotten in England
As a Strong Bird on Pinions Free published

1873 Whitman suffers a stroke on 23 January
Mother dies on 23 May
Leaves Washington for Camden, New Jersey

1874 Whitman's position in Washington terminated

1876 *Leaves of Grass* published by Whitman in Camden
Memoranda During the War and *Two Rivulets* published

1879 *Leaves of Grass* published in an unauthorized reprinting by Worthington in New York
Makes a western trip, going as far as Denver

1880 Summers with Richard Maurice Bucke in London, Ontario

1881 *Leaves of Grass* published by James R. Osgood in Boston, but withdrawn from sale by the publisher after attorney gen-

eral of Massachusetts declares the book obscene
Lectures on Lincoln before the St. Botolph Club in Boston

1882   *Leaves of Grass* published by Whitman in Camden, then by Rees Welsh in Philadelphia, then by David McKay in Philadelphia
Specimen Days & Collect published

1883   Richard Maurice Bucke publishes *Walt Whitman*

1884   Buys house on Mickle Street in Camden

1886   *Leaves of Grass* published by Walter Scott in England

1887   *Specimen Days in America* published by Walter Scott in England

1888   *Complete Poems and Prose* published by Whitman in Philadelphia (limited to 600 copies)
November Boughs published
Democratic Vistas, and Other Papers published by Walter Scott in London
Suffers a stroke in June

1889   *Leaves of Grass* published by Whitman in Philadelphia (limited to 300 copies)

1891   *Good-Bye My Fancy* published

1892   *Leaves of Grass* published by David McKay in Philadelphia
Walt Whitman dies on 26 March

Whitman in His Own Time

WALT WHITMAN.
A VISIT TO THE
GOOD GRAY POET

[Franklin Benjamin Sanborn]

His Philosophy and Way of Life—
His Home in New Jersey—
His New Volumes.
From Our Special Correspondent.

Franklin Benjamin Sanborn was a member of the Concord circle of writers, having moved there in the mid 1850s. As the literary correspondent of the Springfield Daily Republican, *he often contributed interviews and literary gossip to the paper.*

Philadelphia, April 13, 1876

More than ten years ago, when that illustrious statesman and Christian, Secretary Harlan of Iowa, turned Walt Whitman out of his little clerkship in the department of the interior at Washington, one of his eager young friends, Mr. O'Connor, printed a warm defense of Whitman, in which he termed him "the good gray poet." Whitman was then but 46 years of age, or a little older than Thoreau was when he died in 1862, but he had already begun to wear the grizzled beard and silvering locks that have become almost the badge of American poets, since Dana and Bryant and Longfellow have worn them so many years. Emerson, almost alone among the elder poets, has avoided the medieval beard and the insignia of old age—but even he, when 73 years old, as he will be, next month, will have laid aside much of that youthful and alert air that so long have marked him among men and poets. The story of Tithonus is still a parable of the poet,—he is immortal in his love, but loses with years the

3

freshness of his life, and, at last, implores the goddess who made him happy to discharge him from her service and grant him repose among the dead,—

> "Thou seest all things—thou wilt see my grave,
> Thou wilt renew thy beauty, morn by morn;
> I, earth in earth, forget these empty courts,
> And thee returning on thy silver wheels."

Now that Whitman has come almost to his 57th birthday (he was born at West Hills, Long Island, May 31, 1819), and has, for some time, been a confirmed invalid, he has assumed more entirely the grayness that was ascribed to him, and were he inclined to complain, like Tithonius, he might sigh forth, in remembering his former free and joyous life, of which his verses are so full, and contrasting it with his present retirement,—

> "Alas for this gray shadow, once a man,
> So glorious in his beauty and thy choice,
> Who madest him thy chosen, that he seemed
> To his great heart none other than a god.
> . . . . . .
> How can my nature longer mix with thine?
> Coldly thy rosy shadows bathe me, cold
> Are all thy lights, and cold my wrinkled feet
> Upon thy glimmering thresholds.
> . . . I wither slowly in thine arms,
> Here at the quiet limit of the world,
> A white-haired shadow, roaming like a dream
> The ever silent spaces of the East,
> Far-folded mists and gleaming halls of morn."

But, like Thoreau in his later months of illness and retirement, Whitman, though graver than formerly, is none the less cheerful, and has no complaints or reproaches against the Muse or against the power that rules the world. Certain statements made in his name about the neglect of critics and publishers, and the hardships of poverty, have come from him only as a mention of the simple fact, and not as reproaches or entreaties, and they ought not so to be interpreted.

4

Franklin Benjamin Sanborn

"For never poor beseeching glance
Shamed that sculptured countenance."

Whitman has long been a standing text in the newspapers for such wit as Heaven has provided us with, who write, as he once did, for the daily or weekly reader. He provokes jests by his mode of expression and by the contrast he presents to the ordinary and accepted way of life among Americans. He provokes also something more serious than the transient animosity that culminates in a parody or a joke, by the resolute way in which he intrudes, among ideal things, the fleshly and generative forces out of which human life springs, but of which the human soul is reasonably a little shy. This part of his philosophy—for such it is—must not be confounded with the erotic paroxysms of Swinburne, or the cold obscurities of Martial and other elder poets. It is a more ideal phase than those, and, with a little more refinement and modesty in its presentation, would be hardly worse than Shakespeare's treatment of the same matters. It

5

Whitman's birthplace at West Hills, Long Island

is, for all that, a very great stone of stumbling and ground of offense to the better portion of his readers, and especially to women, upon whom of late years, and perhaps always, poets have much depended for their audience. It is by taking advantage of this blot that good Peter Bayne has been able to find so many readers for his dull abuse of Whitman in the Contemporary Review; and it is partly because some cheap and nasty poets in England rave a little too much about Whitman's genius (attracted by this very whim of his) that the virtuous people regard him with so much disgust. In sober fact, his verses are cleaner and his life incomparably more praiseworthy than Burns's,—whose praise is now in all the churches as well as among the people. But Burns had more romance and melody in his composition, and drew the other sex to read his poems by this attraction. Whitman has a broader range of thought than Burns, and touches upon many of the same chords of emotion, but for lack of the poetic form

6

and melody can never, I suppose, be a popular writer, though very popular in his instincts and his topics. But as a moralist, or as a man of wholesome life and influence, no serious charge can be brought against Whitman, and when the balance is struck between him and certain idols of the people—say Beecher, for instance,—the judgment, even of his own time, will not be heavily against the poet, as compared with the preacher.

My first glimpse of Whitman was under such circumstances that I could not easily forget him. It was April, 1860, when I had been seized at night by the United States marshal, under an unlawful warrant from Washington—as thousands have been since,—had then been taken from him by the sheriff and carried before the Massachusetts supreme court on a writ of *habeas corpus.* It was feared by some persons that, even if Judge Shaw discharged me (as he did), I might be again seized by the bailiffs of the slave-power, then in its last days of supremacy at Washington, and hurried away in defiance of the state authority. A large number of friends gathered in the court-room in Boston to prevent this by force, if necessary, and among them came Whitman, who was then in the city, publishing the second edition of his "Leaves of Grass." As I sat listening to the arguments of Andrew and Sewall in my behalf, and of Woodbury against them, and watched with admiration the dark, heavy judicial countenance of old Judge Shaw—as striking as the ugliest and wisest of the English chancellors,—I suddenly became aware of another face, no less remarkable, in the court-room. It was Whitman's,—he sat on a high seat near the door, wearing his loose jacket and open shirt collar, over which poured the fullness of his beard, while above that the large and singular blue eyes, under heavy arching brows, wandered over the assembly, as some stately creature of the fields turns his eyes slowly about him in the presence of many men. I had heard that Whitman was present, and instantly conjectured him to be the magnificent stranger, as indeed he was. A few days afterward, I met him at his publisher's, and heard him expound his new philosophy, as he sat on the counter and listened to my compliments and objections. From that day—16 years ago—I had not seen him nor exchanged letters with him, until to-day. Hearing that he was brought to an anchor by his guardian genius, and owing him much good-will for the incident above mentioned, as well as for his brave work in the world, I thought it a duty as well as a pleasure to go and see him. And a pleasure it certainly proved to be—for I found him, as one would wish to find such a person, master of himself and superior to his circumstances, which, also, are less painful than may have been supposed from the ejaculations of Mr. Robert Buchanan. Whitman could echo the proud words of his friend Tennyson:—

"Turn, Fortune, turn thy wheel with smile or frown;
With that wild wheel we go not up or down;
Our board is little, but our hearts are great.
Turn, turn thy wheel above the staring crowd;
Thy wheel and thou are shadows in the cloud;
Thy wheel and thee we neither love nor hate."

Whitman lives comfortably and pleasantly, as an invalid can, with his brother, Col George W. Whitman, who is inspector of gas-pipes in the city of Camden. This is a populous but quiet place of twenty or thirty thousand inhabitants—in New Jersey, though a suburb of Philadelphia,—and the street where the Whitmans live (Stevens street, near Fifth) is a still, Philadelphia-looking quarter, of long rows of brick houses with white marble door-steps and white wooden shutters, in one of which, at a street corner, Whitman has taken up his abode. This house has a bay-window on the side street, by which I was directed to it from one of the neighboring houses; and through this bay-window the poet pointed out to me a magnolia-tree in a garden across the way, already in bloom at 11 o'clock, though at sunrise, as he said, not a bud upon it had unclosed. This was the second magnolia-tree I have noticed in blossom, yesterday and to-day, the season not being very forward. Eleven years ago, as Whitman says, when President Lincoln was assassinated (to-morrow is the anniversary), the lilac-bushes were in blossom in his mother's door-yard on Long Island; and ever since then the smell of the lilac brings to his mind the tragedy of Lincoln's death. You may reach Whitman's home at Camden in half an hour from the continental hotel in Philadelphia,—taking the street cars down Market street to the Camden ferry-boat (10 minutes), then crossing the Delaware, which takes 10 minutes more, and then driving up Fifth to Stevens street, and walking the short distance to the next corner where Whitman lives. The ferry-boat crosses every 15 minutes, and the street cars run all the time, so that it is easier and quicker to make the pilgrimage from Philadelphia than it is to visit the centennial grounds,

Whitman's mother, Louisa Van Velsor Whitman

where thousands daily throng. Whitman is not thronged with visitors, though many persons come to see him,—and I had a two hours' talk with him alone, to-day,—interrupted only by the coming of a man to bring him a few books, and by the visit of a neighbor's child, a little girl, who told us we could see the baby (Whitman's nephew and namesake, five months old), which we did accordingly.

In the room where I found Whitman, a few books were to be seen in a book-case, and two remarkable paintings hung on the wall. One was the portrait of Whitman himself, painted perhaps a dozen or fifteen years ago, before his hair and beard were gray and before his face had lost the colors of youth. The other is a good painting, perhaps 150 years old, of a Dutch ancestor of Whitman's who he greatly resembles,—both having the ruddy, sensuous and thoughtful face, with strongly-marked eyebrows, and the ancestor, like the poet, wearing his coat open at the neck. The poet now dresses in gray

9

clothes, matching well with his hair and beard, and wears a white scarf or handkerchief loosely tied about his neck above his blue waistcoat—altogether a picturesque and befitting attire, careless but effective. He was sitting by the window as I approached the house, and he opened the door to let me in—walking slowly and with a cane, but not painfully. He suffers much at times from his disorder, which he described as "a baffling kind of paralysis," that first attacked him three years ago, and from which he never expects fully to recover. It not only reduces his strength and affects his power of motion, but also attacks his digestive organs, and thus causes him many miserable hours—some of which he had experienced that morning, he said. But the expectation of my coming had toned him up, he thought, and he then felt well for an invalid, and cheerful, as he always seems to be. He talks gravely and with a melodious, manly voice, now and then affected by a slight hesitation, as if paralysis were giving him a hint not to move his tongue too much; and very simply, using words without affectation, and choosing them for their fitness to express the idea or the picture in his mind. He talked no more about himself than most men do, and what he said on that score was interesting, which is not the case with most men. He is, certainly, a deeply interesting person, and it was easy to see what drew to him the admiration of Emerson, Alcott and Thoreau, who made his acquaintance in the years before the war—now so far remote. He is, indeed, a distinguished and superior person, apart from what he has written, and has an individuality as marked in its way as was that of Thoreau himself, who was but a year or two older than Whitman. Like Thoreau, Whitman spent much of his life with his mother and sister, between whom and himself the closest affection existed. Indeed, his attack of paralysis in Washington in 1873 was aggravated by the death, soon after, of his mother, his sister having died a little while before. His father, who was a farmer on Long Island, died in 1855, when Whitman was preparing to publish the first edition of "Leaves of Grass." Before this he had written sketches for the Democratic Review, and had helped edit several newspapers—among them the "Plebian," the editor of which bore the appropriate name of Levi D. Slamm. Thoreau was also a writer for the Democratic Review in those days before the flood,—so were Hawthorne and, I believe, Bryant.

Whitman does not estimate American literature as most people do, but there is nothing mean or petty in the view he takes of it and of its chief authors. He thought it fortunate for American poetry that it has had for its sponsors four poets so manly, clean and strong as Emerson, Bryant, Longfellow and Whittier. Only one of these was his personal acquaintance, and Longfellow and Whittier I believe he never saw. Lowell he once saw for a few minutes, in the days when he wore his auburn hair long and sat for his portrait to Page, and wrote socialistic and anti-slavery poems for the newspapers. The Cambridge scholar, young, handsome and fat, as Whitman describes him, gave the Brooklyn mechanic-editor, who then saw him at the office of "The Plebian," a high and pleasing conception of Yankee poets,—but he has not since set eyes on him. Emerson he came to know a few years later,—the Concord poet having sought him out in New York. Alcott and Thoreau called upon him at his mother's house in Brooklyn during a visit they were making in New York about 1858, and Alcott had since visited him, perhaps in Washington, where Miss Alcott, like Whitman, was a hospital nurse. He told me how he came to visit the camps,—his brother, the colonel, was badly wounded, and Whitman went down to Virginia to take care of him—perhaps to bring home his body. Though he found him better than was feared, yet other soldiers needed his care, and he never left that kind of hospital service during the war. To my mind the best poems that he has written were inspired by the war—and there are short passages, not so much poems as *sentences*, which are worthy to live, as perhaps they will, among those that Plutarch (and Homer before him) has handed down to immortality. Here are some such,—the first containing his advice to his countrymen in regard to state rights, in which Whitman firmly believes, though he was a strong antagonist of slavery and disunion. He calls it:—

Walt Whitman's Caution

"To the States or any one of them, or any city of The States,
    resist much, obey little;
Once unquestioning obedience, once fully enslaved,
Once fully enslaved, no nation, state, city of this earth ever
    afterward resumes its liberty."

11

Where could you find that doctrine more concisely taught, in spite of repetitions? Here is a portrait of Washington as good as any ever drawn,—Brooklyn Hights being the foreground:—

"And is this the ground Washington trod?
And these waters I listlessly daily cross, are these the waters
        he crossed,
As resolute in defeat as other generals in their proudest triumphs?"

Of a high officer in the civil war Whitman says:—

I saw old General at bay,
    Old as he was, his gray eyes yet shone out in battle like stars,
    His small force was now completely hemmed in, on his works."

And how could the whole connection of slavery with the civil war and its results be better summed up than in this strong poem?—

Ethiopia Saluting the Colors.
[A Reminiscence of 1864.]

I.
Who are you, dusky woman, so ancient, hardly human,
With your wooly-white and turban'd head, and bare, bony feet?
Why, rising by the road-side here, do you the colors greet?

II.
'Tis while our army lines Carolina's sand and pines,
Forth from thy hovel door, thou Ethiopia, com'st to me,
As under doughty Sherman I march toward the sea.

III.
Me, master, years a hundred, since from my parents sundered,
A little child, they caught me as the savage beast is caught,
Then hither me, across the sea, the cruel slaver brought.

IV.
No further does she say, but lingering all the day,
Her high-borne turban'd head she wags, and rolls her darkling eye,
And curtseys to the regiments, the guldons moving by.

V.
What is it, fateful woman, so blear, hardly human?
Why wag your head with turban bound—yellow, red and green?
Are the things so strange and marvelous, you see or have seen?

To return for a moment to the comparison with Burns, here is a poem which cannot be sung like "Scots wha hae," but which is even more startling and moving than that. Whitman's lament for Lincoln also is as touching as most and more sublime than any of Burns's laments for earls and comrades. He, like Whitman, was a true and warm-hearted comrade, and his poetry speaks much of that. But Whitman considers it his mission to have celebrated comradeship in his poems, just as he has idealized democracy in his philosophy. He wishes his works to be regarded (and so they are not published by himself) as a *whole*. So regarded, he believes that the objectionable passages will be found to have as natural a place in them, as the animal life of man has in his whole existence. He considers his philosophy a spiritual one—certainly an ideal one,—and by the maturer judgment of the world he is content to abide, as he must, in regard to his rank as a poet and philosopher. In these years of illness and enforced quiet, he has much considered and revised his books, and now he publishes them as he wishes them to stand and to be read. They make two volumes of about 700 pages in all, with three portraits of the author, and his autograph signature, finely bound, and sold for $5 a volume. The small edition he had prepared is selling fast, and he will print another. Perhaps even some publisher may come forward and offer to print for him, but he prefers now to be his own publisher.

Springfield Daily Republican, 19 April 1876, pp. 4-5; attributed to Sanborn on the basis of his remarks about Whitman's appearance at the former's trial in 1860.

INTERVIEW WITH WHITMAN

Anonymous

This anonymous interview is included as typical of those given by Whitman during his trip to the west in 1879.

Walt Whitman, the poet, is visiting his brother at 2316 Pine street, in this city, resting after his trip to Kansas, and recovering from an attack of sickness. Mr. Whitman is a very remarkable looking man. His long, snow-white hair flows down and mingles with his fleecy beard, giving him a venerable expression, which his grave eyes and well-marked features confirm. Whitman impresses one at once as being a sage, and his thoughtful, original speech confirms the idea.

A *Post-Dispatch* reporter called on the author of "Leaves of Grass" this morning, and after a somewhat desultory conversation abruptly asked him:

"Do you think we are to have a distinctively American literature?"

"It seems to me," said he, "that our work at present, and for a long time to come, is to lay the materialistic foundations of a great nation, in products, in commerce, in vast networks of intercommunication, and in all that relates to the comforts and supplies of vast masses of men and families, on a very grand scale, and those with freedom of speech and ecclesiasticism. This we have founded and are carrying out on a grander scale than ever hitherto, and it seems to me that those great central States from Ohio to Colorado, and from Lake Superior down to Tennessee, the prairie States, will be the theater of our great future. Ohio, Illinois, Indiana, Missouri, Kansas and Colorado seem to me to be the seat and field of these very ideas. They seem to be carrying them out."

"Materialistic prosperity in all its varied forms and on the grand scale of our times, with those other points that I mentioned, intercommunication and freedom, are first to be attended to. When

14

those have their results and get settled then a literature worthy of us will begin to be defined from our nebulous conditions. Although we have elegant and finished writers, none of them express America or her spirit in any respect whatever."

"What will be the character of the American literature when it does form?"

"Do you know that I have thought of that vaguely often, but have never before been asked the question. It will be something entirely new, entirely different. As we are a new nation with almost a new geography, and a new spirit, the expression of them will have to be new. In form, in combination we shall take the same old font of type, but what we set up will never have been set up before. It will be the same old font that Homer and Shakespeare used, but our use will be new."

"Modern poetry and art run to a sweetness and refinement which are really foreign to us, they are not ours. Everywhere as I went through the Rocky Mountains, three weeks ago, especially the Platte Canon, I said to myself, 'Here are my poems, not finished temples, not graceful architecture, but great naturalness and rugged power—primitive nature."

"My idea of one great feature of future American poetry is the expression of comradeship. That is a main point with me. Then breadth, moderness and consistency with science."

"Poetry, as yet given to us even by our own bards, is essentially feudal and antique. Our greatest man is Emerson. Bryant, I think, has a few pulsations. Whittier is a puritan poet without unction—without justice. I hardly know what to say about Longfellow. The best promise in America of those things is in a certain range of young men that are coming on the stage, that are yet voiceless. They are appearing in the Eastern cities and in the West. They have not yet begun to speak because the magazines and publishing houses are in the hands of the fossils."

"There is a great underlying strata of young men and women who cannot speak because the magazines are in the hands of old fogies like Holland or fops like Howells. They are like water dammed up. They will burst forth some day. They are very American. Emerson is our first man. He is in every way what he should be. He is a rounded, finished man, complete in himself. Our living Bancroft and our dead Ticknor I think first-class men."

Whitman's father, Walter Whitman, Senior

"What do you think of Bret Harte?"

"He is smart, facile and witty in the old sense. What a miserable business it is to take out of this great outgrowth of Western character, which is something more heroic than ever the old poets wrote about, to have taken out only a few ruffians and delerium tremens specimens, and make them the representatives of California personality. An artist would have taken the heroic personalities, but Bret Harte and the person who followed him have taken these characters and made them stand for the whole. I think it is an outrage. He seems to me to have taken Dickens' treatment of the slums of London and transferred it to California."

"I think Tennyson the leading man in modern poetry. Nobody has expressed like Tennyson the blending of the most perfect verbal melody with the heart sickness of modern times."

"He has caught that undertone of ennui in a way that will last while men read. I myself have been ambitious to do something entirely different from that, while I can appreciate him. The whole tendency of poetry has been toward refinement. I have felt that was not worthy of America. Something more vigorous, *al fresco*, was needed, and then more than all I determined from the beginning to put a whole living man in the expression of a poem, without wincing. I thought the time had come to do so, and I thought America was the place to do it. Curious as it may appear, it had never yet been done. An entire human being physically, emotionally, and in his moral and spiritual nature. And also to express what seems to me had been left unexpressed, our own country and our own times. I have come now a couple of thousand miles, and the greatest thing to me in this Western country is the realization of my 'Leaves of Grass.' It tickles me hugely to find how thoroughly it and I have been in rapport. How my poems have defined them. I have really had their spirit in every page without knowing. I had made Western people talk to me, but I never knew how thoroughly a Western man I was till now."

"And how about religion?"

"I could only say that, as she develops, America will be a thoroughly religious nation. Toleration will grow, and the technique of religion, sectarianism, will more and more give out."

"Politically?"

"Politically, as far as I can see, we have established ourselves. The basis has been all right. We have nothing to do de novo. I think the theory and practice of American government, without its National and State governments, are stable. It seems to be established without danger, without end."

"And how about Canada?"

"I think Canada and Cuba and Mexico will gravitate to us. We could take the whole world in if it was fit for it, which it is not. There is no danger in enlargement. We can take in all the country from the isthmus to the North pole. Instead of endangering us it will only balance us, give us a greater area of base."

"Our American greatness and vitality are in the bulk of our people, not in a gentry like the old world. The greatness of our army was in the rank and file, and so with the nation. Other nations had their vitality in a few, a class, but we have it in the bulk of the people. Our leading men are not of much account and never have been, but the average of the people is immense, beyond all history."

17

"Lincoln seems to me our greatest specimen personality. Sometimes I think that in all departments, literature and art included, that will be the way our greatness will exhibit itself. We will not have great individuals or great leaders, but a great bulk, unprecedentedly great."

St. Louis Post-Dispatch, 17 October 1879, p. 2; reprinted from Walter H. Eitner, *Walt Whitman's Western Jaunt* (Lawrence: Regents Press of Kansas, 1981), pp. 82-85.

WALT WHITMAN

Anonymous

A Chat with the "Good Gray Poet."
What He has to Say About Himself and Things in General.

When he visited Richard Maurice Bucke in London, Ontario, in 1880, Whitman became something of a local celebrity, and granted several newspaper interviews, of which this is one.

As previously announced in the *Advertiser*, Walt Whitman arrived in this city last evening, in company with Dr. Bucke, whose guest the "good gray poet" will be during his stay in London. The recent lecture of the doctor, and the newspaper discussion that took place subsequently, had excited a good deal of curiousity among the people, and quite a number were on the platform to catch a glimpse of Whitman as he alighted. It was seen that Walt Whitman is a man of about six feet one inch, moderately stout, and weighing probably between 220 and 230 pounds. He wears a full beard, quite gray, and has a very intellectual appearance. A high forehead, large nose, and clear, bright eyes, and a mouth hidden almost from view by a luxuriant growth of beard and mustache, are the marked characteristics of the poet at a first glance, and subsequent conversation fully bears out the idea formed that Walt Whitman, whatever may be the opinion of admirers or detractors, is at least a man more than ordinarily noticeable. A slight lameness is observed, but otherwise he carries well his sixty-one years and seems full of animation. As he stepped off the train he entered the carriage, and was soon conveyed to the residence of Dr. Bucke. An *Advertiser* representative was not long in following, and it will interest the reader to learn some facts concerning the poet who sings the song of the Democrat as given in his own words.

"Yes," he said, "this is my first visit properly speaking to Canada, although I was at Niagara Falls some thirty years ago." He expressed himself as highly pleased with the country through which he had passed coming from the Bridge to London, and although necessarily somewhat fatigued by the journey from Philadelphia was in good spirits and spoke with vivacity.

He was told that his works had excited a good deal of interest in London, and that they had been severely animadverted upon by a clergyman of the city, Rev. Mr. Murray, and that that gentleman was on the platform as he arrived.

"Ah!" said Whitman, "I shou'd have like to have met him. I wish he had come and spoken to me," and the manner in which he spoke showed that he was plainly in earnest.

Whitman speaks freely and unaffectedly of his life and poetry. He said that he was born on the 31st of May, 1819, at West Hills, Long Island, where his father followed the occupation of a farmer. His father was of English descent and his mother sprung from Hollandic stock. His parents having removed to Brooklyn, he, at an early age, learned the trade of a compositor, and when not more than sixteen or seventeen began teaching school. Giving this up in a year or so, he travelled through all the Middle and Southern States, and finally returned to Brooklyn. Here, in 1855, he commenced to put to press, "Leaves of Grass," having set up the type of it himself. He gave this work a great deal of revision, experiencing a difficulty in eliminating the stock poetical touches, if the idea may be conveyed in that way. In 1862 he went to the war, and it was while acting as nurse of the wounded soldiers that he gained the sobriquet of the "Good Gray Poet," that has since clung to him. At the close of the war he received a position as clerk in the Attorney General's office, which he retained till 1874, when he became paralyzed and moved to Camden, N.J., where he at present resides with his brother, Col. Whitman.

Any reference to Walt Whitman would be incomplete indeed that did not have a reference to literature, and the interviewer cannot help but ask his views on the subject.

He reads but little comparatively, so he said, but his favorite works are those of Sir Walter Scott (some of which he has read five or six times), George Sand, Shakespeare, Homer, and "the best of all books, the Bible," the quoted words being spoken with a rever-

George Washington Whitman (by permission of Duke University Library)

ence that one would scarce expect in a man denounced for his immorality.

Whitman says that when quite a youth he began to write in the style which he has made his own. He came to the conclusion that the old forms of poetry, which are well enough in their way, and whose beauty no one appreciates more than himself, were not suited for the expression of American democracy and American manhood. He made many experiments and destroyed his MSS again and again, and as he rejected the old forms, so he threw overboard all the regular stock-in-trade of the poets. It is true generally of all poets, he says, but particularly true of the minor poets, that they have selected only the delicate things, the mere prettiness, for poetic treatment. The noble Greek poets seemed to think only the gods and rulers were worthy of celebration. Shakespeare wrote chiefly of Kings, "but it has been my favorite idea," says Whitman, "to give expression to Nature as we actually find it. The man, the American man, the laborer, boatsman and mechanic. The great painters were as willing to paint a blacksmith as a lord. Why should the poets only confine themselves to mere sentiment? The theologians to a man teach humility, and that the body is the sinful setting of the immortal soul. I wish men to be proud—to be proud of their bodies—to look upon the body as a thing of beauty, too holy to be abused by vice and debauchery.

"The fault I have to find with Tennyson, although he is a master of his art, with Longfellow, Whittier, and all the rest, is that they are too much like saints. Nature is strong and rank. This rankness is seen everywhere in man, and it is this strength and rankness that I have endeavored to give voice. It pleases me to think also that if any of my works shall survive it will be the fellowship in it—the comradeship—friendship is the good old word—the love of my fellow-men. As to the form of my poetry, I have rejected the rhymed and blank verse, I have a particular abhorrence of blank verse, but I cling to rhythm, not the outward regularly measured short foot, long foot—short foot, long foot—like the walking of a lame man, that I care nothing for. The waves of the sea do not break on the beach one wave every so many minutes; the wind does not go jerking through the pine trees, but nevertheless in the roll of the waves, and in the roughing of the wind in the trees, there is a beautiful rhythm. How monotonous it would become—how tired the ears would get of it—if it were regular. It is under-melody and rhythm that I have attempted to catch, and years after I have written a line, when I have read it to myself, or my friends read it aloud, I think I have found it. It has been quite a trial to myself to destroy some of my own pretty things, but I have rigidly excluded everything of the kind from my books."

Speaking of his contemporary poets, Walt Whitman says that Emerson is by far the greatest of American authors, worthy to hold his own with great genius of other lands and other times. Emerson, Bryant, Whittier, (though he does not place the last two on a par with Emerson,) and Longfellow form a very bright and honorable cluster in literature. Whittier he does not regard as great, and the motive of his "Maud Muller" he considers as unworthy of poetic treatment.

"Ah, me! if I could only marry a rich man!" (the expression

placed in the mouth of the heroine,) he regards as unworthy of any American woman. (Query—Why only American?) Bryant he likes. There is about him an odor of out-of-doors, of freedom—the democracy that Whitmanings."

Considering the turn taken by the recent discussion in this city concerning the morality of Whitman's works, his religious views will be of interest. Perhaps we can best give a hint in this direction by transcribing an incident recorded in his diary.

"This afternoon, July 22, 1863, I spent a long time with a young man I have been with a good deal from time to time named Oscar F. Wilbur, company 6, 154th New York, low with chronic diarrhea and a bad wound also. He asked me to read him a chapter in the New Testament. I complied, and asked him what I should read. He said 'make your own choice.' I opened at the close of one of the first works of the Evangelists and read the chapters describing the latter hours of Christ and the scenes of the crucifixion. The poor wasted young man asked to read the following chapter also: how Christ rose again. I read very slowly, for Oscar was feeble. It pleased him very much, yet the tears were in his eyes, and he asked me if I enjoyed religion. I said, 'Perhaps not, my dear, in the way you mean, and yet maybe it is the same thing.'"

The hour was late, and it was not well that the fatigue of the journey should be supplemented by too much conversation, yet it was learned that Walt Whitman is a man with whom any can converse, with decided convictions on literature and religion, and while it is not the province of the reporter to pronounce upon his orthodoxy, there can be no doubt but that he is a reverent man, with no suggestion of irreverence or pruriency in his talk. It is probable that he will remain with Dr. Bucke the greater part of the summer, and possibly he may deliver a lecture in the course of his stay in London.

London Advertiser [Ontario, Canada], 5 June 1880, p. 4.

From WALT WHITMAN

Richard Maurice Bucke

Whitman helped Bucke to write Walt Whitman *(1883) and personally approved most of the material in it. The reminiscences by Helen E. Price are by one whose family were among Whitman's best friends in Brooklyn from the mid 1850s on.*

The memoranda which follow were written for this volume in 1881 by a lady—Miss Helen E. Price, of Woodside, Long Island—whose acquaintance with Walt Whitman, and his frequent temporary residence in her parents' family, make her peculiarly competent to present a picture of the man in those periods of middle life:

My acquaintance with Walt Whitman began in 1856, or about a year after he published the first edition of *Leaves of Grass*. I was at that time living with my parents in Brooklyn, and although hardly more than a child in years, the impression made upon my girlish imagination by his large, grand presence, his loose, free dress, and his musical voice will never be effaced. From that date until the death of his mother, in 1873, he was often a visitor at our house, as I at his, his mother being only less dear to me than my own.

So many remembrances of him in those by gone years come crowding to my mind that to choose what will be most characteristic, and most likely to interest those who know him only from his books, is a task to which I fear I shall prove unequal. On the other hand, *anything* I might write of him, his conversation especially, when deprived of the magnetism of his presence and voice, and of the circumstances and occasions which called forth the words, will, I am painfully aware, seem poor and tame.

I must preface my first anecdote of him with some description of a gentleman with whom many of my early recollections of his conversations are connected. At that time Mr. A. was living with his daughter's family, who occupied with us the same house. A. was a man of wide knowledge and the most analytical mind of any one I ever knew. He was a Swedenborgian, not formally belonging to the church of that name, but accepting in the main

24

the doctrines of the Swedish seer as revealed in his works. Although the two men differed greatly on many points, such was the mutual esteem and forbearance between them, that during the many talks they had together, in which I sat by a delighted listener, it was only on one occasion (at the outbreak of our civil war) that I ever noticed the slightest irritation between them. Each, though holding mainly to his own views, was large enough to see truth in the other's presentation also. The subject of many of their early conversations was Democracy. No one who has even the slightest acquaintance with Walt Whitman's writings need to be told what were and are his ideas on that subject—with what passionate ardor he espouses the cause of the people, and the fervent and glowing faith he has in their ultimate destiny. Mr. A. rather inclined to the Carlylean and perhaps Emersonian idea, that from among the masses are to be found only here and there individuals capable of rightly governing themselves and others, as in myriads of grains of sand, there are only occasional diamonds—or in innumerable seeds, only a very few destined to develop into perfect plants. Some months after our first meeting with Mr. Whitman, my mother invited Mrs. Eliza A. Farnum (former matron of Sing Sing prison) to meet him at our house. In the beginning of conversation he said to her, "I know more about you, Mrs. Farnum, than you think I do; I have heard you spoken of often by friends of mine at Sing Sing at the time you were there." Then turning to Mr. A., who sat near by, he added in a lower tone, half seriously, half quizzically, "Some of the prisoners." This was said solely for Mr. A.'s benefit, as a kind of supplement to their talks on Democracy.

No one could possibly have more aversion to being lionized than Mr. Whitman. I could not say how many times, after getting his consent to meet certain admirers at our house, he has vexed and annoyed us by staying away. At one time an evening was appointed to meet General T., of Philadelphia, and a number of others. We waited with some misgivings for his appearance, but he came at last. Soon as the introductions were over, he sidled off to a corner of the room where there was a group of young children, with whom he talked and laughed and played, evidently to their mutual satisfaction. Our company, who had come from a distance to see Mr. Whitman, and did not expect another opportunity, were quite annoyed, and my mother was finally commissioned to get him out of his corner. When she told her errand, he looked up with the utmost merriment, and said, "O, yes—I'll do it—where do you want me to sit? On the piano?" He went forward very good-naturedly, however, but I knew that his happy time for that evening was over.

A friend of ours, a very brilliant and intellectual lady, had often expressed a great desire to see him—but as she lived out of town it was difficult to arrange a meeting. One day she came to our house full of animation and triumph. "I have seen Walt Whitman at last," she said. "I was sitting in the cabin of the Brooklyn ferry-boat when he came in. I knew it was he; it couldn't be any one else; and as he walked through the boat with such an ele-phantine roll and swing, I could hardly keep from getting right up and roll-ing after him." The next time he called we related this to him; he laughed heartily, and frequently afterward alluded to his "elephantine roll."

Mr. Whitman was not a smooth, glib, or even a very fluent talker. His ideas seemed always to be called forth or suggested by what was said be-fore, and he would frequently hesitate for just the right term to express his meaning. He never gave the impression that his words were cut and dried in his mind, or at his tongue's end, to be used on occasion; but you listened to what seemed to be freshly thought, which gave to all he said an indescrib-able charm. His language was forcible, rich and vivid to the last degree, and even when most serious and earnest, his talk was always enlivened by fre-quent gleams of humor. (I believe it has been assumed by the critics that he has no humor. There could be no greater mistake.) I have said that in con-versation he was not fluent, yet when a little excited in talking on any sub-ject very near his heart, his words would come forth rapidly, and in strains of amazing eloquence. At such times I have wished our little circle was en-larged a hundred-fold, that others might have the privilege of hearing him.

As a listener (all who have met him will agree with me) I think that he was and is unsurpassed. He was ever more anxious to hear your thought than to express his own. Often when asked to give his opinion on any sub-ject, his first words would be, "Tell me what you have to say about it." His method of considering, pondering, what Emerson calls "entertaining," your thought was singularly agreeable and flattering, and evidently an out-growth of his natural manner, and as if unconscious of paying you any spe-cial compliment. He seemed to call forth the best there was in those he met. He never appeared to me a conceited or egotistical man, though I have frequently heard him say himself that he was so. On the contrary, he was always unassuming and modest in asserting himself, and seemed to feel, or at least made others feel, that their opinions were more valuable than his own. I have heard him express serious doubt as to what would be the final judgment of posterity on his poems, or "pieces" as he sometimes called them.

I have, however, seen in his character something that, for want of a bet-ter word, I would call vanity. All through those years he gloried in his health, his magnificent physical proportions, his buoyant and overflowing life (this was in the first ten years of my acquaintance with him), and what-ever so-called oddity there was in his dress and looks arose, I think, from this peculiar consciousness or pride. We all thought that his costume suited him, and liked every part of it except his hat. He wore a soft French beaver, with rather a wide brim and a towering crown, which was always pushed up high. My sister would sometimes take it slyly just before he was

Whitman's brother, Thomas Jefferson Whitman (by permission of the Missouri Historical Society)

ready to go, flatten the crown, and fix it more in accordance with the shape worn by others. All in vain; invariably on taking it up his fist would be thrust inside, and it would speedily assume its original dimensions.

One day, in 1858, I think, he came to see us, and after talking awhile on various matters, he announced, a little diffidently I thought, that he had written a new piece. In answer to our inquiries, he said it was about a mocking bird, and was founded on a real incident. My mother suggested that he bring it over and read to us, which he promised to do. In some doubt, in spite of this assurance, we were, therefore, agreeably surprised when a few days after he appeared with the manuscript of "Out of the Cradle Endlessly Rocking" in his pocket. At first he wanted one of us to read it. Mr. A. took it and read it through with great appreciation and feeling. He then asked my mother to read it, which she did. And finally, at our special request, he read it himself. That evening comes before me now as one of the most enjoyable of my life. At each reading fresh beauties revealed themselves to me. I could not say whose reading I preferred; he liked my mother's, and Mr. A. liked his. After the three readings were over, he asked each one of us what we would suggest in any way, and I can remember how taken aback and nonplussed I was when he turned and asked me also.

He once (I forget what we were talking about—friendship, I think) said there was a wonderful depth of meaning ("at second or third removes," as he called it) in the old tales of mythology. In that of Cupid and Psyche, for instance; it meant to him that the ardent expression in words of affection often tended to destroy affection. It was like the golden fruit which turned to ashes upon being grasped, or even touched. As an illustration, he mentioned the case of a young man he was in the habit of meeting every morning where he went to work. He said there had grown up between them a delightful silent friendship and sympathy. But one morning when he went as usual to the office, the young man came forward, shook him violently by the hand, and expressed in heated language the affection he felt for him. Mr. Whitman said that all the subtle charm of their unspoken friendship was from that time gone.

He was always an ardent lover of music, and heard all the operas, oratorios, bands, and all the great singers who visited New York during those years. I heard him very frequently speak of Grisi, Mario, Sontag, La Grange, Jenny Lind, Alboni, Bosio, Truffi, Bettini, Marini, Badiali, Mrs. Wood, Mrs. Seguin; and I was never tired of listening to his accounts of them. Alboni he considered by far the greatest of them all, both as regards voice and emotional and artistic power. If I remember rightly, he told me that during her engagement in the city he went to hear her twenty nights. Brignoli in his prime he thought superior to Mario. Bettini, however, was his favorite tenor, and Badiali, the baritone, was another favorite. In talking to him once about music I found he had read George Sand's "Consuelo," and enjoyed it thoroughly. One passage he liked best was where Consuelo sings in church at the very beginning of her musical career. He said he had read it over many times. I remember hearing him mention other books of George Sand's, "the Journeyman Joiner" and the "Devil's Pool," which he liked much.

But although he talked of music and books with me, and of politics, patriotism, and the news of the day with Mr. A., it was in talking with my mother on the spiritual nature of man, and on the reforms of the age and kindred themes, that he took special delight. These appeared to be his favorite topics, and she, having similar sympathies and tastes, would take an equal pleasure with himself in discussing them. It was the society of my mother that was certainly Walt Whitman's greatest attraction to our house. She had a nature in many respects akin to his own—a broad, comprehensive mind, which enabled her to look beyond and through externals into the essence of things—a large, generous spirit in judging whoever she came in contact with, always recognizing the good and ignoring the evil—a strong deep faith in an infinite overruling goodness and power, and a most tender and loving heart. How many times has she taken in outcasts who have come to our door, and treated them to the best the house afforded, regardless of dirt, disease, everything but their humanity and suffering. How many times (not always however) has she been most wofully deceived and drawn into much trouble thereby. It makes no difference, the next one that came would be treated with the same hospitality in spite of all remonstrance and argument. She has gone to that unknown world she was so fond of speculating upon, and never will the memory of her unselfish life, her exceeding love and charity, fade from the hearts of her children and friends. It was in her friendship, and in this *women's circle*—a mother and two daughters—that Mr. Whitman passed not a few of his leisure hours during all those years.

Walt Whitman, the most intuitive man I ever knew, had the least regard for mere verbal smartness. When seeing him listening with bent head to Mr. A.'s arguments upon some point on which they radically differed, I have often been reminded of that passage in his book,

> Logic and sermons never convince;
> The damp of the night drives deeper in my soul.

While admitting and appreciating the force of reason and logic, yet if they were in conflict with what he *felt* in the depths of his soul to be true, he would hold fast to the latter, even though he could give no satisfactory reason for so doing. Though he would himself pooh-pooh the assumption, I have no doubt also he had spells of singular abstraction and exaltation. I remember hearing my mother describe an interview she once had with him while we were living in Brooklyn during the early years of our acquaintance. Death was the subject of their conversation. For a few minutes, she said, his face wore an expression she had never seen before—he seemed rapt, absorbed. In describing it afterward, she said he appeared like a man in a trance. Is not this a clue to many pages of *Leaves of Grass?* It would almost seem that in writing his poems he was taken possession of by a force, genius, inspiration, or whatever it may be called, that he was powerless to resist. We all felt this strange power on first reading his book, and that his poetry both was and was not part of himself. So that (as sometimes happened afterward) when he would say things at variance with what he had written, Mr. A. would remark to him, half jokingly, "Why, Walt, you ought to read *Leaves of Grass*." After the interview I have just described, my mother always felt that she had seen him in the state in which many of the earlier poems were conceived.

29

I never took notes of his conversations, and can only recall the general impression they made upon me. I can remember an occasional expression or opinion, but nothing of any importance. My brother and I were starting out one morning to choose a parlor carpet. Hearing of our errand he said, "What a good idea it would be to have the pattern of a carpet designed of leaves—nothing but leaves—all sizes, shapes, and colors, like the ground under the trees in autumn."

I met him once in the Brooklyn street cars, soon after an article appeared in the "the Radical" entitled "A Woman's Estimate of Walt Whitman." He asked if I had read it. I answered that I had, and that I should think he would like to know the lady who wrote it. "No," he said, "that does not so much matter. I do not even know her name." After a pause, he added, "But it was a great comfort to me."

If I were asked what I considered Walt Whitman's leading characteristic, I should say—and it is an opinion formed upon an acquaintance of over twenty years—his *religious sentiment* or feeling. It pervades and dominates his life, and I think no one could be in his presence any length of time without being impressed by it. He is a born *exaltét*. His is not that religion, or show of it, that is comprised in dogmas, churches, creeds, etc. These are of little or no consequence to him, but it is that habitual state of feeling in which the person regards everything in God's universe with wonder, reverence, perfect acceptance, and love. He has more of all this than any one I have ever met. The deeply earnest spirit with which he looks upon humanity and life is so utterly opposed to cynicism and persiflage, that these always chill and repel him. He himself laughs at nothing (in a contemptuous sense), looks down on nothing—on the contrary everything is beautiful and wonderful to him.

One day I called upon his mother in Brooklyn and found him there. When I was going home he said he would cross the ferry with me. On our journey we had to pass through one of the great markets of New York in order to reach the cars running to the upper part of the city. I was hurrying through, according to my usual custom, but he kept constantly stopping me to point out the beautiful combinations of color at the butchers' stalls, and other stands; but above all the fish excited in him quite an enthusiasm. He made me admire their beautiful shapes and delicate tints, and I learned from him that day a lesson I have never forgotten.

One evening in 1866, while he was stopping with us in New York, the tea bell had been rung ten minutes or more when he came down from his room, and we all gathered around a table. I remarked him as he entered the room; there seemed to be a peculiar brightness and elation about him, an almost irrepressible joyousness, which shone from his face and seemed to pervade his whole body. It was the more noticeable as his ordinary mood was one of quiet, yet cheerful serenity. I knew he had been working at a new edition of his book, and I hoped if he had an opportunity he would say something to let us into the secret of his mysterious joy. Unfortunately most of those at the table were occupied with some subject of conversation; at every pause I waited eagerly for him to speak; but no, some one else would begin again, until I grew almost wild with impatience and vexation. He appeared to listen, and would even laugh at some of the remarks that were made, yet he did not utter a single word during the meal; and his face still wore that singular brightness and delight, as though he had partaken of some divine elixir. His expression was so remarkable that I might have doubted my own observation, had it not been noticed by another as well as myself.

I never heard him allude directly but once to what has been so severely condemned in his books. It happened in this way. He had come on from Washington and was stopping with us at that time (it was in 1866), preparing the new edition of *Leaves of Grass* just spoken of. My mother and I were busy sewing in the sitting-room when he came back from a two hours' absence and threw himself on the lounge. He said he had been offered very favorable terms by a publisher down town (we were living in the upper part of New York at that time) if he would consent to leave out a few lines from two of his pieces. "But I dare not do it," he said; "I dare not leave out or alter what is so genuine, so indispensable, so lofty, so pure." Those were his exact words. The intense, I might almost say religious, earnestness with which they were uttered made an impression upon me that I shall never forget.

Here is another authentic personal account of those years—say from 1854 to '60—taken from the New York "World" of June 4th, 1882, and written by Thomas A. Gere.

Thirty years ago, while employed upon an East River steamboat, I became acquainted with Walt Whitman, and the association has ever since been a treasured one by myself and the rest of my companion boatmen. He came among us simply as a sociable passenger, but his genial behavior soon made him a most welcome visitor. We knew somewhat of his reputation as a man of letters, but the fact made no great impression on us, nor did he ever attempt a display of his gifts or learning that would in the least make us feel he was not "of us, and one of us," as he used to express it. In a charmingly practical democratic manner he took great pains to teach many valuable things to a hard-handed band of men whose life had afforded little time for books. In later years I have realized that "Walt"—he would allow no other salutation from us—has done much gratuitous work

Whitman's schoolhouse in Woodbury, Long Island

as a teacher, and in looking back I also realize his excellence as an instructor. A careful choice of words and terse method of explaining a subject were truly peculiar to him—at least the faculty was marvellous to us. In our long watches—he would pass entire afternoons and even nights with us—he would discourse in a clear, conversational sort of way upon politics, literature, art, music or the drama, from a seemingly endless storing of knowledge. He certainly urged some of us into a desire for attainments that perhaps would not otherwise have been aroused.

"My boy," he would often say, after simply but eloquently treating some theme, "you must read more of this for yourself," and then generously put his library at the listener's service. I have seen a youth swabbing a steamboat's deck with Walt's Homer in his monkey-jacket pocket! At all times he was keenly inquisitive in matters that belonged to the river or boat. He had to have a reason for the actions of the pilot, engineer, fireman and even deck-hands. Besides, he would learn the details of everything on board, from the knotted end of a bucket-rope to the construction of the engine. "Tell me all about it, boys," he would say, "for these are the real things I cannot get out of books." I am inclined to think that such inquisitiveness must always have been an industrious habit with him, for his writings abound with apt technicalities.

Walt's appearance used to attract great attention from the passengers when he came on board the boat. He was quite six feet in height, with the frame of a gladiator, a flowing gray beard mingled with the hairs on his broad slightly bared chest. In his well-laundried checked shirt-sleeves, with trousers frequently pushed into his boot-legs, his fine head covered with an immense slouched black or light felt hat, he would walk about with a naturally majestic stride, a massive model of ease and independence. I hardly think his style of dress in those days was meant to be eccentric; he was very antagonistic to all show or sham, and I fancy he merely attired himself in what was handy, clean, economical and comfortable. His marked appearance, however, obtained for him a variety of callings in the minds of passengers who did not know him. "Is he a retired sea captain?" some would ask; "an actor? a military officer? a clergyman? Had he been a smuggler, or in the slave trade?" To amuse Walt I frequently repeated these odd speculations upon him. He laughed until the tears ran when I told him that a very confidential observer had assured me he was crazy!

What enjoyable nights there were when Walt would come to us after a long study at home or in some prominent New York library! He would, indeed, "loaf" and unbend to our great delight with rich, witty anecdotes and pleasant sarcasms upon some events and men of the day. At times he would be joined by some literary acquaintance, generally to our disgust, or perhaps I should say jealousy, for we fancied that in some way we rather owned Walt; but the long classical debates that would occur, and deep subjects that would be dug up, used to waste the night in a most exasperating degree.

Walt's musical ability was a very entertaining quality: he was devotedly fond of opera, and many were the pleasant scraps and airs with which he would enliven us in a round, manly voice, when passengers were few and those few likely to be asleep on the seats: Our best attention was given to his recitations. In my judgment few could excel his reading of stirring poems and brilliant Shakesperian passages. These things he vented evidently for his own practice or amusement. I have heard him proceed to a length of some soliloquy in "Hamlet," "Lear," "Coriolanus" and "Macbeth," and when he stopped suddenly and said with intense dissatisfaction, "No! no! no! that's the way bad actors would do it," he would start off again and recite the part most impressively.

It is believed and asserted that his works will yet rise to meritorious eminence. Of this I do not feel competent to speak. I did not know him as the "Gray-Maned Lion of Camden," or "America's Good Gray Poet," but simply as dear old Walt.

T. A. G.

Here also is a paragraph from the New York "Tribune," by G. S. McWatters, summer of 1880:

While walking in the neighborhood of New Rochelle, Westchester County, a few days ago, I observed a man at work in a field adjoining the road, and I opened a conversation with him. He had served in the Union Army during the Rebellion, and I had no trouble in inducing him to fight some of his battles over again. He gave me a graphic description of how he was badly wounded in the leg; how the doctors resolved to cut his leg off; his resistance to the proposed amputation, and his utter despair when he found he must lose his leg (as they said) to save his life. As a last resort, he determined to appeal to a man who visited the hospital about every alternate day. This man was a representative of the Sanitary Commission [this of course is a mistake], and he described him as a tall, well-built man with the face of an angel. He carried over his broad shoulders a well-filled haversack, containing about everything that would give a sick soldier comfort. In it were pens, ink and paper, thread, needles, buttons, cakes, candy, fruit, and above all, pipes and tobacco. This last article was in great demand. When he asked a poor fellow if he used tobacco and the answer was "no" he would express some kind words of commendation, but when the answer was "yes," he would produce a piece of plug and smilingly say, "Take it my brave boy, and enjoy it." He wrote letters for those who were not able to write, and to those who could he would furnish the materials, and never forgot the postage stamp. His good-natured and sympathetic inquiry about their health and what changes had taken place since he last saw them, impressed every patient with the feeling that he was their personal friend. To this man Rafferty (that was my informant's name) made his last appeal to save his shattered leg. He was listened to with attention, a minute inquiry into his case, a pause, and after a few moments' thought the man replied, patting him on the head, "May your mind rest easy, my boy; they shan't take it off." Rafferty began to describe his feelings when he received this assurance, and though so many years have passed since then, his emotions mastered him, his voice trembled and thickened, his eyes filled with tears, he stopped for a moment and then blurted out, slapping his leg with his hand, "This is the leg that man saved for me." I asked the name of the Good Samaritan. He said he thought it was Whitcomb or something like that. I suggested it was just like Walt Whitman. The name seemed to rouse the old soldier within him; he did not wait for another word from me, but seized my hand in both of his, and cried, "That's the man, that's the name; do you know him?"

WHITMAN IN HIS OWN TIME

Chapter III.
HIS CONVERSATION.

He did not talk much. Sometimes, while remaining cheery and good-natured, he would speak very little all day. His conversation, when he did talk, was at all times easy and unconstrained. I never knew him to argue or dispute, and he never spoke about money. He always justified, sometimes playfully, sometimes quite seriously, those who spoke harshly of himself or his writings, and I often thought he even took pleasure in those sharp criticisms, slanders, and the opposition of enemies. He said that his critics were quite right, that behind what his friends saw he was not at all what he seemed, and that from the point of view of its foes, his book deserved all the hard things they could say of it—and that he himself undoubtedly deserved them and plenty more.

When I first knew Walt Whitman I used to think that he watched himself, and did not allow his tongue to give expression to feelings of fretfulness, antipathy, complaint, and remonstrance. It did not occur to me as possible that these mental states could be absent in him. After long observation, however, and talking to others who had known him many years, I satisfied myself that such absence or unconsciousness was entirely real.

His deep, clear, and earnest voice makes a good part, though not all, of the charm of the simplest things he says; a voice not characteristic of any special nationality, accent, or dialect. If he said (as he sometimes would involuntarily on stepping to the door and looking out) "Oh, the beautiful sky!" or "Oh, the beautiful grass!" the words produced the effect of sweet music.

One evening he spoke quite freely of his British friends, Professor Dowden, Addington Symonds, Tennyson (who had sent him a letter warmly inviting him over there to T.'s house), Professor Clifford, and other and younger ones. I remember his glowing words of esteem and affection for Mrs. Gilchrist, and also for Robert Buchanan (whose denunciations and scathing appeal in the London papers at the time of the poet's darkest persecution, sickness, and poverty, made such a flutter in 1876).[1]

He said one day when talking about some fine scenery, and the desire to go and see it (and he himself was very fond of new scenery), "After all, the great lesson is that no special natural sights, not

35

Walt Whitman, early 1840s

Alps, Niagara, Yosemite, or anything else, is more grand or more beautiful than the ordinary sunrise and sunset, earth and sky, the common trees and grass." Properly understood, I believe this suggests the central teaching of his writings and life, namely, that the commonplace is the grandest of all things; that the exceptional in any line is not finer, better, or more beautiful than the usual, and that what is really wanting is not that we should possess something we have not at present, but that our eyes should be opened to see and our hearts to feel what we all have.

On the evening of the 1st of August, 1880, as we were sitting together on the veranda of the "Hub House," among the Thousand Islands of the St. Lawrence, I said to Walt Whitman, "It seems to me surprising that you never married. Did you remain single of set purpose?" He said, "No, I have hardly done anything in my life of set purpose, in the way you mean." After a minute, he added, "I suppose the chief reason why I never married must have been an overmastering passion for entire freedom, unconstraint; I had an instinct against forming ties that would bind me." I said, "Yes, it was the instinct of self-preservation. Had you married at the usual age, *Leaves of Grass* would never have been written."

The same evening we talked about the use of alcohol, and we agreed that as mankind advanced in a noble individuality they would give up stimulants of all kinds as being always in the long run a mistake and unprofitable. He said, "The capital argument against alcohol, that which must eventually condemn its use, is this, that it takes away all the reserved control, the power of mastership, and therefore offends against that splendid pride in himself or herself which is fundamental in every man or woman worth anything."

One day talking about religious experiences, Walt Whitman said, "I never had any particular religious experiences—never felt that I needed to be saved—never felt the need of spiritual regeneration—never had any fear of hell, or distrust of the schemes of the universe. I always felt that it was perfectly right and for the best."

On the 9th of August we were together at the Falls of Montmorenci, near the foot of the stairs. There had been a good deal of rain, the river was high, and the falls finer than usual. I said, "Now, Walt, put that in a poem just as it is; if that could be done it would be magnificent." He said, "All such things need at least the third or fourth remove; in itself it would be too much for nine out of every ten readers. Very few (he said, a little mischievously, perhaps), care for natural objects themselves, rocks, rain, hail, wild animals, tangled forests, weeds, mud, common Nature. They want her in a shape fit for reading about in a rocking-chair, or as ornaments in china, marble, or bronze. The real things are, far more than they would own, disgusting, revolting to them. This (he added, half quizzically) may be a reason of the dislike of *Leaves of Grass* by the majority."

Walt Whitman, however, never mentions *Leaves of Grass*, unless first spoken to on the subject; then he talks about it, and his purpose in writing it, as of an ordinary matter. I have never heard him myself say much on the subject, but I will give here some of his words taken from the "Springfield Republican," reported, I have reason to know, as they were said impromptu:

"Well, I'll suggest to you what my poems have grown out of, since you want to know so bad. I understand as well as any one they are ambitious and egotistical, but I hope the foundations are far deeper. We have to-day no songs, no expressions from the poets' and artists' points of view, of science, of American democracy, and of the modern. The typical war spirit of the antique world, and its heroes and leaders, have been full depicted and preserved in Homer, and since. Rapt ecstasy and Oriental veneration are in the Bible; the literature of those qualities will never, can never, ascend any higher. The ages of feudalism and European chivalry, through their results and personalities, are in Shakespeare. But where is the work, where the poem, in which the entirely different but fully equal glories and practice of our own democratic times, of the scientific, the materialistic, are held in solution, fused in human personality and emotions, and fully expressed? If, for instance, by some vast instantaneous convulsion, American civilization were lost, where is the poem, or imaginative work in any department, which, if saved from the wreck, would preserve the characteristics and memories of it to succeeding worlds of men?"

"You speak of Shakespeare and the relative poetical demands and opportunities, then and now—my own included. Shakespeare had his boundless rich materials, all his types and characters, the main threads of his plots, fully ripened and waiting to be woven in. The feudal world had flourished for centuries—gave him the perfect king, the lord, all that is heroic and graceful and proud—gave him the exquisite transfigurations of caste, sifted and selected out of the huge masses, as if for him, choice specimens of proved and noble gentlemen, varied and romantic incidents of the military, social, political and ecclesiastical history of a thousand years, all ready to fall into his plots and pages. Then the time comes for the evening of feudalism. A new power has advanced, and the flush, the pomp, the accumulated materials of those ages take on the complex gorgeousness of sunset. At this point Shakespeare appears. By amazing opportuneness, his faculty, his power, the feudalistic demands on him, combine, and he is their poet. But for my poems, what have I? I have all to *make*—have really to fashion all, except my own intentions—have to constructively sing the ideal yet unformed America. Shakespeare sang the past, the formed; I project the unformed, the future—depend on the future, and have to make my own audience."

"Most of the great poets are impersonal; I am personal. They portray their endless characters, events, passions, love-plots, but seldom or never mention themselves. In my poems all concentrates in, radiates from, revolves around myself. I have but one central figure, the general human personality typified in myself. Only I am sure my book inevitably necessitates that its reader transpose him or herself into that central position, and become the actor, experience, himself or herself, of every page, every aspiration, every line."

In our family groups and sociable company, he was fond of telling little funny stories, bringing in comical sayings, generally trivial in themselves (sometimes quite venerable), deriving most of their charm—and they were very amusing—from special aptness to the case, and from his manner of telling them. In St. Louis, where he was a half invalid, one winter, he was in the habit of visiting, twice a week, the kindergarten schools, and spending an hour at a time among the young children, who gathered in swarms about him to listen to "The three Cats who took a Walk," or some other juvenile story. Lingering with us all at the table after tea was a favorite recreation with him. The following are some examples of his dry anecdotes, generally told to groups of little or larger children:

> There was a very courageous but simple old woman, and some chaps agreed upon a plan to frighten her. One of them dressed up in black, with horns and tail, and made himself very frightful. In this rig he appeared to the old woman at night and said in a terrible voice, "Look at me!" The old lady calmly put on her spectacles, looked him steadily all over and said, "Who are you?" "I am the devil!" said he, in a deep voice. "You the devil, are you?" said the old woman composedly; then calmly, after a pause—"*poor creetur!*"

He was fond of the well-known story about a sailor shipwrecked upon a strange coast, who wandering inland after a long jaunt saw a gibbet holding a murderer's corpse, and immediately burst out, "Thank God, at last I am in a Christian land."

A dry expression of his, talking about some one was, "Well he has the good sense to like me." He used to tell about some man who said, when it was alleged that a certain fact was historical, "Oh, it's in the history is it? then I *know* it must be a lie." He would often

39

give the following as "the wise Frenchman's reason": "Do you say it is impossible? then I am sure it will come to pass."

One day he said: "Among the gloomy and terrible sights of the Secession War were often extremely humorous occurrences. It was a sort of rule in many hospitals when certain that a patient would die, to give him almost whatever he wanted to eat or drink. Under these circumstances some of the men would ask for whisky, and drink it freely. One man, a rough Westerner, whose life was limited to a few hours, used to wake up in the night and call out to the watchman, 'Come, Bill, give me some whisky; you know we are going to die. Come, give me some whisky, quick!'"

He had many dry idioms from his old intimacy with omnibus drivers in New York and other cities. (He always "took to them" and they to him—and the same to this day; at Christmas, in Washington, Philadelphia, Camden, or where residing at the time, he has for years a custom of dispensing to these drivers, on quite a large scale, presents of the strong warm buckskin gloves so serviceable in that occupation). One little story was of an old Broadway driver, who, being interrogated about a certain unpopular new-comer, answered with a grin, "Oh, he's one o' them pie-eaters from Connecticut."

Walt Whitman was so invariably courteous and kind in his manner to every one, it might have been thought he could have easily been bored and imposed upon, but this was not at all the case. He had so much tact that he always found a way of escape. He had a horror of smart talkers, and particularly of being questioned or interrogated. He had a very dry manner of dismissing intruders, or correcting those who went too far—not surly, but a peculiar tone of the voice, and glance of the eye, and sometimes a good-natured anecdote. A gentleman said to him one evening at tea-time, "I should not think, Mr. Whitman, that you were at all an emotional man." "Well," he replied drily, "there is an old farmer down in Jersey, who says nothing, but keeps up a devil of a thinking; and there are others like him."

He once told me he had read a good many different translations of Homer, and that the one he liked best, after all, was Buckley's literal prose version. He did not care for either Lord Derby's or Bryant's. I was reading the "Iliad" one day as we sat on the veranda together, and I made some remark to the effect that it was praised on account of its age and scholarly associations rather

40

Whitman's house at 106 Myrtle Street in Brooklyn

than its intrinsic merit, and that if it was first published now, no one would care anything about it. "Well," he said, "perhaps not, but not for the reason you say. See," he said—the subject seemed to inspirit him, for he rose and walked slowly up and down, leaning on his cane, occasionally pausing—"See how broadly and simply it opens. An old priest comes, oppressed with grief, to the sea-shore. The beach stretches far away and the waves roll sounding in. The old man calls his divine master, Apollo, not to permit the foul insults and injuries put upon him by the leader of the Greeks. Almost at once in the distance an immense shadowy form, tall as a tree, comes striding over the mountains. On his back he carries a quiver of arrows, and his long silver bow. Just think of it," he said, "so daring, so unlike the cultivated prettiness of our poets—so grim, free, large. No, no," he continued, "don't make light of the 'Iliad.' Think how hard it is for a modern, one of us, to put himself in sympathy with those old Greeks, with their associations." These are the words that he used, but to see them in print will convey only a faint impression

41

of their effect, or of the man as he said them—the manner, the deep, rich melody of the finest voice I believe in the world.

He thinks much of Dr. John A. Carlyle's translation of Dante's "Inferno," has had the volume by him for many years, reads in it often, and told me he had learned very much from it, especially in conciseness—"no surplus flesh," as he describes it.

He said very deliberately to me once that he believed he knew less, in certain respects, about *Leaves of Grass* than some of the readers of it; and I believe (strange as it may seem) that this is true. There are things in the book I am sure could never be fully appreciated from the author's point of view.

He said one day that he considered the most distinguishing feature of his poetry to be "Its *modernness*—the taking up in their own spirit of all that specially differentiates our era from others, particularly our democratic tendencies."

Another time he said:

"The unspoken meaning of *Leaves of Grass*, never absent, yet not told out—the indefinable animus behind every page, is a main part of the book. Something entirely outside of literature, as hitherto written; outside of art in all departments. Takes hold of muscular democratic virilities without wincing, and puts them in verse. This makes it distasteful to technical critics and readers. I understand those shrinking objections," he said, "and consider them in one sense right enough; but there was something for me to do, no matter how it hurt or offended; and I have done it."

He said further:

"I don't at all ignore the old stock elements and machinery of poetry, but instead of making them main things, I keep them away in the background, or like the roots of a flower or tree, out of sight. The emotional element, for instance, is not brought to the front, not put in words to any great extent, though it is underneath every page. I have made my poetry out of actual, practical life, such as is common to every man and woman, so that all have an equal share in it. The old poets went on the assumption that there was a selection needed. I make little or no selection, put in common things, tools, trades, all that can happen or belongs to mechanics, farmers, or the practical community. I have not put in the language of politics, but I have put in the spirit; and in science, by intention at least, the most advanced points are perpetually recognized and allowed for."

He said to me once, "I often have to be quite vehement with my friends to convince them that I am not (and don't want to be) singular, exceptional, or eminent. I am willing to think I represent vast averages, and the generic American masses—that I am their voice; but not that I should be in any sense considered an exception to ordinary men."

Another time he said, "I have always considered the writing and publication of *Leaves of Grass* as experiment. Time only can tell how it will turn out."

"Remember, the book arose," he said, another time, "out of my life in Brooklyn and New York from 1838 to 1853, absorbing a million people, for fifteen years, with an intimacy, and eagerness, an abandon, probably never equalled— land and water. I have told you how I used to spend many half nights with my friends the pilots on the Brooklyn ferry-boats. I sometimes took the wheel and steered, until one night a boat I was steering nearly met with a bad accident. After that I would not touch the wheel any more."

Walt Whitman and Rev. Mr. R. had a long conversation on the veranda one beautiful summer evening. Mr. R. wanted to get at the sources and birth of *Leaves of Grass* from its author. The latter spoke as he always does, without any *arrière pensée*. Among other things, he said he had tried to do something that would on the one hand give expression to deepest religious thought and feeling, and on the other be in accord with the last results of modern science. He said, "I do not know that I have succeeded, but at all events I have indicated what needs to be done—and some one else may accomplish the task."

Another day Mr. R. said, talking of Colonel Robert Ingersoll: "He takes away what we have, and gives us nothing in its place—is there any good or service in that?" He pressed Walt Whitman for an answer, to find out his opinion about Ingersoll's argument and about Christianity. Walt Whitman said at last: "Well, I think the main and final point about the whole or any of these things is—is it true?"

He several times spoke of President Lincoln, whom he considered the most markedly national, Western, native character the United States has yet produced. He never had any particular intimacy with Mr. Lincoln, but (being a personal friend of John Hay, confidential secretary) saw a good deal of L.—was much at the White House (1863 and '64), and knew the President's character behind the scenes. In after years he desired to keep the anniversary of Mr. Lincoln's death by a public lecture he had prepared (see *Specimen Days*), but he could get neither engagements, audiences, nor public interest,[2] and after delivering this lecture in 1879, '80, and '81, to small gatherings, he stopped it.

He said one Sunday morning after a previous merry evening: "God likes jokes and fun as well as He likes church-going and prayers." Once, after some conversation, he went on to speculate whether Luther was really as original and central a man as generally supposed, or whether circumstances ought not to be credited with a good deal that seemed to flow from him—and whether his Reformation was of such value to the world as most Protestants think. He talked of great men generally, and how their apparent greatness is often due to the force of circumstances—often because it is convenient for history to use them as radiating points and illustrations of vast currents of ideas floating in the time, more than to any qualities inherent in themselves—and ended by discussing Renan's opinion of the relative greatness of Jesus, Jesus son of Sirach, and Hillel.

One evening he said he wondered whether modern poets might not best take the same "new departure" that Lord Bacon took in science, and emerge directly from Nature and its laws, and from things and facts themselves, not from what is said about them, or the stereotyped fancies, or abstract ideas of the beautiful, at second or third removes.

He once said no one but a medical man could realize the appropriateness (jeered at by the "Saturday Review," as proof positive that W.W. was no poet,) of his putting in the word "diarrhœa" in one of his hospital poems; a malady that stood third on the deadly list of camp diseases. In the same connection, he said that several pieces in *Leaves of Grass* could only be thoroughly understood by a physician, the mother of a family of children, or a genuine nurse.

He never spoke deprecatingly of any nationality or class of men, or time in the world's history, or feudalism, or against any trades or occupations—not even against any animals, insects, plants, or inanimate things—nor any of the laws of Nature, or any of the results of those laws, such as illness, deformity, or death. He never complains or grumbles either at the weather, pain, illness, or at anything else. He never in conversation, in any company, or under circumstances, uses language that could be thought indelicate. (Of course, he has used language in his poems which has been thought indelicate, but none that is so.) In fact, I have never known of his uttering a word or a sentiment which might not be published without any prejudice to his fame. He never swears; he could not very well, since as far as I know, he never speaks in anger, and apparently never is angry. (I know that he himself will emphatically contradict me—that he will refuse to accept this, and a great many more of my outlines, as a true portrait of himself, but I prefer to draw and color for myself.) He never makes compliments—very seldom apologizes—uses the common forms of civility, such as "if you please," and "thank you," quite sparingly—usually makes a nod or a smile answer for them. He was, in my experience of him, not given to speculating on abstract questions (though I have heard others say that there were no subjects in which he so much delighted). He never gossips. He seldom talks about private people even to say something good of them, except to answer a question or remark, and then he always gives what he says a turn favorable to the person spoken of.

His conversation, speaking generally, is of current affairs, work of the day, political and historical news, European as well as American, a little of books, much of the aspects of Nature, as scenery, the stars, birds, flowers, and trees. He reads the newspapers regularly (I used to tell him that was the only vice he had); he likes good descriptions and reminiscences. He does not, on the whole, talk much anyhow. His manner is invariably calm and simple, belongs to itself alone, and could not be fully described or conveyed. As before told, he is fond of singing to himself snatches of songs from the operas or oratorios, often a simple strain of recitative, a sort of musical murmur,—and he sings in that way a large part of the time when he is alone, especially when he is outdoors. He spends most of his time outdoors when the weather permits, and as a general thing he does not stay in for rain or snow, but I think likes them in turn as well as the sunshine. He recites poetry often to himself as well as to others, and he recites well, very well. He never recites his own poetry (he does not seem to know any of it). Yet he sometimes reads it, when asked by some one he wants to gratify, and he reads it well. I do not know whether or not he can be said to sing well; but whether he does or not, his voice is so agreeable that it is always a pleasure to hear him.

From Richard Maurice Bucke, *Walt Whitman* (Philadelphia: David McKay, 1883), pp. 26-34, 37, 59-70.

1. He who wanders through the solitudes of far-off Uist or lonely Donegal may often behold the Golden Eagle sick to death, worn with age or famine, or with both, passing with weary waft of wing from promontory to promontory, from peak to peak, pursued by a crowd of prosperous rooks and crows, which fall screaming back whenever the noble bird turns his indignant head, and which follow frantically once more, hooting behind him, whenever he wends again upon his way. The rook is a "recognized" bird; the crow is perfectly "established." But for the Eagle, when he sails aloft in the splendor of his strength, who shall perfectly discern and measure his flight?—ROBERT BUCHANAN, *London Daily News*, March 13, 1876.

2. In one of the principal cities of the United States, the 15th anniversary of President Lincoln's death (April 15, 1880) was commemorated by this public address. The next morning the discriminating editor of the leading daily paper relegates all report of "the Death of Abraham Lincoln," as described and commented on by Walt Whitman, to a half-supercilious notice of five or six lines—and fills two columns of his journal with a lecture by a visiting English clergyman, on "the Evidential Value of the Acts of Apostles"!

WALT WHITMAN AT HOME

"Quilp" [George Johnston?]

A Visit to The Good Gray Poet of Camden

This interview, probably by George Johnston of Iowa, is typical of the "pilgrimage literature" that was to spring up and eulogize Whitman during his later years. Much as a generation visited Concord to meet Emerson, so did people go to Camden to "experience" Whitman.

Saturday, December 12th, 1885, was a bright sunshiny day, the memory of which will linger long in the mind of the writer, and to which he will look back with feelings of reverence and respect for the destiny which threw him in contact with the good white-haired poet of Camden, the world-renowned Walt Whitman; the poet par excellence of the nineteenth century, the exponent of the millennial splendors and harmonies which greeted the prophetic vision of Holy John in the Patmian Isle; the interpreter and expounder of that which is to be, when the latter day glories of modern civilization and development have been brought to perfection, and science and poetry and religion shall have been blended into an intellectual trinity, for the enlightenment and elevation of mankind; Walt Whitman, the hoary-headed poet and priest, who for a quarter of a century, in spite of the jeers and frowns of humanity, has kept bright the flame of the true poetic fire which he himself kindled in the long ago beneath the altar in the new temple, which he in early manhood dedicated to the worship of the phantasms that the next generation may see resolved into a sublime and glorious reality. We, for the writer was accompanied by a friend, found the old sage in a small frame tenement in one of the thoroughfares of Camden, N.J., where he has resided for some years. His house is not large, and is quite as unpretentious as the man himself. A few gentle taps brought his housekeeper, who is also maid of all work, to the door, and we were ushered into the presence of the friend of Lord Tennyson; the unknowable, the incomprehensible, the undefinable Walt Whitman. He occupied an easy chair in the northeast corner of the room, which was apparently about twelve by fourteen feet. His hair and beard, both of which were white as the driven snow and of great length, blended beautifully with the hair on a robe made of the hide of a prairie wolf, which covered the chair in which he sat, and differed little from it, except that some of the hair on the robe was slightly flecked with black. Indeed, the hair of the man was so much like the hair of the beast, that it was difficult to distinguish the one from the other; and his face, as he greeted us kindly and shook us warmly by the hand, would have seemed, had we been a little farther away from it, as the broad, bright sun shining through a halo of the thinnest vapor which its rays were powerless to dispel, but in doing so irradiated it with an unearthly glory, so bright and genial was the good-natured smile that played upon the old man's countenance, and so warm and captivating and magnetic were the glimpses we now and then caught of the inner part of the man that was hidden behind this strange exterior.

On the wall over the mantel-piece was suspended a portrait of one of the poet's ancestors, who came from Holland about a century and three-quarters ago. It was well preserved, and had as meek an expression of countenance as Moses may have been supposed to have had when he stood on the mountain top and looked across Jordan into the promised land, after the toils and trials of forty years in the wilderness. In the recesses on either side of the chimney were portraits of the poet's father and mother. They looked as if they might have been good-natured, mild-mannered people who were in love with nature and with themselves.

We didn't think of it at the time, but it appears to us since that there might have been just a little resemblance between the portrait of the poet's mother and the poet himself, but we are sure there was not much.

Scattered over the mantel-piece and the table and suspended on the walls were photographs of the poet's friends. They lay around loose, like snow flakes in winter time; sometimes they were piled up in drifts, and possibly some of them were on the floor. Of books there were many, and, like the pictures, they were scattered everywhere around the room; on the chairs, on the sofa, on the floor; most of them shut, but some of them open as if they sought

The Brooklyn Freeman, *which Whitman edited*

to drink in the wild, weird music of their owners' voice, and were trying to catch the words of wisdom that fell from his lips and made the little room where he dwelt an intellectual Mecca for the poets of all nations and all climes.

Shortly after we entered, two other visitors came into the room. They were young ladies just ready to bloom into early womanhood—pupils from Bryn Mawr College. They walked straight up to the venerable figure in the chair and, gently laying one arm on the old man's shoulder, reverently kissed his cheek.

Pretty soon the writer made an incidental remark about the growth of the new Philadelphia City Hall, and the old man remarked that he often gazed upon it from a distance, and it always seemed to him like the airy fabric of a vision, and even its unfinished tower as it pointed skyward was a shape of beauty, notwithstanding Gosse, the English poet, had said it was the ugliest thing he had seen in America.

After a casual remark by one of the young ladies which led the old man to say that it wasn't a nice thing to be a literary hack and write for people whenever they ask you, one of the girls rejoined, "But doesn't it make you feel good to think of what will come after

49

you?" This pointed question, which may be pardoned in consideration of the artless innocence and inexperience of the questioner, the
sage seemed to think demanded something more than a categorical answer, and he proceeded to make a deliverance upon the subject of
the implied implication of writing for posthumous fame, and in his curiously quaint and philosophical manner proceeded to say that no
great writer thought of the future, but wrote as the guiding spirit of
his inner manhood prompted him at the moment, without any regard to futurity, and that he didn't believe Shakespeare wrote the
half of the sonnets attributed to him, for the reason, as he seemed
to wish us to think, of their intense egotism. Continuing, he said,
"Some of the wilder or more daring of the poets, such, for instance,
as Hugo and Keats, may have written for futurity, but not so Tennyson; he wrote to please himself and his family, and accepted his lord-
ship for that reason. The trend of his early writings was radical, but
he had become conservative like Emerson, who left his pulpit and
evoluted from a priest into a philosopher. Whittier," he continued,
"is rather radical, but most of them are conservative as they should
be. Nature is conservative, but her power for breaking down the mysti-
cal is amply provided for. The reason is good, but there is something like Socrates' demon behind it. His demon did not command
him to do things, but not to do things; for instance, not to escape
from the death penalty. This," said the sage, "was the spirit which impelled me to write the 'Leaves of Grass,' wherein I have sought to em-
body the lessons it taught me." Just here the writer ventured to ask
if that wasn't the same idea expressed by Shakespeare when he says
there is a divinity which shapes our ends? "Yes," he replied, "possibly it may be," but, while his voice said yes, his manner of saying it
meant no, and we could not resist the conclusion that in the deepest recesses of his soul he referred to something grander, and higher, and
nobler, and better, than the divinity to which the immortal dramatist
referred. What it may have been we cannot tell, for the conversation
of the poet is as hard to comprehend as his poetry. His attempt to express his own opinion of the spirit which guided him, seemed like
the vain effort of a bird with broken pinion trying to rise and soar
heavenward. Frequently he hesitated and halted for a word, and
then his thoughts went back as it were along the pathway he had
trod to look for it, and while doing this he repeated himself and
went on, only to do the same thing again and again. It was like the fi-

nite attempting to grasp the infinite; it was mortality trying to express the immortal emotions and gorgeous conceptions that struggled for an outlet but failed to find it; but his conversation, with all its incomprehensibility, impressed the writer with a consciousness of his own insignificance, as compared with the gigantic intellect of the intellectual giant in whose presence he stood, and left a pervading sense of the indescribable pleasure like that produced by reading his poetry, the intellectual essence of which may be felt, but the effect of which cannot be described.

At the conclusion of the interview, which we have tried to describe, the young ladies took an affectionate leave of the venerable philosopher, one of them leaving the prints of her fresh young lips on his cheek, and the other taking the print of his lips which he impressed upon her cheek away with her.

There may be parts of Walt Whitman's poetry so incomprehensibly common, so deeply obscure, as to suggest the idea that they are immoral, but no one can see the author of them face to face and hear him talk, and not be convinced of the purity, the wisdom, and the goodness of the man. He that in the chilling midnight air and amid the falling dew on the bloody field of battle lay beside the wounded soldiers that the warmth of his body might warm them into life, and did it so frequently that he became a hopeless paralytic, can't have a bad heart; can't be amenable to the charge of intentional immorality.

Cecil Democrat [Iowa], 23 January 1886; text from Ernest J. Moyne, "Whitman and Folger McKinsey," *Delaware Notes*, 29th series (1956): 107-110.

A VISIT TO WALT WHITMAN

William Summers

Unlike the rapture of George Johnston's interview, Summers's discussion with Whitman about politics is relatively objective; yet it is clear that he is impressed by his subject.

It was on a clear, bright, sunny day in the month of September that I crossed by the ferry the Delaware river for the purpose of seeing for the first time in my life the "good, gray poet" Walt Whitman. Whitman is now seventy years of age—he was seventy on May 31 of the present year—and he is living in poverty and retirement at Camden, in the State of New Jersey, over against the Quaker city, Philadelphia. On reaching Camden I made inquiry of all and sundry as to which was the house of Walt Whitman, the poet. Nobody seemed to know anything either of the man or his works. "Does he live in Mickle-street?" I asked. "I don't know, but I dare say he does," was the only reply I could get. So true is it of the poet, as well as of the prophet, that he is not without honour save in his own country. However, after much fruitless search, I succeeded in finding the abode in which the poet dwells—a two-storied cottage, No. 328, in "long, unlovely" Mickle-street. Armed with a letter of introduction from an intimate acquaintance and friend of Whitman, I inquired whether it would be possible for me to see him. After a brief delay I was informed that the doctor forbade too much talking and excitement, but that the poet would be glad to see me for a short space of time. I was then ushered into his bedroom, where I found him seated amid a litter of books, manuscripts, and papers. He was dressed in a loose-fitting blue serge coat, and wore the large, soft drab hat with which those who are acquainted with the portrait in "Specimen Days and Collect" are familiar. His reception of me was most kind and cordial. Without any unnecessary delay, or any beating about the bush, he proceeded at once to talk with the utmost freedom and ease about himself and the world at large:—

52

"I am still very sick," he said. "For the last twenty years I have had attacks, what I call 'whacks,' of paralysis. In all I have had six of these 'whacks'; the others have lifted off after a while, but this is the most serious and obstinate of all: it has not lifted off yet, and does not seem like as if it would lift. My first attack came upon me when I was at Washington in one of the Government offices nearly twenty years ago. By the way, few people realize how near this country was to going to the devil twenty years back. What many people call slavery, and what, I suppose, even I call slavery, found much greater favour at the North, and especially in New York, than is usually believed. There was a sort of impalpable movement, an undercurrent, a subterranean something, which militated against the rapid triumph of Lincoln. I remember hearing Lincoln himself say, with much force and emphasis, how cautious he was obliged to be, because he had to contend with an enemy at the rear as well as with the enemy in front. I was myself in favour of the Union and the war, but I had friends at the South of whom I was fond, and whom I liked very well. I went first of all from Brooklyn to Washington to nurse some of my friends. I went as a sort of amateur volunteer. We have a phrase, 'on his own hook.' Well, I went just like that: I went 'on my own hook.' All around Washington there were towns, or rather clusters of hospitals, for the sick and wounded. At one time there would be as many as fifty or sixty thousand sick and wounded in that district. I remained there during the war, and I guess it was there that, as a consequence of the exposure and fatigue, I laid the seeds of my malady."

"I came originally," continued Whitman, "from Long Island. Paumanok, you know, is the old Indian name of the island. It was settled first by the Dutch, and then by the English. I was born here, at Huntingdon" (saying which Whitman drew with his stick a map of Long Island, and pointed out the relative positions of Huntingdon, Brooklyn, and New York). "From Long Island I went with my parents and settled at Brooklyn. I set up a paper of my own, and afterwards contributed to a larger newspaper. Well I continued to live there for many years; in fact, till I went to Washington at the time of the war. But I made journeys, excursions, detours. I went to New Orleans and lived there awhile, and afterwards returned to Brooklyn by way of the great Lakes, Michigan, Huron, Erie and the Niagara Falls. It is at the West, in the States that border, or rather edge,

Whitman in 1854

on the Mississippi, that the future of this country lies. The seaboard, Atlantic States retain English habits and traditions; it is at the West that the true America is to be found."

"But how are you getting on on your side?" asked Whitman, pulling himself up at this point, as if he were conscious that he had for the present done quite enough talking about himself. I answered his question as well as I was able, speaking hopefully of the prospect in the old country, but saying that the Irish difficulty was of course the great obstacle that lay in our path. For my part, I said, I thought Mr. Gladstone had got the root of the matter in him, as I could not for the life of me see why the Irish should not be permitted to manage their local affairs, as the thirty-eight States of the Union were permitted to manage theirs. "But," I continued, "I should like to hear your opinion. What do you think, Mr. Whitman? Are you able to follow our English politics?"—"No," he replied, "I am not able. I'm

54

'bluffed' just as much as you are. I don't think one way, and I don't think another way. I'm just puzzled. Some of my friends are very certain about it, but I am not certain. I can't say that I am sure Mr. Gladstone knows what he would be at. Let me see, what is the poet's phrase? It seems as if there was no 'leaf, herb, or medicine' that would cure Ireland's disease. However, if I were a young man as you are, I would certainly throw myself into the conflict on the side of the Irish. I have many kind friends who write to me from Ireland in favour of Mr. Gladstone's policy; and my wish, my desire, my animus, would certainly be on the side of the just, wise, brave, and sensible Irish people. Still, as I said, I am puzzled. It seems as if nothing would help Ireland at all. The country appears to be under a spell— an incantation. For the last thousand years or so no good appears to have come out of anything on Irish soil." "If that is the case, what is the reason?" I asked. "Is it the land, or the people, or the treatment to which the people have been subjected? You remember your own verses to 'Old Ireland'?"

Yet a word, ancient mother, You need crouch there no longer on the
    cold ground with forehead between your knees,
O you need not sit there veil'd in your old white hair so dishevell'd,
For know you the one you mourn is not in that grave.
It was an illusion; the son you love was not really dead.
The Lord is not dead; he is risen again young and strong in another
    country.
Even while you wept there by your fallen harp by the grave,
What you wept for was translated, pass'd from the grave.
The winds favour'd and the sea sail'd it,
And now with rosy and new blood, moves to-day in a new country.

"Do not the Irish prosper when they come to the new country?"
"Yes," said Whitman "That is so, especially in the matter of politics. Politics," he continued, with a merry twinkle in his eye, "politics in this country means getting anything from one to ten thousand a year, so that there is plenty of scope for the Irishman here. Politics with us, the same as with you, is in a very mixed and chaotic condition just now, but no doubt good will issue out of all this agitation and discussion and simmering of thought. With us the mugwump is the most promising element in politics, but it is afraid to speak out its whole mind quite fearlessly on all public questions. Many people

are afraid of the newspapers. Still, as I said, the mugwump element is the best we have got."

"I noticed, Mr. Whitman," I here interposed, "that you were writing when I came to see you."

"Yes," he said; "I was writing to a friend."

"Do you think you will be able to give us any more poems like these?" I asked, pointing to the volume of "Leaves of Grass" which I carried in my hand.

"I guess not," he replied, with a mixture of sadness and resignation.

I felt that I had trespassed quite long enough on the old man's time and attention, so with many thanks for his kindness, and with the expression of a hope that he might speedily recover from his affliction, I bade him a friendly adieu. It was with regret that I parted from him—his talk was so eloquent, so free, and so flowing, and there was withal an air of genius and distinction about him. He is, I should say, in some respects, fit to take rank with men like Victor Hugo and Thomas Carlyle, and is beyond question one of the most striking personalities and one of the most typical and representative characters that the great Republic of the West has hitherto produced.

Pall Mall Gazette, 18 October 1888, pp. 1-2.

WALT WHITMAN

C. Sadakichi Hartmann

Notes of a Conversation
with the Good Gray Poet
by a German Poet and Traveller.

OPINIONS ON MEN AND THINGS

The Ideas Expressed in Whitman's Books—
Criticisms of Bryant, Emerson, Holmes, Hawthorne, Lowell,
Stedman, Poe and Byron—
Bismarck, Washington and Lincoln—
Thoughts on Women and on Government

This somewhat bizarre and almost stenographic report may be more indicative of the interviewer than the interviewee. C. Sadakichi Hartmann later published Conversations with Walt Whitman *(1895), a book of dubious accuracy.*

One cannot say much about women. The best ones study Greek or criticise Byron—they are no women.

The Greek nation is the most remarkable one, after all.

I excuse a great deal of tyranny, even cruelty in the government of a nation.

There is a certain idea in my works—to glorify industry, nature and pure instinct.

The American nation is not much at present, but will be some day the most glorious one on earth. We are now tuning the instruments, afterward comes the music.

The old countries have also their destiny; there is no such thing as decay.

There is no worse devil than man.

Choice literature, I think, is empirical.

57

Taine's English Literature is one of the productions of our age. Man is like a star, every one standing for himself.

I always remember that my ancestors were Dutch.

Sensuality I have done with. I have thrown it out, but it is natural, even a necessity.

I can hardly say that I had ever the idea to better mankind. I grew like a tree and the poems like fruit.

Bryant and Other Writers.

Bryant! He is our greatest poet. He has a smack of Americanism, American individuality, a smack of outdoor life, the wash of the sea, the mountains, forests and animals. But he is too melancholy for a great representative of American poetry.

Emerson's deficiency is that he doubts everything. He is a deep thinker, though he had hardly any influence on me; but people say so, may be, without any knowledge. He has much of the Persians and Oriental people. He is only the offspring of other suns tumbling through the universe.

Men should do as they please. Nobody has the right to interfere with another man's business, religion or habit. This I have said to Ingersoll.

Our time? We must settle a little more. But there seems to be a demand for this hurly burly time.

Poe has a tendency for the gloomy side of life.

About Hawthorne I have nothing particular to say. The multitude likes him. I have read his novels. In my opinion they do not amount to much. His works are languid, melancholy, morbid. He likes to dwell on crime, on the sufferings of the human heart, which he analyzes by far too much.

Byron became bitter through the ups and downs of his career, his life—especially the downs. A desperate fierceness is predominant in his works. But I like something more free—Homer, Shakespeare, Walter Scott, Emerson.

Bismarck and Washington

Bismarck's work of life is to make Germany strong and powerful.

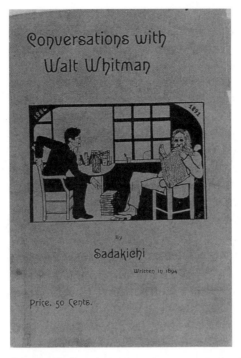

Front cover of C. Sadakichi Hartmann's Conversations with Walt Whitman *(1895)*

It doesn't matter much who is there in Washington. Certainly, they must have one and I think Harrison tries to do his best. He is sufficient.

Lincoln was our greatest man. I sometimes ask myself what would have become of us if he hadn't been President during those terrible years 1862-65.

The theory of our government is to give to every man the freedom of his activity—to work, study, electrify.

Our literature will come! The newspapers indicate it, miserable as they are. Miserable and grand, too, as they are.

If the common consent of people think churches a necessity, then they ought to be.

Everybody who reads novels not for mere pleasure will admire Walter Scott. He had a Shakespearian variety of subjects. He did not analyze and anatomize his characters.

George Washington had the power of organization, the ability to identify the power of the State. He was an Englishman, an English Franklin, wealthy, well educated, with high morals.

To write the life of a human being takes many a book, and after all the story is not told.

Holmes and Others.

O. W. Holmes! Very witty, very smart, not first rank and not second rank; man of fine culture, who knows how to move in society; he takes the same place in modern society as the court singer and troubadours in the Middle Ages, who had a taste for castles, ladies, festivals, &c., who knew exactly how to move among kings and princes, but something was failing, that very thing that had made him a poet.

J. R. Lowell, cute, elegant, well dressed; somewhat of a Yankee; student, college.

Paul Hayne, I don't know much about him; quite a poet, genteel, &c.; nothing dazzling.

Some persons think they are poets if they have a feeling for jewels, paste gems, feathers, birds, flowers, perfume, &c. In a barbaric country among uncivilized people they would deserve some praise, but not in our time, when everybody can imagine these things.

Whittier was a strong poet, the favorite of Horace Greeley—as good and powerful in his old days as in his young. Much earnestness and fierceness bends all his Quaker peace.

Stoddard is fair, but many are like him.

In Denver I would like to live.

Never forget to study the old, grand poets, but do not imitate them. We want something which pays reverence to our time.

In New York, Boston, &c., they eat their bread and beef and digest it for the Western world, but in the Valley of the Mississippi is quite another life.

I am no worshipper of beauty. I think there is not such a thing as abstract beauty.

Stedman is, after all, nothing but a sophisticated dancing master. If Hercules or Apollo himself would make their appearance he would look at them only from the standpoint of a dancing master.

If anything has a destiny the English language has a destiny. In my books, in my prose as well as my poetry, are many knots to untie.

"Leaves of Grass" are the reflections of American life and ideas which reflect again.

Rousseau I have never read, of Voltaire now and then a quotation.

I don't know why some men compare my book with the Bible.

Verdi, I think, is one of the best musicians; he is a storm with the intention of being a real storm. Mendelssohn is my favorite. I always like to hear him. Music is the only art where we get something.

I live very economically, but you don't know what support I get of my friends; besides I write for the magazines and get well paid. The state of my affairs is at present very bright. Why should I trouble myself. I have only a few years more to live.

New York Herald, 14 April 1889, p. 10.

WHITMAN'S REMINISCENCES

Anonymous

The Old Poet Talks Entertainingly—
His Contempt for Harrison

As Whitman became older, reporters from Philadelphia and New York regularly dropped by to hear his opinions on current literature and political events. This interview, first published in the Philadelphia Times, *is typical of such reports.*

Walt Whitman, who was seventy-one years old on May 31, was found yesterday sitting at the window of his two-story cottage in Camden, 329 Mickle Street, in a comfortable old armchair presented to him by the son and daughter of Tom Donaldson of the Smithsonian Institution.

When the good gray poet was asked about his health, he cheerily replied: "I feel these sudden changes of the weather, but, God be praised, I am feeling bright and cheerful, and am blessed with a good appetite and a reasonably good digestion, and what more can an old man ask who, as the Methodists say, is still on 'praying ground and pleading terms?' "

"Every fine day I have my stalwart attendant wheel me out, often to the Federal Street Ferry, where, sitting on the long wharf, I enjoy the mellow light of the sinking sun, and the pleasant sight of the eager crowd hurrying off and on the ferryboats."

Mr. Whitman was asked what foundation there was for the statement contained in Woodbury's recent "Life of Ralph Waldo Emerson" that the Concord philosopher had described an interview with the old poet at the Astor House in New York at which Mr. Whitman appeared without any coat. He said: "I think it was Sam Bowles, the father of the present editor of the Springfield *Republican*, who said, when offered an astounding piece of pretended news: 'Thanks, but we employ an able-bodied liar of our own.' I would not for an instant say that Mr. Woodbury was a falsifier, but do say that in that statement he makes with so much verisimilitude that this biographer of the great sage of Concord is conspiciously intact and the author has been imposed upon."

"To be plain and explicit, which is the thing you newspaper men demand, I never called on Mr. Emerson without a coat, which would certainly have been, at least, seemingly disrespectful to the sweet-tempered and gracious old man. We were always on the best of terms, and I well remember his kindly but earnest invitation to come to his home at Concord, and how I enjoyed every moment of the two days I spent there; how sitting before a fire of hickory logs in his well-appointed study, surrounded by countless books, he told me many interesting incidents in his life, many of them disclosing his inner life and too sacred to put into cold type."

"The last time I saw Emerson I met him in Boston at a supper at Young's restaurant. J. Boyle O'Reilly and Joaquin Miller, the poet of the Sierras, were present."

Pausing, the poet's eyes glistened as he said, with deepest pathos, "Poor O'Reilly! He had a spirit touched to fine issues, and in heart and mind and imagination he lived to redress the wrongs of 'that most distresed country' as Napper Tandy called old Ireland. Ah! how I miss O'Reilly. As Carlyle says in his life of John Sterling, many of my seances with O'Reilly are written in star fire. They can never see the light of publicity."

"Our meeting at Young's was a most memorable one, and Emerson was kind enough to select the passages from my 'Leaves of Grass' which pleased him the most, and I remember how the old philosopher enjoyed the pleasures of the table both *ebendi et bibendi*, and with what pleasure he listened to Joaquin Miller's recitations of some passages from unpublished poems, descriptive of his early life, when Miller was a 'Forty-niner' in California."

"I never saw Emerson again, but we corresponded for many years and up to the last year of his noble life."

"Do you hear now from Edwin Arnold?" the poet was asked.

"Indeed I do," he answered, "and I am overjoyed at the latest news I have from Edwin Arnold, at Tokio, in Japan, that his new book, after the style of his 'Light of Asia,' will net him the handsome sum of $25,000. He is enamored of his pleasant life in Japan, and, while loth to leave the country, says: 'My engagements in En-

Ralph Waldo Emerson

gland are imperative, and I must soon sail for merry England, and after a short stay I will keep my promise to visit you and to renew my pleasant memories of the Pacific slope."

"What do you think of the political situation?"

The old poet promptly replied: "A plague on both your houses. I can't keep up with the sinuosities of American politics. Nor do I want to. I am reminded of what Emerson said to me—quoting from one of his essays: 'The Democrat is the young Conservative; the Conservative is the old Democrat; the aristocrat is the Democrat ripe and gone to seed, but all stand on the same platform—the supreme value of property which one endeavors to get and, the other to keep.'"

"As to Harrison, he seems to me to be vapid and to have inaugurated the day of small things. If there is any bigness in the man or his methods I fail to 'observantly distill it out.' What has he done! What will he do! He seems to have divided his own party and run

wrapped in the triple brass of his own selfishness, hugs to his breast the delusion that he can again be named for President of the United States. I am not a politician, one of those who pretend 'to see the things they see not' but I can see nothing in the President that the masses can catch on to or enthuse over."

"And taking the Administration in its entirety after two years of public trial, judged by the light that beats upon the throne, I can only recall the criticism a celebrated English writer made about the literature of the hundred years he had been asked to give a comprehensive opinion about. He wrote: 'If I have described this period in English literature as vapid and insincere, and found it productive of no great results in intellect or in morals, it is simply because there is not great underlying thought in it; but patches, promising much, in fulfillment nothing.'"

"So this Administration strikes me, though it may be because I am withdrawn from the current political thought and may judge the lines as out of joint, and may expect too much of an Administration which evidently seeks first and last to perpetuate its lease of power."

"I write little now, occasionally for the *Century* and recently for our mutual friend, Mr. Stoddard, at his request, a poem for *Lippincott's*. I am an old man now, and write only as the spirit moves me. Whittier is eighty-four, but he writes better than he ever did. Tennyson is eighty-one, but finds time to enjoy semi-occasionally and kindly correspondence with his old friends. One of my latest and most lasting regrets is that I never was strong enough to make a visit to Tennyson, in England, as he has often urged me to do."

New York Times, 1 September 1890, p. 3; originally published in the *Philadelphia Times*.

THE LOUNGER

[Jeannette L. Gilder]

Jeanette L. Gilder, an editor of the Critic, *published Whitman's writings in her journal. Through articles such as this, and by publishing portions of his letters to her, she kept the public informed about Whitman's activities and his health.*

I lived within thirty miles of Walt Whitman all summer but it was not until the week before I returned to town that I determined to make a Camden pilgrimage. There were four pilgrims—two little girls, a young lady and myself. The day was a beautiful one, cold, crisp and clear—just the day for a visit to a poet. There is that about Camden which dissipates any poetic preconceptions one may have in visiting that Jersey town. One would as soon expect to find a bard in Long Island City. Even the poet's house has no outward appearance of sheltering any but an ordinary tenant beneath its roof. A two-story-and-a-half frame building, painted a dark brown, with the upper shutters closed and the edges of the loose-fitting lower window-sashes stuffed with newspapers to keep out the wind beating down from the north greets the searcher after No. 32 Mickle Street. At the curb-stone is a block of white marble with the initials 'W. W.' cut into it and the door-plate imparts the further information that 'W. Whitman' can be found by pulling the bell-handle. I pulled it, and a young man in his shirt-sleeves, with a short pipe in his mouth, opened the door. 'Walt' was not down stairs yet, but if we would wait in the parlor he would be told that we were there.

———

The room in which we found ourselves was comfortable enough, but suggestive of anything rather than poetry. The only things that relieved its prosaic aspect were a violin and a music-stand with a few sheets of music lying on it. After a while the young man re-

66

turned and said that 'He' was not able to come downstairs, but that we might go up if we would. The first door at the end of the hall, front, was the one we were to pass through. We climbed a narrow stairway and knocked for admittance. 'Come in,' said a feeble but familiar voice. I opened the door, and stood for a moment on the threshold before I could find my voice to speak. Seated in a big rocking-chair with a grey fur rug thrown over the back, wrapped in a gown made of a grey blanket, sat the 'good grey poet.' I had not seen him for three or four years, and he was very much changed. His body was thinner than I had ever seen it, but the fine head crowned with its white hair was unaltered.

What had startled, not to say shocked, me upon opening the door was the appearance of the room as much as the appearance of its occupant. The blinds were closed and there were no curtains at the windows, and it was no easy matter to pick one's way across the sea of old newspapers that surrounded the poet. The office of the exchange reader on a daily paper was never so littered. These papers were the accumulation of years, to judge by their dates; and so was the dust upon them, to judge by its thickness. A table stood opposite Mr. Whitman, and this too was stacked, as high as it would hold, with newspapers. A little space had been left, just big enough to hold an inkstand but not big enough to use as a desk, for when the poet wrote his name in a book for me, he had to hold it on his knee. A hot wood fire burned in an old-fashioned 'air-tight' stove, guiltless of blacking, and on the opposite side of the room stood a big double-bed that had not yet been made up. Any one with the bump of order even half developed would have been driven wild by the appearance of the place; but the poet did not seem to mind it at all; and what surprised me greatly was, that amid all this confusion he seemed to know just where to lay his hand upon anything he wanted. He would dive into the enormous pile of newspapers at any angle, and always fish out the book or the picture or the manuscript that he wanted. He spoke quite feelingly of the comfort of his surroundings and of the good care that was taken of him but spoke very despondently of his health. His mind, he said, was generally very clear, but every now and then his head would feel 'like an apple-

First edition of Leaves of Grass *(1855; from* The Collection of American Literature
In the Library of Pauline and Howard Behrman *[New York, 1973])*

dumpling,' and he would have to stop reading or writing and rest.

———————

I had a small camera with me, which I had brought 'with intention,' and I asked Mr. Whitman if I might take a picture of him. He
was good enough to say that I might, so I opened one of the blinds
and asked him to sit quietly for a moment as it would take some
time to get a picture, the room being so dark. 'Now,' said I, 'sit just
as you are—don't move'; and I took off the cap. What was my horror when, right in the midst of the exposure, the old bard waved his
hand majestically, and turning towards the window exclaimed, 'The
sun is coming out now!' Luckily I had another plate, with which I

got a fairly good picture—one that will at least serve as a memorandum of the poet amid his unique surroundings. But the first one was nothing but chaos with a ghostly shape in the foreground that bore little resemblance to anything human.

Critic, n.s. 16 (29 November 1891): 307-308; Gilder was the regular editor of "The Lounger" column in the *Critic*.

WALT WHITMAN

William H. Garrison

William H. Garrison's account is interesting because it demonstrates Whitman's genuine affection for the common people, and especially for children.

Walt Whitman the poet has suffered during the period of his literary activity every form of critical calamity, from adulation that would exalt him above all the world-poets of the past, to detraction that denied him even ordinary sanity. Walt Whitman the man has a different record: his personality was potent, and no one who came under the influence of its spell could fail to be impressed with his power.

The story of his career has been written at by many hands, and material for a complete biography has been furnished by the poet himself to his friend and admirer Dr. Bucke, but it may be worth while to set down what Whitman would call "a few hints, a few diffused clews, and indirections," covering an acquaintanceship of about twenty years, during the greater part of which I was his neighbor in Camden.

My first meeting with Walt Whitman occurred when I was a boy and had occasion to ask for a certain residence on his street. I did not know who or what he was, but on his answering my question I was so struck with the quality of his voice, which was musical and resonant, that I took the earliest opportunity to make inquiry as to the new-comer, and received the information that it was a man named Walt Whitman, who had written what some people called poetry and others nonsense. Had the present city directory of the town been in existence, I could have found it authoritatively stated that the gentleman was "Walt Whitman, *poet*"! My first visit to him occurred some years later, in the little house on Mickle Street which has been the scene of the closing years of his life. When I entered the room the poet was sitting in his great chair by the window, in front of him a table heaped up at least to the height of four feet with books of all sorts, old and new, gift-editions from men famous in letters, and cheap second-hand purchases; the floor was knee-deep in newspapers, manuscripts, and books, among the last a well-thumbed Latin lexicon. The decorations of the room were insignificant, with the exception of two portraits, one of his father and one of a Dutch ancestor, and it was upon these pictures that the conversation turned. The portrait of the father showed the thoughtful Puritan face of which Emerson is the type, and indeed the resemblance to Emerson himself was so strong that Sidney Morse, the sculptor, presented Whitman with several small busts of the New England seer, in which the likeness was very striking. The Hollander, on the other hand, had the full lips and sensuous features of the man of pleasure, and Whitman's comment was that physically and mentally he had often recognized what he owed to these antecedent forces of which he was the resultant. This idea seems to have impressed him, for he repeated it to Mr. Gilchrist in 1887, when the latter was painting his portrait.

The most interesting talk that I ever had with Walt Whitman was on one winter afternoon some five years ago, when I dropped in and found the poet ready and eager "to gossip in early candle-light of old age." His theme was himself and his book, and he told the story not at all to me, as it seemed, but as though he were taking a backward glance o'er travelled roads, alone. The starting-point was an answer to the question,—

"Mr. Whitman, how did you come to write poetry?"

And in his reply he said that at the time when he was a carpenter-builder in Brooklyn he would buy a bit of property in the suburbs, erect a little house upon it with his own hands, sell the place at an average profit of about two hundred dollars, and, taking the money thus earned, go down to Long Island and lie out on the rocks, reading, dreaming, and watching the ships.

"I think the first time I ever wanted to write anything enduring," he said, "was when I saw a ship under full sail and I had the desire to describe it exactly as it seemed to me. I tried then and failed, and I have tried since, but have never yet been satisfied with the result. I have been able to describe a locomotive so that I shall never want to change or add to what I have written; but the ship at sea has always eluded me. Years later, when I was living in New York, I used to go to the Battery of an afternoon and sit and watch the sailing-

71

Frontispiece engraving of Whitman in Leaves of Grass *(1855), left, and the spine of the second edition (1856)*

vessels by the hour; but I could never put down on paper any words about them that entirely pleased me."

In the course of the same talk Whitman said that at one time he had been a voracious and omnivorous reader, not alone in English, but also largely in French, which he learned during his residence in Washington, and to a limited extent he had read Spanish.

As a general rule, Whitman talked in the most objective way, and preferably on commonplace, non-literary topics.

All writers, whether classic or modern, were in his phrase "fellows,"—a word of which he was very fond,—and not the least characteristic of the man was his use of conversational English. His vocabulary was a singular mixture of old words used with unexpected meanings (as when he spoke of his book having been published under the "umbrage" of a certain firm), commingled with such picturesque and useful passing slang as caught his fancy, as for instance the word "sculp," which he habitually used when his bust was being made.

Whitman seemed to have the keenest enjoyment of bright colors. On one Sunday afternoon while entertaining some half-dozen callers he halted the general talk to call attention to the bright red dress of a little girl whom he spied out of his window. "How that color brightens up the whole street!" he said. And on another occasion, when he had driven out to a horse-race (his first appearance at a race-track), he told me he lost all interest in the sporting event to sit in admiration of a clump of green trees that outlined themselves against a white fence. "Isn't that beautiful?" he said. "How the white background sets off the many shades of the green leaves!"

One of the most satisfying qualities that Whitman possessed, as a man, was the dignified, unruffled demeanor that he never lost, whether he was hobnobbing with a deck-hand or a 'bus-driver or entertaining some guest who was a celebrity in two continents. Always he seemed to be realizing in action his own ideal when he says,—

> I think I could turn and live with animals, they are so placid and self-contained.
> I stand and look at them long and long.
> They do not sweat and whine about their condition;
> They do not lie awake in the dark and weep for their sins;
> They do not make me sick discussing their duty to God.
> Not one is dissatisfied, not one is demented with the mania of owning things;
> Not one kneels to another, nor to his kind that live thousands of years ago;
> Not one is respectable or unhappy over the whole earth.

In general society Whitman never lost this poise that was characteristic of him in smaller circles. Often silent for an hour or two, barring an occasional interjected remark, he was always an attentive listener, and, when some topic was broached that engaged his atten-

73

tion, a careful and a ready talker. I have known him to sit at a dinner-table for the best part of an evening without opening his lips, and suddenly to warm into a theme on which he spoke fluently and without interruption for a half-hour or more. But his talk, while always thoughtful, was almost invariably remembered not so much because of its intrinsic intellectual worth as because of the striking personality of the speaker who uttered it.

One word as to the care which Whitman bestowed upon even the smaller fugitive pieces which he published in the local and other newspapers. In the matter of the accuracy with which these productions were printed he was scrupulously exact. Each bit when it had left his hands in manuscript was sent to a quaint old printing-establishment in the town, where it was set up in type. It was then returned to the author, who made such corrections as seemed to him desirable, and after this a revised and re-corrected copy was struck off and sent out as the matter to be used *punctatim et literatim*. At times he was critical even to the verge of whimsicality in the matter of punctuation, and it was a source of annoyance to find the title of his latest book, "Good Bye My Fancy," so printed that a comma or any other mark separated the four words into two groups.

This sensitiveness was doubtless due to the experience he had had at the printer's case; but if this be so it is difficult to explain the "copy" that he furnished for some of his prose bits. I have seen a manuscript, a part of "November Boughs," a single page of which was composed of at least a dozen kinds of paper, written in black pencil, blue pencil, black ink, and red ink. Some of the parts of this manuscript were written on bits of brown straw paper, others on manilla paper, others on the blue paper that had once formed a part of the cover of a pamphlet, and each piece of a different size, shape, and color, suggesting the idea that as a thought or a sentence had come into the mind of the writer he had made a note of it and pasted the whole together without thinking it worth while to give to the total result coherence or form.

His nickname, Walt, he told me himself he had received from the 'bus-drivers in New York, with whom he rode as constantly when he lived in that city as he did with those in Camden when he made the latter place his home.

To those who knew him, Walt Whitman was such a straightforward man that the apparent eccentricity of costume which he affected seemed almost inexplicable, as indeed it was to me until he told me that he had once worked at carpentering, and then the idea suggested itself that, after all, the loose rolling collar exposing the chest and the turned-back cuffs were only a conventionalized form of the laboringman's ordinary garb; and when I asked Whitman whether this was so he said he supposed that was the case.

In a gift-volume of the "Gypsies" Charles Godfrey Leland addresses Whitman in a poem in which he says that Walter, his first name, means a warrior, and this the poet has always been, that the "Whit" may either be the Saxon "wit" or "wisdom" or "white" in the sense of his being a "white" man, but that the essence of the whole name lies in the last syllable,—he is a "man"; and this is the testimony of all who have ever come to know Walt Whitman personally.

Lippincott's Monthly Magazine, 49 (May 1892): 623-626.

WALT WHITMAN IN BOSTON

Sylvester Baxter

Sylvester Baxter, a Boston journalist, met Whitman in 1881, when he was see-ing Leaves of Grass *through the press. He gives a vivid portrait of Whitman's interaction with the Boston journalists of the day.*

In the course of the eventful life that covered nearly three-quarters of the century now almost at its close, Walt Whitman, in his journeyings, wove himself pretty thoroughly into the texture of the land that formed the grand themes of his verse. The central prair-ies, the high plains of the far West, the Rocky Mountains, the shores of the Atlantic and of the Pacific, the Mississippi, the great lakes, the Gulf of Mexico, cities and towns in all parts—the spirit of all these he absorbed in his wanderings up and down in the United States, distil-ling its essence in his great book, "Leaves of Grass."

There are, however, four great cities with which he is peculiarly identified. New York, of course, first of all—Manhattan he always called it, with that curious insistence of his upon naming things in his own way. Whitman was a New Yorker of New Yorkers. Born al-most in its outskirts, he passed the greater part of his life in and about the vast city, which he loved with an affection such as has been accorded it by few of its children, singing its praises, characteriz-ing and depicting it in his verse with a wholeness, a universality, a sympathy, and a delicacy of perception such as no other city has re-ceived from any other poet. If all American literature down to date save two books should be destroyed—Whitman's "Leaves of Grass," and Howells' "Hazard of New Fortunes,"—a remote posterity might be able to gain a very accurate idea of the New York of the nine-teenth century.

Whitman's relations with Boston were of quite another kind. From Boston came his first recognition from an authoritative source; the recognition of one grand spirit by its peer, in the shape of the hearty and unreserved greeting of the great Emerson. In Boston "Leaves of Grass" was first regularly published, and nearly a generation later Whitman's poems received in the New England metropolis that form of indorsement which, with a book, is comparable to the reception of a person into the best society,—publication by a house that ranked among the first in the country. In Boston, too, his work found a larger number of admirers than probably in any other place in the country. The poet spent less time in Boston than in any other of the four cities. His visits were three in number, the first and the last of several weeks each, and the second of but a few days. But these visits were notable occasions in his life. Whitman was also ancestrally connected with the Boston neighborhood. The Whitman stock in America originated in the Old Colony, and the family is numerously represented in the towns on the south side of Boston Bay. What was formerly South Abington became the town of Whitman a few years ago.

The third of the great cities with which Whitman had to do ranks next to New York in the important bearing which it had on his life. It was in and about Washington that he spent most of the Civil War period and the several years of his service as a department employee.

Last comes Philadelphia,—for Camden, though in New Jersey, is essentially a part of that city. So long as health permitted, Whitman was wont to cross the Delaware in the ferry-boats, repeating his favorite East River experiences, immortalized in "Crossing Brooklyn Ferry." He was bound to Philadelphia by strong ties of personal friendship and by the Quaker element in his blood that left characteristic marks upon his personality and even affected to a notable extent his literary style. It was to a Philadelphia publisher that he transferred his "Leaves of Grass" after the unfortunate outcome of its Boston publication; the several subsequent editions were issued there by David G. McKay, besides his volume of prose and his supplementary poems.

It was on his second visit to Boston, in April, 1881, that I first met Whitman, beginning a friendship that will always form one of the pleasantest memories of my life. Whitman had been invited to Boston by a number of his younger admirers connected with the Papyrus Club—prominent among them John Boyle O'Reilly—to read his paper on Lincoln; a sort of memorial service which the poet made it a point to observe somewhere every year on the anniversary of the death of the great President, whom Whitman honored as the most rep-

Walt Whitman, circa 1860 (Feinberg Collection, Library of Congress)

resentative of Americans,—an incarnation of the spirit of modern democracy. As a member of the Boston *Herald* staff, I had been requested to write an article on Whitman—not an interview, but one of those personal sketches of literary and public persons that had become a feature of that newspaper and of which I had contributed a number. The task in question, however, would naturally have fallen to my colleague and intimate friend, Frederic Russell Guernsey—now resident in Mexico and prominent in journalism and business there—for Guernsey was an old admirer of Whitman and had written charmingly about him. When John Burroughs came to Boston—the summer before, I believe—he dropped in upon Guernsey at the *Herald* and introduced himself with the words: "My name is John Burroughs. We are both friends of Walt Whitman, and that is enough to make us friends,—so let's take a walk together. I don't care anything for the sights of the city; I want to see the people."

But Guernsey had other work on his hands at the time of Whitman's visit, and so the assignment came to me. It was about noon, and I found Whitman in an easy-chair in the parlor at the Revere House. Several friends were with him, among them Trueman H. Bartlett, the sculptor. Making known my errand, he greeted me cordially. His hand, which was rather small, but relieved from any effect of daintiness by an unusual hairiness, had a warm, magnetic touch, like that of a man of strong physical nature. His peculiar attire agreed so perfectly with his appearance that it seemed as if any other must have looked out of place. It had that effect of entire appropriateness, of perfect adaptation to personality, that all dress, considered from the ideal point of view, should have. Therefore the idea of its eccentricity hardly entered one's head, so comfortable did he look. It clothed Walt Whitman as a tree is clothed by its bark, or an animal by its fur. With all its apparent carelessness, it was evident that Whitman was very scrupulous about his dress. It had the look of perfect adaptation to his person—very much as his rough-seeming verse, as the poet confessed, was brought into conformity with an adequate expression of himself only after most careful study and continuous experiment. In the easy-setting garments of Quakerish drab, in the flowing collar and loosely-knotted handkerchief, and the large, broad-brimmed hat, there was evident a consummate neatness, as of a person instinctively clean and with an innate aversion to slovenliness.

As he sat there with his big stick, it seemed to me that if I should come across him in just that position, seated on a gray, lichen-covered boulder in the depth of a wood, under old trees draped with moss that flowed like his hair and beard, and with rabbits and squirrels sporting over his feet in entire fearlessness, it would not be in the least surprising. He talked about himself, not loquaciously nor with egotism, but with a quiet, matter-of-course candor. His voice was high-pitched, but agreeable and without twang; a sort of speaking tenor—a Middle State voice, Guernsey called it. He had just come in from a drive to Cambridge to call on Longfellow, and expressed great pleasure over his visit and a sincere admiration for Longfellow's verse. He found Longfellow most beautifully and aesthetically surrounded, but Whitman declared that he himself could not possibly work in a luxurious environment; it would oppress him, as if for lack of breathing space.

Various callers came in; among them John T. Trowbridge. There was a most joyous meeting between the two poets, who were intimate friends of long standing, and they had been much together in the Washington days. Trowbridge called him "Walt," in the comrade-like way in which Whitman preferred to be addressed by his friends, old and young, and it seemed quite the thing to speak to the Poet of Democracy thus familiarly. Trowbridge was an old admirer of Whitman's verse, and could recite from "Leaves of Grass" by the page, with genuine eloquence and deep feeling. The two had not met for a long time, and the talk was largely reminiscent. Whitman said that he was about ready to give up in discouragement, feeling that perhaps there could not be anything in his poetic mission after all, when Tennyson's magnificent letter came, almost taking his breath away with its surprising heartiness, and filling him with new cheer and courage. "And Tennyson has shown his admiration for you in no more genuine way than in being directly influenced by you in his later style," said Trowbridge. "Do you think he has?" asked Whitman simply. "Most undoubtedly," said Trowbridge.

It was the morning after the reading (the sixteenth anniversary of Lincoln's death) which took place the evening before, April 15,—a sort of semi-drawing-room occasion, in the pleasant Hawthorne Rooms on Park Street, before a representative and distinguished audience. There was considerable talk about the affair, and what Whitman said of his impressions was afterwards included in the memoranda of his "Specimen Days." I particularly remember how struck he was by seeing so many fine-looking gray-haired women, and in his notes he says:

"At my lecture I caught myself pausing more than once to look at them, plentiful everywhere through the audience—healthy and wifely and motherly, and wonderfully charming and beautiful—I think such as no time or land but ours could show."

Whitman was strongly impressed by the growth of Boston, not only materially but in the higher aspects. He compared the change to the facts revealed by Schliemann in his excavations, where he found superimposed remains of cities, each representing either a long or rapid stage of growth and development, different from its predecessor, but unerringly growing out of and resting in it. "In the moral, emotional, heroic, and human growths (the main of a race in

Frontispiece engraving of Whitman in Leaves of Grass *(1860)*

my opinion), something of this kind has certainly taken place in Boston," he wrote.

"The New England metropolis of to-day may be described as sunny (there is something else that makes warmth, mastering even winds and meteorologies, though these are not to be sneez'd at), joyous, receptive, full of ardor, sparkle, a certain element of yearning, magnificently tolerant, yet not to be fool'd; fond of good eating and drinking—costly in costume as its purse can buy; and all through its best average of houses, streets, people, that subtle something (generally thought to be climate, but it is not—it is something indefinable amid *the race*, the turn of its development) which effuses behind the whirl of animation, study, business, a happy and joyous public spirit, as distinguish'd from a sluggish and saturnine one. Makes me think of the glints we get (as in Symond's books) of the jolly old Greek cities. Indeed, there is a good deal of the Hellenic in B., and the people are getting handsomer, too—padded out, with freer notions, and with color in their faces."

The contrast with the Boston that he knew on his two former visits must indeed have been remarkable. It was then in the last stages of its hereditary and traditional Puritanism; it was now the least Puritanical of all the great American cities so far as the native social element, that which distinguishes them as American, was concerned. The ferment of its intense radicalism, generated by its very Puritanism, had liberalized and transformed it.

One of Whitman's pleasantest experiences during his short stay was a visit with the sculptor, Bartlett, to the house of Mr. Quincy A. Shaw in Jamaica Plain, where two hours passed quickly in looking at Mr. Shaw's superb collection of the pictures of J. F. Millet. He was profoundly moved by the work of the great Frenchman, and he declared that never before had he been so penetrated by that kind of expression. The scenes of homely peasant life told him the full story of what went before, and necessitated, the great French revolution:

"The long precedent crushing of the masses of a heroic people into the earth, in abject poverty, hunger—every right denied, humanity attempted to be put back for generations—yet Nature's force, titanic here, the stronger and hardier for that repression—waiting terribly to break forth, revengeful—the pressure on the dykes, and the bursting at last—the storming of the Bastile—the execution of king and queen—the tempest of massacres and blood."

He found the true France, base of all the rest, in these pictures. "If for nothing else, I should dwell on my brief Boston visit for opening to me the new world of Millet's pictures," he wrote, and he asked: "Will America ever have such an artist out of her own gestation, body, soul?" At the end of his visit he wrote: "It was well I got away in fair order, for if I had staid another week I should have been killed with kindness, and with eating and drinking."

The next August, Whitman wrote me asking if I could find him a quiet boarding-place where he could stay several weeks while he was overlooking the publication of the complete edition of his poems by the house of James R. Osgood & Company, in accordance with a proposition made by the firm at the time of his visit in the spring. I found him a pleasant room in the Hotel Bulfinch, on Bulfinch Place, a quiet and characteristic old West End street, a few steps back from the Revere House. The Hotel Bulfinch is one of several in Boston which have the reputation of being the original of "Mrs. Harmon's Hotel" in Howells's novel, "The Minister's Charge." But that celebrated hostelry is a "composite," and Lemuel Barker was not running the elevator, which proved a great convenience to the venerable poet, with his difficulty of locomotion. Bulfinch Place, even if it cannot lay exclusive claim to "Mrs. Harmon's," deserves to rank among Boston's historic streets, for, on the other side of the way, near the corner of Bulfinch Street—the name was given in honor of the architect of the State House—is the old boarding-house, celebrated and beloved among actors; for many of the famous figures of the American stage have known it, and William Warren, the great comedian, lived there for many years, until the end of his honored life.

Whitman arrived about the middle of August, and during the two months of his stay felt himself comfortably at home. He passed the time leisurely, and many pleasant attentions were paid him in an informal way. Not being hurried for time, these attentions did not fatigue him. A large portion of the day he spent in his sunny room on the south side of the house, reading over his proofs, which littered the table in characteristic disorder, carefully marked in his firm, strong, and somewhat crabbed hand. Friends dropped in on him for a chat, now and then, and of an evening he enjoyed having one of the young men of the *Herald* countingroom, who lived in the house, come to his room and play the violin for him.

Walking at that time was not painful or particularly fatiguing for him, and a favorite diversion for him was to go out to Scollay Square, near by, where he would take an open car for South Boston, going to City Point and back, sitting on the front seat and occasionally talking with the driver, something after the manner of the old-time days on the Broadway stages in New York. He enjoyed the water-front at City Point exceedingly; the views of the harbor and the swarms of yachts, and the democratic aspect of the place, with the crowds resorting there.

Another favorite spot was the Common. In "Specimen Days," under date of October, 10-13, he wrote that he spent a good deal of time there, every mid-day from 11.30 to about one o'clock, and almost every sunset another hour. "I know all the big trees," he wrote, "especially the old elms along Tremont and Beacon Streets, and have come to a sociable, silent understanding with most of them, in

the sunlit air (yet crispy-cool enough), as I saunter along the wide un-
paved walks." And he told how, on a bright and sharp February mid-
day, twenty-one years before, he walked for two hours up and down
the Beacon Street mall with Emerson, listening to his argument
against a certain part in the construction of his poems, "Children of
Adam"; while each point of Emerson's statement seemed unanswer-
able, he felt at the end more settled than ever to adhere to his own theory. "Whereupon we went and had a good dinner at the American
House." This most interesting account, in which he lifts the veil
from a most important episode, appears to be about the only thing
in Whitman's works relating to his earlier visits to Boston.

An episode that gave Whitman rare pleasure was a visit to Concord as a guest of Frank B. Sanborn, meeting Emerson for the first
time after many years. It was delicious autumn weather, and that
evening many of the Concord neighbors, including Emerson, A.
Bronson Alcott, and Miss Louisa M. Alcott, filled Mrs. Sanborn's
back parlor. The next day, Sunday, September 18th, he dined with
Emerson and spent several hours at his house. He also visited the
"Old Manse," the battle-field, the graves of Hawthorne and Thoreau
in Sleepy Hollow Cemetery, and the site of Thoreau's hermitage at
Walden Pond. Another pleasant incident was a roadside chat with
Dr. William T. Harris, the scholar and philosopher, as he halted in
front of his house on the drive back from Walden Pond. This Concord visit is charmingly described in "Specimen Days."

One evening I took Whitman to the Globe Theatre to see Rossi,
the celebrated Italian tragedian. A feature of Rossi's art was to depend for effect upon the naturalness of his impersonation, the sub-
tlety of his delineation, the fineness of his shading—all of which was
remarkable—and to dispense, so far as he could, with the aid of extrin-
sic things, like the simulations of "make-up." The man, Rossi, was
therefore in evidence in all that he did. The piece was "Romeo and Ju-
liet," and Rossi played his part with much ardor, as well as delicacy.
Whitman sat quietly through the performance, but at one point—I believe it was in the midst of an impassioned love-scene—he gave a little involuntary laugh. I think the sight of a middle-aged Romeo,
slightly bald on the back of his head, was a bit too much for his
sense of the ridiculous. At the close his only comment was: "I'm
afraid an old fellow like me is not so impressionable as he was in his
old theatre-going days."

With all his progressiveness, his enthusiasm for the modern, for the great inventions of the age, a bit of conservatism cropped out concerning the electric light, which was just coming into general use. Passing under some arc-lights in the street, on our way back from the theatre, he remarked: "This white, intense glare is too cold and harsh; over on the Common I noticed some new gas-burners shedding a full, rich, mellow radiance; that light is very pleasant." Garfield's death occurred while Whitman was in Boston. The analogy to Lincoln's death, which had affected him so profoundly and which he had celebrated with one of the noblest odes in the English tongue, seemed to bring it peculiarly near the poet. The next day, when it was mentioned, he simply said that he had heard the bells in the night. He contributed, however, the following lines to the Boston Sunday Globe:

> The sobbing of the bells, the sudden death-news everywhere,
> The slumberers rouse, the rapport of the People,
> (Full well they know that message in the darkness,
> Full well return, respond within their breasts, their brains, the sad reverberations.)
> The passionate toll and clang—city to city, joining, sounding, passing,
> Those heart-beats of a Nation in the night.

A memorable evening was one spent in Bartlett's studio with a little company informally gathered in honor of Whitman. The studio was a most unique and picturesque place at the very end of the wharf of the Boston Terra-Cotta Company on Federal Street, bordering the river-like Fort Point channel—one of the most interesting portions of the water-front. The room was spacious and hall-like, something like twenty or twenty five feet high, with a quaint stairway in one corner, leading to rooms in a clerestory. The walls and ceiling were unfinished; the walls of brick, and ornamented with relief-casts and large cartoons. About the place stood sculptures—cast in plaster, or unfinished in the clay and muffled in mysterious-looking wrappings. The recesses of the great room were dim in the flickering gaslight, which but sparsely penetrated into the corners, and the shadows danced among the beams of the ceiling. If the scene could have been painted it would have made a real picture, with some notable portraits. Among the company were John Boyle O'Reilly, Joaquin Miller, Francis H. Underwood, Arlo Bates, Frank Hill Smith,

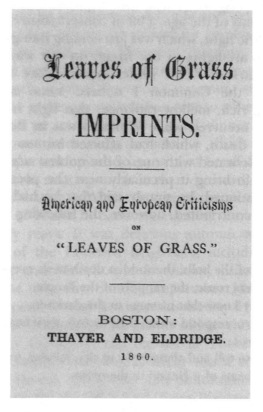

Title page of Leaves of Grass Imprints *(1860), which Whitman edited and contributed to*

Fred Guernsey, and myself. The evening was one of quiet sociability. There was a bowl of good punch, some lager beer, and crackers and cheese. There was no formal conversation, and talk ran on at random. I believe Joaquin Miller's play, "The Danites," was having a run in Boston at the time, and that was why "the poet of the Sierras" happened to be in the city. Boyle O'Reilly spoke of the play which he had in mind, part of whose scenes were to be in Australia. Miller was much interested in the idea, and he dilated with enthusiasm upon the great effect that might be produced by an Australian forest scene, with huge snakes squirming among the trees! Miller had then none of the frontierish eccentricities of costume, long hair, etc., that had distinguished him a few years before. He was quiet and somewhat retiring in manner, gentle in speech, and manifestly of a romantic cast of thought.

There was a picturesque contrast between Whitman and Underwood. Both were white-haired and full-bearded—Whitman of a rough hewn type, rugged as an ancient oak; Underwood—"the Assyrian" of that unassuming but idyllic and thoroughly charming little book, "A Summer Cruise Along The Coast of New England," written a generation since by Robert Carter—with classic features, clear cut as a cameo.

Whitman sat quietly through the evening, not saying much, but keenly observant and attentive, fully a part of the occasion and absorbing it all in the way his friends knew so well. There was always sociability in the very silence of the dear old man. Towards the end of the evening, Bartlett announced that Whitman had consented to recite something for us. We sat in expectant hush as he began; but it was not one of his own poems that he gave us in tones strikingly natural and eloquent with deep feeling; it was a translation from the French of Murger's beautiful verses on death, "The Midnight Visitor," closely akin to Whitman's noble treatment of the theme. It was profoundly impressive; an episode that must remain memorable with all of the little company.

Whitman returned to Camden shortly before the publication of his poems. The appearance of "Leaves of Grass" under such conditions was generally received as a literary event of exceptional importance. The criticisms and reviews were naturally of the most divers character. It was, of course, to be expected that certain lines would be seized upon most eagerly by certain critics, but in all the comment that was made there was little, or nothing, to prepare Whitman's friends for the unfortunate occurrence that ruined the sale of the book when prospects were most promising. A storm of indignant protest followed the notification from the attorney-general of Massachusetts to the publishers. A most scathing letter from William Douglas O'Connor was published, consigning Mr. Marston, who filled the office at that time, to the depths of infamy. Mr. O'Connor was unjust to Mr. Marston, however. The attorney-general's act was simply an official one; his attention having been called to the subject, under the law, there was no other course left for him. It turned out, some time after, that the incentive came from a certain clergyman, well meaning enough, no doubt,—but it may be questioned if a keen scent for impurity is a corollary of a pure mind. It was extremely improbable that the attempt at suppression could have been successful in court, but the publishers did not care to run the risk; Whitman firmly and consistently declined to change a line and he took over the plates himself.

Whitman had made many true friends in Boston, and from time to time he received pleasant remembrances from them. Learning how confined he was to his house, by reason of his growing infirmity, Boyle O'Reilly, Bartlett, and a few others, started very quietly a subscription for a horse and carriage to enable him to take an outing in pleasant weather. The handsome new team was driven up to his door in Camden one fine day, taking him completely by surprise. The gift added immensely to his comfort and pleasure for several years.

An attempt to secure him a pension by reason of his hospital services, which was the cause of his crippled condition, was made, Congressman Lovering, of Lynn, interesting himself actively for the measure. Pensions had already been given to nurses, but somehow the project failed; possibly because Whitman had not been regularly employed, but was a volunteer in the work. Whitman firmly refused to become an applicant for a pension, but would probably have accepted it had the efforts of his friends been successful.

Probably the most intimate and devoted of Whitman's younger friends in Boston was William Sloane Kennedy, the essayist, whose studies of Whitman are of the finest quality. Kennedy was away from Boston at the time of Whitman's last two visits. Returning from a visit to Whitman at Camden, in 1887, he reported the uncomfortable life that the poet led in the summer weather in the hot and close atmosphere of an inland city. What a blessing it would be, he said, if he could have a little cottage in the country somewhere, amid the natural surroundings that he loved. The idea was favorably received, and so, the next year, Boyle O'Reilly, Kennedy, and I endeavored to realize it. Our original project was to raise the money quietly, build the cottage, and have somebody drive Whitman out there and take him by surprise. But the matter leaked out and got into the newspapers, causing us to change our plans. We found little trouble in raising the modest sum required. Two or three subscriptions came from outside Boston, among them a handsome one from "Mark Twain," who wrote:

"What we want to do is to make the splendid old soul comfortable and do what we do heartily and as a privilege;" and he added, "There couldn't and wouldn't be any lack of people ready and willing to build a cottage for Walt Whitman; and as long as a rope-walk if he wants it."

Frank Hill Smith, who is an architect as well as a painter and decorator, contributed an artistic design and plans for a simple cottage of the kind needed, and John G. Low gave the tiles from his Chelsea works for a handsome fireplace. Mr. Montgomery Stafford, the owner of the land at Timber Creek, in Kirkwood, New Jersey, the idyllic spot where Whitman went when so ill at the end of his Washington life, and where he was restored to comparative health, offered to give the site for a cottage.

But, when we raised the money, we sent it to Whitman for him to build how and where he pleased, thinking he would take delight, as an old builder, in looking after the matter himself. He intended to do this, but he never got round to it. I think the lethargy of age was creeping over him fast, and he lacked the energy to make a beginning.

At his death, we learned that he had built a tomb for himself and his parents in the Camden Cemetery, taking much interest in the work and supervising the construction himself. Perhaps he finally used the means we raised for a summer cottage in thus preparing for himself a last resting-place.

New England Magazine, 6 (August 1892): 714-721.

THE LAST SICKNESS AND THE DEATH OF WALT WHITMAN

Daniel Longaker

Daniel Longaker, a Philadelphia physician, attended Whitman in the months preceding his death. His detailed account chronicles Whitman's physical decline and reports the results of the autopsy that followed his death.

Walt Whitman's last sickness in reality dates from his years of hospital work in 1863-5, and originated at that time in two causes—the first, the emotional strain of those terrible years; the second, blood-poisoning absorbed from certain gangrenous wounds in patients whom he at that time closely attended. In 1864 and 1865 he had temporary break-downs, and these culminated, in January, 1873, in an attack of paralysis, which was greatly aggravated during the same year by the death of his mother. This paralysis more than once brought him to death's door. It let up a little in the late seventies and early eighties, then settled down thicker than ever in the late eighties, and steadily deepened until the end.

Early in 1891 my friend Horace L. Traubel asked me to see Whitman professionally. It was only after some persuasion, I believe, that Whitman had agreed to accept the services of a physician, although his friends had for some time been quite solicitous about his declining health.

I shall not forget my first sight of and interview with him. Seated on the great arm-chair, the back covered with a wolf robe, he told me the particulars of his case. What especially impressed me was the manner in which he spoke of his various spells of sickness and of the functional troubles annoying him at that time. It was a connected and methodical recital, so that there was little occasion for questions on my part. I regret not having made any notes of this and the subsequent visits during the early period of my attendance on him; which mis-chance makes it impossible for me to record here the full particulars of this history, given me by him at that time with some completeness.

As usual with old persons, Whitman's memory of remote was better than of recent events. He dwelt more fully on the details of his blood-poisoning from the gangrenous wound of his hand, and of the paralysis which had occurred almost twenty years before, than on those of his last serious attack, in 1888. Speaking of his personal habits, he told me he had always been temperate though he had not been a total abstainer; that he did not use tobacco; that he had never had any venereal disease. He feared, sometimes, that he ate too much. Locomotion was difficult. He moved about awkwardly with the aid of his cane, yet declined assistance. Sensation was little if at all impaired in the arms or the legs. The grip of his hand was good and with not more than the normal difference in strength between the left and the right. Examination of heart and lungs showed these organs in good condition. He had some slight trouble in the upper respiratory tract, and this he denominated his old attack of "grip." His arteries were in fairly good condition, which surprised me. There was little or no atheromatous degeneration ascertainable in the temporals or radials, which, from the history of paralysis, I had expected to find.

In spite of the absence of evidences of gross organic disease, his apparent age was greater than his real years. His present trouble, he said, was a "torpor, want of peristalsis," and difficult and insufficient evacuation of the bowels. There were also frequent calls to void urine. For this purpose he would have to arise several times during the night. The trouble was due to an enlargement of the prostate gland—a condition existing in many men past the age of sixty years. It usually entails much suffering and distress, and admits, except by surgical interference, only of palliation.

In addition to these functional disturbances Whitman complained of great lack of energy. "Inertia," he explained—"as though a great wet, soggy net were spread out over me and holding me down." More or less constantly present, it was unaffected by atmospheric changes or conditions. For some months now he had left his room but seldom and had not been out of the house at all. He promptly passed a soft rubber catheter, and expressed surprise that the operation was so easy and painless. No arguing or coaxing was required, as is almost always necessary when this procedure is instituted. I finally prescribed for him a stomachic and laxative pill, and

Whitman and his nurse, Warren Fritzinger, in 1890

told him I saw no reason why he should not soon again be going out into the air, which I felt very necessary to the re-establishment of his former energy. His nurse, Warren, I was assured, was quite proficient in the art of massaging, and this treatment was ordered to be continued.

At subsequent visits of this time Whitman would hand me memoranda similar to the notes usually kept by nurses. These were in ink, often on the inside of an opened-out envelope, or on the reverse of a sheet bearing a request for his autograph from some distant collector, or on some similar odd bit of paper.

On March 20th, the day following my first visit, he wrote (in part): "Took the pills—had a couple of slack-roasted oysters for breakfast, with a little coffee and small biscuit of Graham meal; have now taken eight of the pills." On the 21st he wrote: "Took a pill first thing this morning; a passable night past, must have slept five hours." Monday, March 23d, he continued: "Extra heavy, inert condition—listlessness, deaden non-volition—sweat rather easily, eat almost nothing—no appetite—no bowel action at all. Void water

92

fairly, used the catheter last evening, it worked fairly. 2:30 P.M., limited (but sort of decided) bowel voidance, bronze color, consistence of dough, no watery discharge, no flatulence. Continued the pills—taken two to-day." Wednesday, March 25th: "Took the fifteenth pill first thing this morning early. Breakfast;—farina, roast apple and two or three mouthfuls of broiled steak. Must have had a passable night's rest." Saturday, March 28th: "A pill first thing this morning; a little oatmeal porridge for breakfast, small cup of cocoa at noon. No bowel impulse this forenoon—head heaviness—dullness extra last evening and to-day. Must have slept off and on from 11 to 6 with some waking." "Head heavy and some distress," he writes on March 30th, "but a shade of improvement in general strength and poise (less horrible inertia and weakness, bad enough tho' yet)."

These are mere extracts from his daily notes. They evince a remarkable degree of coöperation and reveal at the same time powers of observation and description of the minutest details that would be a credit even to a physician.

The following observation is as interesting as it is unique. He styled it *"A Crude Notion"*:

"My great corpus is like an old wooden log. Possibly (even probably), that slow vital, almost impalpable by-play of automatic stimulus belonging to living fiber has, by gradual habit of years and years in me (and especially of the last three years), got quite diverted into *mental* play and *vitality* and attention, instead of attending to normal play in stomachic and muscular and peristaltic use. Does this account for the stomachic non-action, non-stimulus? Or what is there in this, if anything?"

A great deal, I was obliged to confess. "April 15th, 1 o'clock," he writes in a letter: "Went out in wheel chair fifteen minutes; warm, bright sun, flustered, headache—eyes badly blurred—(first time out in four months)."

Again: "May 10th. Am feeling this deadly lassitude and weakness to-day the same still. One favorable item at 10, a *bowel movement* (the first in ten days), viscid quite definite mostly formed, brown, no g't straining (no use of the syringe). If this is the result of the new pills they are very welcome for *that obstinate* deep-set-in constipation is the back and bottom of all our woes (and seems come to stay). I got the pills soon after 1 yesterday afternoon and took one—then near 5 another—then at 9 this morning another. Had a tolerable night. A rare egg on Graham toast for breakfast—coffee; have been moist—skin half sweating the last 15 or 20 hours. Am sitting here in the big chair in my den as usual."

Again: "June 7, 1891, Sunday ev'ng, 4:30—Have just had my 2d meal, mutton and rice stew, wet Graham toast, &c.; relished fairly—drank a little of the Rhine wine—take the granules (3 to-day). No motion of the bowels now, I think, five perhaps six days. To-day easier (negative)—freer from the horrible deathly sinkiness of yesterday and Thursday—have been sitting up reading and writing all day—had one or two visitors, excused myself.

"Horace Traubel still in Canada, having a good time I guess. Expect him back last of the coming week. A half-medical acquaintance was in—said, 'You look all right—surely there's nothing the matter with your health!' Didn't know whether to take it as compliment or the other thing. (Ah! this immovable block of constipation.)"

These extracts give a more realizing sense of his condition during these days than could any words of mine. I was informed in a letter received from Dr. R. M. Bucke at this time: "Mentally Mr. W. is failing a good deal. Makes slips now that would have been impossible for *him* a very few years ago. For instance, I have a post card from him, dated 23d inst., on which he says: 'Dr. Torkaner came yesterday. I like him.'" Then Dr. Bucke says: "A *name* is something he *never* went wrong in." This singular name thus quoted was meant for mine.

At almost every visit I would urge the beneficial effects of fresh air, of sunshine, and of a little exercise, but all to little avail. His experience of outdoor exercise was quite bad. As he says in his letter, it flustered him— "blinded and deafened" him. He was loth to repeat it. A very few outings were all he took during the entire spring, summer and autumn. He preferred his bedroom—his den, he called it—to the rest of the house, and here I nearly always found him. Never idle, he sat surrounded by a vast heap of books, papers, manuscripts and what not, in apparently hopeless confusion, always busied in something, always interested in anything I chanced to say of men or women, medical men and matters medical always seeming to interest him especially. The severest thing I could make him say of any one was that many of the women visitors at summer resorts cared more for the exhibition of their jewelry and dress, the men, more for whiskey, than for the wonderful beauties and grandeurs of nature to be seen at so many of these places. All of which he de-

Walt Whitman, early 1860s (Feinberg Collection, Library of Congress)

plored. He had more faith in the generality—the common average man and woman—than in the majority of these erring seekers after pleasure.

Several times we discussed woman. In his opinion she was man's superior in every way; she bore pain and suffering with more fortitude. On one occasion he told me he thought it a grand thing to grow old gracefully. He used to tell me that my visits did him good, and would say to others that my visits did him as much good as my medicine.

While he did not regain sufficient strength, during this time, to leave his room often, he lost none of his interest in men and the affairs of the day, not only all through the long months of this confinement, rendered doubly tedious by the physical burdens he bore, but all through the dark days that followed the invasion of the fatal sickness which appeared on the seventeenth of December; and this in spite of the mental failure spoken of by Dr. Bucke.

In the early afternoon of the date just named he was seized with a severe chill. He termed it an incipient rigor. The second annual visitation of grippe was prevailing extensively at this time. Returning home about midnight, after an exhausting day of professional work, I had the first intimation of the change in my Camden patient. The note left by my friend Traubel, who had waited in my home until patience gave out, was urgent. And yet, because of my numerous involvements, I was able to respond only late in the afternoon of the following day—more than twenty-four hours after the chill. A cursory examination sufficed to reveal the gravity of this case. The chill had been attended and followed by a rise of temperature—the thermometer showing 102 F.; his pulse was 100; respirations, 30. A very troublesome cough, slight hoarseness, and, already, pretty free muco-purulent expectoration was established. There was complete loss of appetite and marked prostration, so that he voluntarily remained in bed. He did not admit having headache or any special pain, complaining in fact of nothing. He thought his friends had been unduly anxious about him, and he apologized to me because they had brought me over to Camden, needlessly, and so late in the day: he could have waited until the time of my usual visit on the next day. Not intended as reproof for deferred duty it was yet a keen rebuke, and gladly would I have made amends for this temporary neglect.

On the following day, the third of his illness, there was no improvement. The areas of dullness, especially over the right lung, found on the preceding day, had increased. All the physical as well as rational signs indicated a widely diffused broncho-pneumonia. Air entered the lungs very imperfectly. Cough was very troublesome, and expectoration quite free. With his bad general condition, the marked prostration and the hints of heart failure that I had heard, there seemed to me no chance of ultimate recovery or even of a temporary rally. There was a complex of symptoms which in all my previous experience in men of his age had been of fatal, even rapidly fatal, significance. On the next day, Sunday, I saw him twice, the second time late in the afternoon, and in consultation with Dr. Alexander McAlister, of Camden, whose residence in the immediate neighborhood would assure his presence should a physician be suddenly needed through any serious change in the patient's condition. At neither visit was much change in his general condition noted from the previous day, although his strength seemed slowly ebbing. He could take no nourishment and was disinclined to use the stimulants that seemed to us appropriate and necessary. For the first time in my knowledge he made objections to taking his medicine; but he took it nevertheless. The lungs were distinctly worse; very little air was entering the left and less still the right. The respiratory movements were very limited indeed, and tracheal rales, known usually as the death-rattle, were heard with each of the movements. There was some cyanosis, the end of the nose being slightly, and the finger-tips markedly, blue. Clearly, there was not enough lung tissue left functionally active to oxygenate the blood satisfactorily. The heart's action was regular and not intermittent, and the pulse continued at one hundred, with the respirations as on the first day, thirty. There was less fever. He fully realized his critical condition, but gave not the slightest evidence of anxiety or fear of its probable outcome. He was, indeed, cheerful and complained of nothing, admitting that he had pain or suffered in any way only when he was especially asked. I may say here, this state of mind (this lack of anxiety for the future, this absence of complaint, this cheerful attitude) was maintained to the last hour of his life.

The first part of this, Sunday, night, was passed with sleep at short intervals, but at one A.M., December 21st, his attendants thought the end was near. He took a milk punch and rallied from this very low condition. When I saw him later in the day, he was somnolent; skin relaxed and leaky; the *large rales persisting*. He wished to be left alone, would not talk— indeed, refused to see his near friends. Very remarkably, however, on one occasion, when Warren, his nurse, had left a few minutes, he raised himself in and sat up on the side of the bed. He was unable to get back unaided. Dr. R. M. Bucke arrived late in the day. He fully shared our belief that the end could not be far off.

The somnolency and the cyanosis continued on the 22d; also some irregularity of the pulse (the first noticed), and greater frequency. He preferred still to be left alone, saying, "My friends seem not to realize how weak I am, and what an effort it is for me to talk." More favorable was his taking food—a small mutton chop in the morning, and several milk punches during the day. His attendants reported a fair night, but on the 23d I found him again in a somnolent state, the heart's action very irregular, the pulse small and averaging one hundred and ten beats to the minute. The right lung seemed less solid and more pervious to air. Several raw oysters were eaten during the day, and this was all. He *could* not take milk punch or stimulants.

December 24th, Dr. McAlister saw the patient with me at five P.M. It was evident that the slight improvement of the preceding day had not continued. More careful examination disclosed quite extensive involvement of the left lung, with the right practically useless. Generally he seemed much weaker. At ten P.M. my colleague was hastily summoned. He found the patient generally cyanosed, with labored respiration; a weak, rapid and irregular pulse; the surface of the body covered with a cold, clammy sweat. He was exhausted. It was believed by all present that he could not live through the night—so complete was the collapse. On the 25th I saw him twice. Not only had he rallied from the collapse by morning, but there seemed a slight amelioration of the bad condition of the previous day. All were quite hopeful. The promising condition continued only a short time. On the 26th he was as bad as ever. He lay all day long in what appeared to be a semi-conscious state, but very curiously replied promptly to any question put to him. His hearing, not good of late, was now especially acute. Lowering my voice purposely to test this, I uniformly observed that he heard me. My colleagues agreed with me that this was so. "No pain," said he, "but so very miserable!" His heart seemed failing—irregular and intermittent—the pulse, however, still averaging one hundred. All nourishment was refused. Dr. Bucke, watching at the bedside late in the evening, declared the end near at hand, and that he would remain now until all was over. None of us had the faintest idea that the end was yet three months off. But low as was the ebb, life continued. At the consultation on the 27th, Drs. McAlister and Bucke present with me, a very careful examination of the chest was made. The patient was supported for a short time in the sitting posture, in order that the bases and posterior surface of the lungs could be examined. Improvement was indicated by the presence of some resonance on percussion and by the existence of some breath sounds—though these were feeble. The left side was more impaired than we had believed. The respiratory movements were still entirely abdominal, thirty-three to the minute. Expectoration of muco-purulent matter continued. There was little if any fever, but loss of flesh was evident. That we were not mistaken in our conclusion that there was some improvement the next few days abundantly proved. By January 7th there had been re-established a normal pulse respiration ratio, the former seventy-two and the latter eighteen. I had in my attendance during the previous year found the pulse very uniformly at sixty-four. This was, there-fore, but little above the normal for him. At this time there was complete abatement of all the alarming symptoms. The tracheal rale—or death-rattle—had been survived; one attack of complete collapse, with cyanosis and irregular and intermittent heart action, that all thought the sure precursor of death, was not such. Altogether, this was one of the most remarkable experiences of my entire professional life. While all alarming conditions and signs were now gone, there was never any establishment of real convalescence. Badly as he must have felt, he had already settled down to a routine of daily life little varied from this on to the very last.

The curious mental condition of which I have spoken, and which I at first supposed to be a sort of stupor or semi-consciousness, was not such at all, as I found upon a more careful investigation. Had it been coma, or partial coma, hearing, with the other special senses, would have been dull; but his hearing at this time was, for him, remarkably acute—was even abnormally so. He was often supposed to be sleeping when he was without doubt perfectly aware of all that was going on about him. All that was necessary to secure his attention was a word uttered in the lowest tones or a touch on the hand or arm. Once, when I supposed him asleep, and placed my finger on his wrist in the lightest manner possible, he looked up and greeted me. He preferred to be left entirely alone. Often the presence of his best friends seemed to worry him. When he was at his lowest, and when his end was hourly looked for, we were requested to induce him, if possible, to see one of them for a few moments on a matter of some importance to himself. "No, no, I cannot! Tell them to wait until I am better." And he continued: "My friends seem not to realize how it tires me to talk." But we said: "You may never be better." All the same his decision was made, and he would not abate from it.

He preferred his attendants in the room adjoining his own, and had a bell-pull fixed within easy reach of his hand as he was lying down. When he desired help, he rang.

He must have suffered greatly, but he made little complaint. All the pain and soreness was referred to the left side, the splenic re-

Walt Whitman, 1862

gion, the sigmoid flexture of the colon; and near the end of life there was some pain in the left foot. The cause of the pain was not clear until the post-mortem. Hiccough was a very persistent symptom from before Christmas up to within a short time of the end. At first it lasted hours without intermission, and finally troubled less continuously. Much cough and muco-purulent expectoration showed that the pneumonia had undergone partial resolution only. Some of the consolidated areas were undergoing softening. Only very late were occasional night sweats noticed, and the fever, if present at all, was very moderate. There was a continual loss of flesh in spite of a fair amount of nourishment taken daily.

As a rule, he would awake about nine A.M. after a restless night. Hourly or oftener he would ring or call the nurse to change his position. Soon it was possible for him to lie on the left side only, and finally this tortured him. Said he: "I have to choose between two evils: lying on the left side tortures me, on the right the phlegm chokes me." However, after each change of posture he was supposed to fall promptly asleep. Between nine and ten in the morning he would have his breakfast—a simple meal of Graham toast, coffee and usually either an egg or a small piece of steak. Then between four and five in the afternoon a second meal, consisting of bread and butter, mutton broth and rice, and occasionally including some raw oysters. Milk, either plain or as milk punch, was taken very moderately, and the same was true of stimulants in general. Every few days three or four ounces of champagne were taken. This with the view of securing its effect on the alimentary canal. It acted pretty uniformly as a laxative, and only a few times was it necessary to resort to enemata. There were only three or four days during which no food was taken, and then he said he did not want to be bothered with it. Whenever he felt unusually restless at night, he would attribute it to having eaten too much. In the vain search for a remedy to control the hiccough, ice-cream, suggested by one, was tried. Its effect was indifferent, and several times harmful, in that a diarrhœa followed its use. The digestive function was, as a rule, fairly well performed. The moderate quantities of food taken were digested. The tongue remained moist and clean throughout. The excretion of urine was much below normal. It varied from eight to twelve ounces in the twenty-four hours.

After his morning meal Whitman would have the curtain opposite his bed raised. He would then obtain the daily papers and his mail and these would engage him for hours. There were very few days when they were neglected. When they were, all hope would sink in the breasts of his attendants, to be as quickly revived by their resumption. Ocassionally, some writing was done. On January 10th he signed two of the Johnston etchings for his attending physicians.

To the very last day of his life this interest in the news and affairs of the day was maintained. Little as he said, even in the way of necessary communications, he would occasionally surprise us by referring briefly to a bit of news. "Dr. Parker's dead," said he to me on the day following the death of Dr. Andrew J. Parker.

He did not, as is usual with consumptives, entertain any hopes of recovery. Some days he would say he felt much better, but only once during this long period did he apparently allow himself to be deluded by the hope that he would get well. About the middle of February, one morning after breakfast, some one said to him: "We hope soon to see you in your chair again." His prompt negative—"Never!

never!"—showed conclusively that he had no such hope. At another time the nurse told him they were thinking of getting a new bed for him. "You slip away from us so in this one." He rejoined: "Some of these fine mornings I shall be slipping away from you forever." "Well, doctors, what is the verdict?" was a question asked us more than once. In explanation of the reason for the question he said he thought "it would be a satisfaction to know how the cat was going to jump." Then, too, he was of the opinion that "what the doctors can't tell you about yourself no one else can." The exception referred to, when he apparently allowed himself to be misled by a false hope, was when he declared to Warren one morning that "he was going to beat those doctors yet." Once he gave us the account of the famous two-hour talk on Boston Common with Emerson, who, he said quaintly, "talked the finest talk that ever was talked." At the conclusion of the narration he promptly extended his hand, and, as Dr. McAlister said, "dismissed us with his blessing."

We were much in the dark as to the extent and real nature of his trouble. The large pleural effusion, which must have existed for weeks, entirely escaped our recognition. Repeatedly the question of cancerous disease came up, but it was always decided against. He continued to lose flesh and strength so gradually that one failed to observe the decline.

March 11th he was again reading the daily papers. For several days they had been neglected. His attendants were greatly cheered.

I have already spoken of the necessity for frequent changes of posture. In the twenty-four hours from the 21st to the 22d of March he was turned just forty-one times. On the 23d his hearing was dull. It had all along been quite acute. Respirations were now relatively too frequent—twenty-three to the minute. The pulse was eighty-four. The tracheal rale—"death-rattle"—was again heard, but it disappeared as soon as he turned to his left side from the position on the back. March 26th, although we realized that our patient was extremely weak, we were hardly prepared for the end, then near at hand.

At 12.30 P.M. there was a little dyspnœa—he felt short of breath. The respirations had gone up to thirty a minute. His pulse was small and irregular—eighty-four to ninety-two. Some tracheal rales were noticed.

This was his last day, and ere the darkness of night had gathered his emaciated body was without life.

Mr. Traubel sends me this brief statement of the last hour:

"The end came so suddenly this day's evening between six and seven, even after all our anticipation, that we had no time to summon you. Harned, McAlister, Fritzinger, and Mrs. Davis were present already when I arrived. There was no sign of struggle on the part of the patient. The light flickered, lowered, was quenched. He seemed to suffer no pain. His heart was strong to the last, and even may be said to have outbeat his life, since for some minutes after the breath was gone, the faint throb at his breast, though lessening, continued. He needed no help—indeed, help was past avail. A few minor attentions which we fairly reasoned might give him comfort were shown. Elsewise we sat or stood and watched. He said nothing. He lay on his back—the one hand which he had reached out to me when I came, and which I held, on the coverlet. He passed away as peacefully as the sun, and it was hard to catch the moment of transition. That solemn watch, the gathering shadow, the painless surrender, are not to be forgotten. His soul went out with the day. The face was calm, the body lay without rigidity, the majesty of his tranquil spirit remained. What more could be said? It was a moment not for the doctor, but for the poet, the seer."

The wonder, that life had continued so long, grew as one by one of the revelations of the post-mortem examination were made.

To this examination he had assented months before his death. "Yes," he said, "if it will be of interest to the doctors and of any benefit to medical science, I am willing."

The following are the notes of the post-mortem performed on the body of Walt Whitman, March 27, 1892, by Henry W. Cattell, demonstrator of gross morbid anatomy, University of Pennsylvania:

The autopsy was made in the presence of Dr. Daniel Longaker, Prof. F. X. Dercum, Dr. Alexander McAlister and Horace L. Traubel. The brain was removed by Dr. Dercum, and is now, after having been hardened, in the possession of the American Anthropometric Society. This Society, which has been organized for the express purpose of studying high-type brains, intends to first photograph the external surfaces and then make a cast of the entire brain. After this, careful microscopic observations will be made by competent observers.

Both the head and the brain were remarkably well formed and symmetrical. The scalp was thin, and practically no blood was lost

Walt Whitman, 1864

when the incisions were made. The calvarium was white and the muscular tissue pale. The dura mater was very adherent to the skull cap and showed recent pachymeningitis on both sides, but especially on the right. The blood in the longitudinal sinus was fluid. The bone was well ossified, and there was little or no diploic substance remaining. The pia and arachnoid were very œdematous, and considerable cerebro-spiral fluid escaped during the removal of the brain. Numerous milky patches, especially over the vertex, were seen, but no miliary tubercles were discernible. The membranes were not adherent to the cortex, and the brain substance was excessively soft. The blood vessels of the circle of Willis were very slightly atheromatous. The brain weighed forty-five ounces, two hundred and ninety-two and one-half grains avoirdupois. While this is a medium weight for a brain, it must be remembered that the brain decreases in weight one ounce for every ten years in a person over fifty, and that it is much more important for intellectual and physical well being that the convolutions are well formed, the sulci deep and the cortical substance wide. Large allowance must also be made for the extreme emaciation of the whole body, involving of course the brain. It is likely the brain had shrunk (from this cause) six to eight ounces in the last months of life. Taking these elements of the problem into account, it seems likely that at mental maturity Walt Whitman's brain weighed at least fifty-six ounces.

The body was emaciated, post-mortem lividity was slight, and there was no rigidity. On attempting to remove the skin of the left side a little to the left of the median line at the sixth rib laudable pus escaped. On careful examination there was found here an elevated area the size of a fifty-cent piece, which was situated over but slightly to the left of the center of the manubrium and had eroded that bone to the extent of a twenty-five-cent piece. The abscess had burrowed into the pectoralis major and had commenced to erode the superficial fascia. It had not broken inwardly, though it could be plainly seen from the posterior surface of the sternum.

About half an ounce of pericardial fluid was found. The heart, which weighed about nine ounces, was very flabby and well covered with epicardial fat, except a small portion in the center of the right ventricle. The pulmonary valves were slightly thickened but competent. Aortic valves in good condition, closing completely. The mitral valves good, the tricuspids perfectly good.

There were three and one-half quarts of serous fluid in the left pleural cavity, and the lung, the size of the hand, was completely pressed against the mediastinum, so that it was absolutely impossible for air to enter. A few bands of recent lymph extended across an injected pleura, which was hemorrhagic in spots. On the plueral surface at a point just below the nipple was an abscess the size of a hen's egg, which had completely eroded the fifth rib, the longest diameter of the abscess being in the vertical direction. There was no external mark on the skin to lead one to suspect the presence of the abscess, though there was some bulging and distinct fluctuation, and the two ends of the rib could be plainly felt grating against each other. Only about one-eighth of the right lung was suitable for breathing purposes. The upper and middle lobes were consolidated and firmly bound down to the pleura. There were about four ounces of fluid in the cavity. Large tubercular nodules and the areas of catarrhal pneumonia were everywhere to be found. Those portions of the lung not tubercular were markedly emphysematous, this being especially marked at the free edges of the lungs.

The spleen was soft and weighed about eight ounces, the capsule thickened and fibrous; on section pulpy. It was matted down to the diaphragm and showed old peritonitis and perisplenitis. Numerous tubercles occupied this region, extending to the anterior wall of the stomach and to all of the neighboring viscera. The diaphragm was pushed downward by the fluid.

The kidneys were surrounded by a mass of fat. The left suprarenal capsule was tubercular and contained a cyst the size of a pigeon's egg. In this was found a darkish fluid. The capsule strips readily; the kidney weighed about six and one-half ounces, and showed some parenchymatous change. The kidney substance was soft, red, and swollen, and somewhat granular. The right kidney was a little the smaller and the better of the two.

A huge gall stone almost entirely occupied a rather small gall bladder to which it was firmly adherent. The outer surface of the stone was covered with a whitish deposit.

The pancreas was hemorrhagic. The common iliacs were but very slightly atheromatous.

Over the whole of the mesentery, especially in its lower portion, were hundreds of minute tubercles varying in size from that of a fine needle-point to the head of a good-sized pin. These whitish points were surrounded by a hemorrhagic base. The serous surface of the intestines was injected and dotted with tubercles. The bladder was empty and the walls thickened. The prostate was enlarged. The rectum was swollen and filled with semifluid feces. A few hardened masses were found in the tranverse colon. The stomach was small. The vermiform appendix was two inches long and patulous, containing two small hardened fecal masses of an irregular outline. The sigmoid flexture was unusually long.

The above macroscopic lesions of the various organs were confirmed by microscopic sections.

It would seem very probable that the extensive adhesion of the dura mater to the calvarium was due to an old sun-stroke.

The cause of death was pleurisy of the left side, consumption of the right lung, general miliary tuberculosis and parenchymatous nephritis. There was also found a fatty liver, gall-stone, a cyst in the adrenal, tubercular abscesses, involving the bones, and pachymeningitis.

It is, indeed, marvellous that respiration could have been carried on for so long a time with the limited amount of useful lung tissue found at the autopsy. It was no doubt due largely to that indomitable will pertaining to Walt Whitman. Another would have died much earlier with one-half of the pathological changes which existed in his body.

To medical ears, at least, it may seem strange that physicians of even average diagnostic skill should overlook a large pleural effusion like this. There were two reasons for it—the first was the lack of complaint of pain; the second, our respect for his disinclination to be disturbed. It seemed a rudeness, almost, to subject him to a searching examination. Practically, this failure of discovery made little difference, since it is doubtful if the removal of the fluid would have added much to the comfort or succeeded in prolonging life. This pleurisy was due to deposit in the membrane of the tubercles, the same as were found about the spleen and the peritoneum of the left side of the abdomen in general. Here they originated peritonitis, and thus accounted for the pain. The abscess eroding the sternum must have existed a long time. It also was tubercular, and in all probability was the original point of development of the disease and the focus of subsequent infection. It is a fact now pretty generally known that individuals in apparently perfect health may have tuberculous mediastinal glands, and such this, in all likelihood, was originally. How long it and the other abscess eroding one of the ribs had existed is a matter of surmise, not of certainty. It might have been several years. It certainly antedated the outbreak of pneumonia in December by months. No wonder, now, that he felt a "deadly lassitude and inertia!"

I wish to silence forever the slanderous accusations that debauchery and excesses of various kinds caused or contributed to his breakdown. There was found no trace or reason to suspect, either during life or after death, either alcoholism or syphilis. This statement is in justice due the memory of one whose ideal of purity was high.

But he had a ruddy face; and he despised not the "despised persons"—therefore he must be one of them! The accusation is as old at least as the time of the Man of Nazareth, against whom it was charged that he mingled with publicans and sinners.

About his (Whitman's) indomitable will there can be no disagreement. And yet I do not share the opinion that it was exercised in a struggle against the inevitable. Perhaps, if he willed at all, it was to die sooner. But bodily pangs and tortures seemed not to perturb him; he lived out his last days as he had lived his last forty years, with senses alert and keen and emotions under perfect control. His mind was bent on higher things than those passing about his inert and out-worn body. Who, indeed, shall trace for us the mysterious labyrinths of its wanderings, and record its experiences throughout those long days and weeks and months? We are certain they had not the complexion of fear, and it seems likely that his lifelong faith in continued existence did not desert him (was probably confirmed) in this last supreme experience and agony. This much, at least, is certain, that at the very end, as all through his life, the act of dying had no terrors for him who had passed

. . . . "death with the dying and birth with the new-washed babe."

In *In Re Walt Whitman*, ed. Horace L. Traubel, Richard Maurice Bucke, and Thomas B. Harned (Philadelphia: David McKay, 1893), pp. 393-411.

WALT WHITMAN, SCHOOLMASTER: NOTES OF A CONVERSATION WITH CHARLES A. ROE, 1894

Horace L. Traubel

Charles A. Roe was a student of Whitman's when the latter taught school in Flushing, New York, in the late 1830s. His account is one of the few we have of this early period in Whitman's life.

[Charles A. Roe was born at Little Bay Side, in the town of Flushing, Long Island, February, 1829. He lived there for nearly forty years, and moved into Flushing village in 1867.

He was elected supervisor of the town of Flushing in 1860, serving six years. In 1866 he was made Treasurer of Queens County, continuing in that capacity through two terms of three years each. In 1874 he moved out on a farm at Westbury, Long Island, among the Quakers, where he remained three years, making his next place of residence Brooklyn.

While residing in Brooklyn he was in business in New York City. On the last day of 1889 he removed to Lakewood, New Jersey, where he has since resided and where this interview took place, October, 1894.

I report Mr. Roe practically in his own words. Some repetitions have been eliminated and the matter has been redeemed from the inconsecutiveness of an unpremeditated conversation. Otherwise, Mr. Roe speaks for himself, without interferences or interlineations on my part. Certain editing was necessary.

Whitman says, "Specimen Days," page 16: "1836-7 worked as compositor in printing offices in New York City. Then, when little more than eighteen, and for a while afterwards, went to teaching country schools down in Queens and Suffolk counties, Long Island, and 'boarded round.' This latter I consider one of my best experiences, and deepest lesson in human nature behind the scenes, and in the masses."]

You want to know what I remember about Walt Whitman? Well, put it down your own way. But I do not suppose that I can tell much you can use. And I will have to talk in a rambling sort of fashion, just as the things come to me.

I went to school with him in the town of Flushing, Long Island. He taught the school at Little Bay Side. His boarding place was with a widow lady. We became very attached to him.

His ways of teaching were peculiar. He did not confine himself to books, as most of the teachers then did, but taught orally—yes, had some original ideas, all his own. I know about that, for I had heard of others who tried oral teaching. But the plans he adopted were wholly of his conception, and most successful.

He was not severe with the boys, but had complete discipline in the school. Before and after school, and at recess, he was a boy among boys, always free, always easy, never stiff. He took active part in games of frolic. It seemed to be his object to teach even when he played. He had a game of twenty questions. He would mentally select an animal, or some other object, and then give us twenty chances to guess what it was. We combined a good deal of fun and instruction in this game.

Walt never was trifling. I could see that he always kept in mind the serious nature of his task and its responsibility. At the same time he would never betray by anything in his manner that he felt above us, or condescended, or wished in any way to put on a tone or an air of superiority.

Every day of a certain hour we would go out in an unoccupied room together, to practice in mental arithmetic. He made a prominent feature of this. At that time it was a new method of instruction—since then it has become more or less general.

Walt was very fond of describing objects and incidents to the school. He would not do this privately, but to all hands. He would give quite a good deal of time to any subject that seemed worth while. He was always interesting, a very good talker, able to command the attention of scholars, of whom, by the way, there were seventy or eighty. Our ages ranged sixteen, seventeen, eighteen years old—yet many, too, were young shavers like myself.

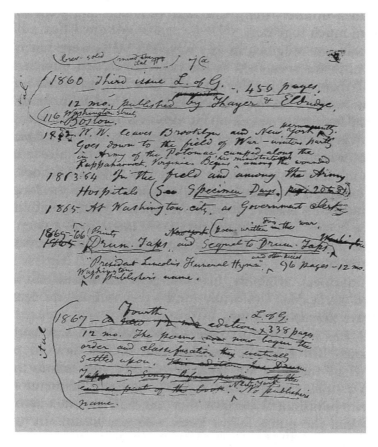

Portion of Whitman's manuscript outline of his life

I never had the least complaint of Walt from any scholar or from the parents of any scholar. We were all deeply attached to him, and were sorry when he went away.

The girls did not seem to attract him. He did not specially go anywhere with them or show any extra fondness for their society.

He would call over at our house and spend an evening. He did not prefer to talk of books. Nearly any every-day subject attracted him. My father had been a great reader, however, and naturally they would converse on books, too.

He spent his Sundays mostly at home. I never remember his going out to any of the churches. If he took walks, I did not know it. He had a brother, then, who was with him and went to school. They were much together.

He was not religious in any way. His views were not of a religious turn. It was remarked by the lady he boarded with that he was rather off from anything like church. This fact produced no feeling that I saw except with this one old lady. She had four young daughters. I had heard her speak of his views on religion as being rather atheistic. Very friendly to him otherwise—just a trifle suspicious, or sorry, that was all.

It is my impression that he was at Bay Side one school year—it was not longer. I was thinking perhaps it was only the long winter term. I cannot be positive about it. Yet there's hardly anything which took place in that time I do not recall. He made such a deep impression upon me, that even insignificant things became important and long-remembered.

His kindness, affability, his close association with us, were unusual and agreeable. Uniformly kind—yes: without the least variation; always exactly the same.

Walt was a good story-teller—Oh! excellent: was both funny and serious. Did I say he had his own notions how to punish a scholar? If he caught a boy lying he exposed him before the whole school in a story. But the story was told without the mention of any names. No punishment beyond that. He had such a way of telling his story that the guilty fellow knew who was meant. He would do this in the case of any ordinary offence. But if the offence was grave enough, the whole school was taken into the secret.

He was the soul of honor. If anyone attempted anything dishonorable he would be out on it at once. There was an examination or something. I had a paper with names on. I did not use it but he saw the paper. After examination was over, and the school was about to be dismissed, he said that he was sorry any scholar should do such a thing as this he had seen me do. He did not mention my name, but I know I never committed the offence again.

He did not take walks with the scholars. The school hours were long, and we only had the one hour recess in the middle of the day. The school was held in the basement of a building put up by Samuel Leggatt, who formerly had been President of the Franklin Bank, New York. This building was intended for a church. Before Whitman came we only had an ordinary schoolhouse. He was among the first teachers in that school. The building still stands. It was designed for a free church for all denominations—located about a mile and a half from the village of Whitestone.

My parents liked Whitman very much as a teacher. Though Episcopalians, themselves, they had no feeling about his being an infidel.

He was not aggressive—did not talk of his religion. His not attending church, or some chance observation, probably to Mrs. Powell, may have caused some persons to remark his heterodoxy. Mrs. Powell only spoke of it casually, was sorry, wished it might have been otherwise, and so on. Walt always boarded with her as long as he had the school.

He was above anything of the woman kind. Did I say that before? He did not care for woman's society—seemed, indeed, to shun it. Young as I was, I was aware of that fact. I do not think he became very closely acquainted even with our young men of his own age. He seemed retiring, diffident, yet he was friendly to everybody—was not offish—made no enemies.

My memory of Walt is cute—unusually cute—probably because his personality had such a powerful and peculiar effect upon me, even as a boy. I had other teachers, but none of them ever left such an impress upon me. And yet I could not mention any particular thing. It was his whole air, his general sympathetic way, his eye, his voice, his entire geniality. I felt something I could not describe. What I say, others will also say. I think he affected all as he did me. They have admitted it—yet, like me, can give no definite reasons. No one could tell why. Their memory of him is exactly like mine. There must be something in it—it is not imagination.

Walt always dressed in black—dressed neatly—very plain in everything—no attempt at what would be called fashion. He wore an old style frock coat, vest and pants black. I judge he wore a white shirt. He dressed mainly as other people dressed. My impression is that his shirt was cut low. His hat not out of the usual at that time. There were only soft hats and silk hats and I know he never wore a silk hat.

Walt's face was entirely beardless. He was never sick; did not smoke; never, that I saw or heard of, drank any liquors. As to his eating, I never knew him to have had any peculiar habits. He was a hearty eater—ate simple foods, being so healthy and strong.

I was talking a while ago of his ways of punishing us. I should have said that he would sometimes stand the scholar up before the school—perhaps put a fool's-cap on him. But he never inflicted corporal punishment. He never asserted himself in a brutal way. Gentle—yes, but firm.

All they taught in schools at that time, was reading, writing, arithmetic, grammar. It was a very primitive district school. Walt had no assistant. I remember no celebrations during his stay and no ceremonies when he left. We lived in what was strictly a farming district, and such things, even sociables, were infrequent, or did not occur at all. We were not close-settled.

School hours were from eight to four: in the winter they were just as long as we could possibly see.

We played ball, but I don't think Walt ever took part in it. He associated more with the younger scholars, frolicing rather than playing games. We had a fine ball ground. He was active as a boy—very quick, agile, supple in all his movements. His complexion? It was ruddy, clear, beautiful.

Whitman's boarding place was a mile and a half from the school. He carried his lunch with him, in a basket. On pleasant days he ate outside with the pupils. As long as it was anyways comfortable at all, even in cold weather, they would eat out of doors. It was his custom to be out every possible moment of his time. He always walked to and from his boarding place, stormy weather or clear. Sometimes we would walk together. He talked a great deal—was always calling our attention to this thing or that—some tree, bird, the sky, rock, or what-not. He was talkative, then—seemed let loose—and our enjoyment was great. There was a walk through the wood that we almost always took. It was almost direct from his boarding place to the school. He liked the fresh air: liked to be alone, also liked to be with people.

Whitman had dignity and yet at the same time he could descend down to sociability. The very moment he stepped across the school door-sill he was master. He had authority, but was not severe. We obeyed and respected him.

He was well proportioned, physically. Did not seem unusually big. Very rugged and healthy. A fine red in his face. Eye clear, lips firm. I could not speak of his strength from any particular circumstance or incident. We all understood it, however, from his genera[l] carriage.

The Powell folks told me that he had written poetry. I knew nothing direct. He wrote something that he called "The Fallen Angel." It commenced:

Walt Whitman, circa 1867 (Feinberg Collection, Library of Congress)

> Oh he was pure! the fleecy snow
> Sinking through air to earth below
> Was not more undefiled!
> Sinless he was, as fleeting smile
> On lip of sleeping child.

We had at that time speaking lessons, and he would give the scholars verses to recite. This was one lesson. They said it was his own composition. That was the rumor. The poem was quite long, having a number of stanzas. My version is very faulty, no doubt, but the lines I have given you are substantially correct.

My father was a good conversationalist. He and Walt were very friendly. Walt would have remembered me in later life by remembering my father. They were uncommonly congenial. I can recall very little or nothing of their conversation. My father was a man of very liberal views. This would have made him interesting to Walt. They were much together.

Now, this has been a rambling sort of talk, but you are welcome to all that can honestly be made of it.

One thing is sure. As far as Walt's goodness and character goes, you can report me pretty full and as strong as you choose. Even back in the school-days, those of us who knew him, his scholars there on Long Island, felt, somehow, without knowing why, that here was a man out of the average, who strangely attracted our respect and affection.

Walt Whitman Fellowship Papers, 14 (April 1895): 81-87.

From REMINISCENCES OF WALT WHITMAN

William Sloane Kennedy

William Sloane Kennedy, a writer for the Philadelphia Saturday Evening Post, *became one of Whitman's public champions, beginning in February 1881 with "A Study of Walt Whitman" in the* Californian, *and continuing through his detailed study of the composition and reception of* Leaves of Grass *in* The Fight of a Book for the World *(1926).*

> "Publish my name and hang up my picture as that of the tenderest lover."
>
> — *Leaves of Grass.*

Philadelphia, November 22, 1880.—A delightful call on Walt Whitman last night. There is a kind of sweet and pathetic resignation in the tones of his voice; he seems patient and pain-chastened; has a proud but kindly, native-aristocratic temper and carriage. It appears that he has never dipped into the Greek language; said he had not. But I never knew any one show profounder insight into the Greek *al fresco* spirit than he in the course of a few broken and hesitating sentences. (Walt Whitman's syntax is always much broken in conversation, until he warms up to his theme.) He said, "The Greeks tested everything by the open air." I can't tell how it was, but the large personality of the man so vivified the few words he spoke that all the majesty of Greece—especially her sculpturesque art-idea— seemed to loom up before me as never before in my life, although the study of Greek literature had been a specialty of my collegiate and post-collegiate years. Whitman dwelt enthusiastically on the remarkable perennial purity of the great St. Lawrence River, which he had seen during the past summer. We both thought that this translucid purity would have deep influence upon the art and the ethical natures of the people who are to dwell along the St. Lawrence and the chain of the Great Lakes.

February 17, 1881.—At the close of the evening Whitman spoke of the Adamitic element in his poetry, saying, "I know that other writers excel me in intellectual gifts, etc., but my contribution, that which I bring into literature for the first time, is the brawn and blood of the people, the basic animal element, virility, the pure sexuality, which is as indispensable to literature as its finer elements. Hitherto the blackguards have had this field to themselves." He expressed himself as immensely pleased with Denver, Colorado; said he would rather live there than anywhere else in the world; New York City was his next choice, and had been his first in youth; but its feverish life was too much for him now, in his old age. He spoke with delight of the purling streams of water that he had seen flowing through the streets of Denver,—the pure melted snow of the mountains; said he used to get up in the morning, when there, and go out on purpose to see it. I introduced a remark of John Burroughs about the low and degraded quality of American humour, which deals with its characters as if they were despicable inferiors, and not as do the great humourists,—with genial and generous sympathy. Whitman heartily agreed with Burroughs, and said, with warm indignation, that the men out in the mountains and mines and plains of the West were the equals of the Homeric heroes or the old gods, and are so treated by Joaquin Miller, and a few others; but our newspaper scribblers spy around to pick out small sources of ridicule and burlesque. He told me a little anecdote of Carlyle. Mrs. Lowell, of Boston, had loaned Carlyle the "Harvard Memorial Biographies" (of those who fell in the war). After reading in them, Carlyle said to Mrs. Lowell, "Well, I dinna ken but I have got on the wrang track about your America." Whitman remarked that perhaps literature was not of such importance in itself, except as it helped us to look with more pleasure and profit on life,—its shows and duties. As he sat there on the sofa (in the little parlour of the Stevens Street house in Camden), with his enormous, long-used hat on his head (the rim pushed up from the forehead to an almost perpendicular position, as is often his wont when at home—the same habit is noticeable in the portraits of Montaigne), I was impressed by his large personality,— the rich, supple-sweet fulness of flesh, delicacy on a basis of rugged strength.

Walt Whitman, circa 1870

February 22, 1881.—Met Whitman strolling along the sunny side of Market Street. When Gulliver was placed on his mistress's hand before the Brobdignagian looking-glass, he actually seemed to himself to have dwindled in size. So it is with me when I meet Walt Whitman,— partly on account of his imposing presence. But then, after one has talked with him for a while, he imparts his own stature (momentarily), and one goes off feeling seven feet high, like Bouchardon after reading the Iliad. Walt had on a huge ulster. In winter he always dresses warmly in thick gray clothes, which somehow seem to have a certain fulness, perfume, comfortable warmth, peculiar to him. March 8, 1881.—Had a delightful call with Mr. G. P. Lathrop on Whitman. Lathrop's ostensible errand was to get Walt to read his Death of Lincoln piece before the St. Botolph's Club of Boston. (Satisfactorily arranged; Walt Whitman went on and gave his reading at the Hawthorne Rooms).[1] I was amused at Whitman's account of a talk he had years before with philosopher Alcott. He said: "Yes, he talked,

119

and I listened; I talked a little; I liked his atmosphere." This struck me as droll, who knew so well the amiable weakness of my good old friend of Concord for monopolizing conversation.

Belmont, Mass., January, 1885.—Spent several hours of January 2 with Whitman (on my way home from New Orleans). A young son of Thomas Donaldson came in for a call, and on going away bashfully kissed the old poet. Walt Whitman read us his as yet immature "Fancies at Navesink," which appeared in the *Nineteenth Century* the next August.

Philadelphia, June 3, 1886.—Spent an hour or so with Walt Whitman at his little Mickle Street "shanty," as he calls his house (No. 328). He sits there "anchored" in his great chair by the front lower-floor window (scarcely able to get up and down stairs now, since his sunstroke a year ago), and holds what seems like a simple democratic court, receiving all who come to him,—bores and all,—only now and then having courteously to assert his right to some of his own time. To-day I found a young artist present, who reverently asked (what was cheerfully granted) permission to come and sit quietly in the back part of the room, for a few hours, in order to record with the pencil, if he might be able, what even the photograph could not catch. Another acquaintance was (bad-manneredly) questioning Whitman, and taking notes of what he said before his very face. Whitman said he was grown quite lethargic, taking little live interest in anything. The morning papers, which he dozed over a couple of hours or more every day, occupied his mind without making any demand upon his intellectual or sympathetic nature. He had promised and promised, and "re-re-promised" to write for the *Century* a paper on the War Hospitals; but there the bundle of materials lay (at his feet under the table), waiting until the inspiration should come—if it ever did. (The article was afterwards written for the *Century*.) As Whitman sat there talking, his gray suit and white hair and beard were outlined against a huge grizzly wolf-skin, thrown over the high-backed chair, and half surrounding the entire upper half of his body; his feet rested on a salmon-coloured rug; and here and there—on the window-sill, on the floor, and on the table—were bright-red roses and other flowers, the gifts of his lovers. After his wont, he greeted everybody who passed on the sidewalk, little children and all, with a "How d'y'do!" Through his friend, Mr. Edward Carpenter, of England, he had just received a gift of £50, and at the close of my call his young friend "Warry" brought his horse and phaeton to the door, and drove him over to Philadelphia to bank the money. He spoke in the warmest terms of Mr. Carpenter, and of two English ladies, who, as I gathered, had made him (Carpenter) the medium of their tribute of admiration and gratitude to the poet. Walt Whitman spoke, indeed, with invariable kindness of everyone whose name came up during our talk,—Stedman, Symonds, Conway, and others. It is evident that he cherishes no ill-will (and never has cherished any) against either his half friends or no friends. He had also just received from one of two charming Quaker ladies—dear friends of his, to whom he had given a note of introduction to Tennyson—a letter giving account of their cordial reception by the Laureate and his family, who constrained them to stay to lunch, and showed them every attention. At Farringford, Tennyson's study, to which they mounted, is a sunny room at the top of a winding staircase, and commands, through green cedars of Lebanon, a lovely view of Freshwater Bay. To pass suddenly from the poetical to the practical,—Whitman said that he was extremely annoyed by the habit the women of his neighbourhood had of coming out two or three times a day with their brooms and stirring up the water in the gutters. He thought it caused malaria. "If they would only leave it alone!" he said. I learned accidently, and from several sources, that Walt Whitman still keeps up his work of ministering to the sick and suffering. His housekeeper coming in, as I sat there, informed him that Mrs.— was not expected to live; he received the news as would a physician a report from one of his patients, and yet with a deep compassion which few physicians genuinely feel. Calling again unexpectedly one day, I found by his side, a bottle of cordial destined, he said, for a sick neighbour. Whitman's friends know that he is extremely sensitive about receiving gifts, in cases where he thinks there has been no *quid pro quo*. I learned that, after his Lincoln reading in Philadelphia, in the spring of 1886,—a reading which was, in part, a complimentary benefit on the part of friends and disciples,—Mr. Whitman insisted on handing two dollars apiece all around to the attendants behind the curtain and in the lobbies of the Opera House where the entertainment was given.

Walt Whitman's friends rarely visit him without having a hearty laugh with him over something or other. This is for the benefit of those enemies of his who are so ignorant of his nature as to assert that he is destitute of humour. On the other hand, he has his stern as well as his sad moods; in the former there is a look of power in his face that almost makes one tremble. All his nerves are well covered: he never exhibits, facially, the least emotion on hearing important or startling news; composure is his most apparent and constant trait. This immobility of feature he clearly derives from his Dutch ancestry.

June 6, 1886.—Sunday Evening.—Found Whitman sitting on his front stoop, talking with a negative-pugnacious reformer. The poet entertained his ideas without a trace of impatience or severity of judgment, and yet was capable of quietly chloroforming him if he became disagreeable. He reprehended any measures that might be taken to punish the expression of even the most violent anarchistic sentiments; for the right of free speech is inviolable. He is very much annoyed by the pestiferous brood of autograph-hunters, and by weak-headed poetlings who send him manuscripts for his kind judgment. The manuscripts he almost always throws into the wastebasket, which is indeed capacious enough in all conscience, being nothing less than one of the great wicker-work clothes-baskets employed by housekeepers on wash-days.[2] The poet seems to carry on his small mailing and publisher's business downstairs now, in the little parlour where he sits. By his side, amid a litter of paper, is to be seen a pile of copies of the two-volume centennial issue of his works.

A peculiar feature of Walt Whitman's personal rooms—those, I mean, which his housekeeper is not allowed to "put in order"—is the chaos of confusion in which his papers are coiled. The bump of order does not appear to exist in his cranium. He has a huge book of addresses of Whitmanites and book customers (probably several hundred names), but the entries in that plethoric and much-thumbed old volume are not indexed at all, nor are they in alphabetical order! The disorder of the dear old fellow's in-door dens (they have been to him in past years little more than sleeping places; his real study, the sky-domed vault of the earth) is, of course, apt commentary upon the loose arrangement of the prose and poetry of his books. But the habit of getting things into confusion about their rooms is one which many old bachelor-authors fall (especially invalids), and is by no means necessarily typical of any looseness or vagueness of the logical faculties. Whitman said he considered "Drum Taps" as an attempt to express the emotional element of the Civil War. He asked me very emphatically to make a note of this,—that in *Leaves of Grass* his intention had been, among the rest, to put on record a complete individual; make a clean breast of it, give a true pic-

Walt Whitman in 1869

ture of the nineteenth-century man; his effort had been distinctively a liberative one,—to make a full sweep, for once, as by the fierce whirl of a child's carlacue in the dark, right through the manacling conventions which fetter the expression of man's real soul. He said he considered that his study of the trades, and the facts of practical life, had served to give proportion, or balance, to his writings, redeeming them from the too common fault of literary work,—namely bookishness. He emphatically denied that his efforts in poetry were the outcome of culture, or the result of wide reading of books. He said that, among Mr. E. C. Stedman's mistakes about him, was that which he made when he asserted of him that he did not include within the range of his sympathies the wealthy, or so-called higher classes. He has since created enemies among anarchists by sympathetic little poems on the old Emperor William and Queen Victoria. He spoke of the late Mrs. Anne Gilchrist as one in conversation with whom you did not have to abate the wing of your thought downward at all, in deference to any feminine narrowness of mind. Her articles on Whitman are proof enough of this, which is also strikingly evident from her letters to the poet, which I had the pleasure of reading one July day in John Burrough's summer-house overlooking the Hudson.

From *Reminiscences of Walt Whitman* (London: Alexander Gardner, 1896), pp. 1-9.

1. Mr. Sylvester Baxter, in the *New Englander* for August, 1892, gives details of this visit. It was there and then that Osgood & Co. saw Whitman, and made overtures to publish *Leaves of Grass*. In August, 1881, he came on for a two months' stay to see the new edition through the press. Took room in Hotel Bulfinch; often rode down on horse-cars to the sea at City Point; passed an evening in Bartlett's studio, down on water-front—Joaquin Miller, Boyle O'Reilly, and others being present. It was at the Hotel Bulfinch he wrote his lines "The Sobbing of the Bells."

2. I suppose there is no doubt that the following whimsical stanzas refer to Walt Whitman, and that the Phildelphia bard, their author, has had verses of his consigned to that vast and terrible waste-basket, although he says in the preface to his volume of "Poetry" that he can "confidently state that these poems are original"!:—

I saw a poet with a shaggy mane
And features leonine;
I strove to deem him great, and fain
Would love a thing divine.

But, lo! he won no mortal soul,
And loafed within his own;
His sullen mien, his eyeball's roll,
Were of the sad and lone.

From THE LEGACY OF AN OCTOGENARIAN

James R. Newhall

James R. Newhall worked with Whitman when both were newspaper reporters in New York in the early 1840s, and his account is one of the few firsthand ones we have of Whitman's journalistic career.

In 1842 I again found myself in New York, and at this time was chiefly engaged in the editorial department of a daily paper; two or three weeklies being likewise issued from the same establishment.

It was at this time that I became a co-worker with Walter Whitman, who was then only known by his undocked name, but who, when he became a member of the Bohemian conclave, chose to reduce the baptismal part to Walt. Mr. W. and myself occupied chairs at the same table, and of course saw much of each other. He was modest and companionable; though what he might have been had he possessed power to see the position he would attain as one of the leading poets of the age, can only be imagined. The association was extremely agreeable in many respects. Though affable and unassuming in personal intercourse, he was occasionally so trenchant with his pen that the proprietors had, now and then, to broadly hint that some restraint would be desirable. His style at that time somewhat resembled Dickens's, having nothing of the rough, ragged, and sometimes uncouth features that so marred it after he had fraternized with the Bohemians. As the writer knew him he was more than commonly free from vicious habits or inclinations, and it was never learned that he afterward, when surrounded by roistering associates, became tainted by their indiscretions.

Poet like, however, Mr. Whitman had even at that time gained a reputation for indolence. I remember his coming in one pleasant spring morning and asking if I would fill his place, as well as my own, on the next morning's paper. Without any hesitation I assented. An hour or two after, one of the proprietors came in and asked where Whitman was. I replied that he said he wanted to take a stroll on Long Island, and that I had agreed to fill his place on the morning paper. "Lazy d---l!" he exclaimed; "but then, if you choose to do his work and your own, too, and make an accommodating turn-about, I have no objection." It never seemed to me, however, that it was laziness, as the term is commonly understood, in Whitman, but rather a desire for the stimulation of a free and airy ramble, with the opportunity to indulge uninterruptedly in some train of thought, the fruit of which might soon appear in print.

Why Mr. Whitman was always poor it is not easy to tell, for at one time, while in the vigor of early manhood, he certainly earned a good deal of money, and apparently had no expensive habits. He appeared to enjoy good health, and loved to take long walks about the city and far into the suburbs. But for many of his latter years he was sadly paralytic, almost entirely deprived of the use of his lower limbs. His exposure during the war was considered to be the cause of his suffering.

The "Bohemians" were an interesting though not an exemplary class. Henry Clapp, who finally became a leader among them, was at one time a resident of Lynn, and very zealous in stirring up the people of Essex County on the temperance and anti-slavery questions. He edited a weekly paper, was a writer of much vigor and pungency, and an eloquent speaker. After leaving this section he roved about Europe for a time, became quite prominent among the Bohemians of London, and finally returned to New York, where he attained the pre-eminent title of "King of the Bohemians." He had charge of one or two newspapers. But though a forcible writer, he was so uncertain and so unsteady in his course as an editor, that he was by no means successful. He died in 1875.

One or two brief narrations will very well illustrate the readiness with which Mr. Whitman was able to wield the pen, as well as afford a glimpse at other traits. The first relates to the time when his writings were beginning to be known and appreciated, and before he had fallen into those vagaries of style which characterized him, and in the minds of many damaged him in after life. He was then about twenty-five years of age.

I was one day, during a temporary residence in New York, passing down Broadway, when I met a friend who informed me, with much feeling, of the recent death of his endeared wife, and added

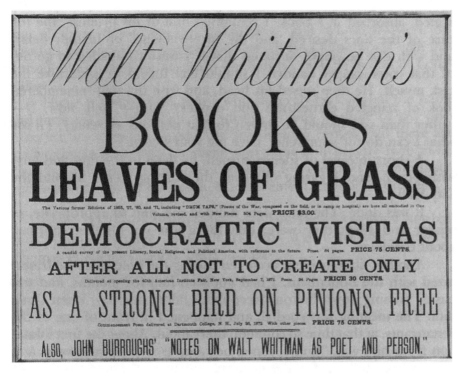

Broadside advertising poster written by Whitman for his books

that he was having prepared a monument to mark her burial place, and wished I would furnish some suitable poetic lines to accompany the formal part of the inscription. I told him that such composition was not exactly in my line, but that I knew one who could do it in a most acceptable manner; that I should see him in the course of an hour or two and would not hesitate to ask the favor. The person to whom I alluded was Mr. Whitman.

I saw him during the evening, made my request, and was assured that the lines should be ready in due season. Some weeks passed and, though we met about every day, nothing was said regarding the matter, probably both of us allowing it to drop temporarily out of mind.

When I again met my friend he was quite impatient, saying that the workman was actually waiting for the lines. I told him I would see to it forthwith; and knowing where Mr. Whitman could usually be found at that hour, I hastened to see him. He was comfortably seated, absorbed in a book. I reminded him of his promise, the nature of the lines desired, and the inconvenience of further delay; and with due emphasis declared that if I were compelled to go out of that room empty handed I should feel forced to undertake the task myself. He then raised his head, and with the well-remembered look of mingled earnestness and drollery said:—"Well, now, N— rather than you should be driven to that perilous extremity, I'll see what I can do for your relief. Give me your pencil."

A short interval of silence ensued, he deep in thought and busy with pencil, and I gazing out over the stirring scenes around the City Hall.

It was done. The lines were handed me, and so appropriate, so tender and sweet they were, that there was not another murmur about the delay.

Another little incident occurred during the time when he fraternized with the Bohemians. I had not seen him for months, and was hastily passing down Fulton street about noon, one day, when I met him. The meeting was cordial, and happened in front of one of the restaurants, at that time so common thereabout. About the first salutation from him was, "Come, come, now, let us step right in here, and I'll order something for the encouragement of the inner man; and over the supper we will have a talk." My reply was, that as I was hastening to take a steamer, I must decline his kind invitation. "Well, then, good-by," he said, as we shook hands; but with an air of mock gravity added, "and perhaps it was as well that you declined my generous invitation, for six cents is the sum total of my funds."

The last time I ever saw Mr. Whitman was some fifteen years ago. His condition was then pitiable, such that even with the assistance of a muscular attendant he found it difficult to mount a few steps. To my remark that rheumatism must be a very painful affliction he rejoined, "Rheumatism! I wish it was rheumatism; it is paralysis; hopeless paralysis."

Of the quality of Mr. Whitman's literary productions it would be unseemly here to enlarge. He was extolled as poet by some of the English publications to a degree that to many confirmed the idea that distance lends enchantment. It is hardly likely to be conceded with anything like unanimity, that the reviewer who placed him at the head of all American poets—naming Bryant and Longfellow especially—could have so written after mature consideration. Perhaps he was greater than all in the sense that everyone is greater than others in something. But supposing the works and memory of one of those three—Bryant, Longfellow, and Whitman—were decreed to be blotted out of existence, which would the world vote that it should be? I seriously question whether it would be Bryant or Longfellow.

There are, doubtless, many who sincerely believe that the name and fame of Mr. Whitman will survive as long as those of any poet America has ever produced. And it is equally certain that there are many who believe that his name and fame will rapidly fade away. That he himself had an ardent longing for the poet's immortality, and believed it to be his destined achievement, cannot be doubted.

From *The Legacy of an Octogenarian*, ed. Israel Augustus Newhall and Howard Mudge Newhall (Lynn, Mass.: Nichols Press — Thomas P. Nichols, 1897), pp. 130-135.

A VISIT TO WALT WHITMAN IN 1877

[Edward Carpenter]

An Englishman, Edward Carpenter first read Whitman's poetry in Rossetti's 1868 edition. Moved by it, he began a correspondence with Whitman shortly afterwards. His visit to Whitman was the highlight of his American trip of 1877, later expanded as Days with Walt Whitman *(1906).*

It was on the 2nd of May, 1877, that—crossing the water from Philadelphia—I knocked at the door of 431, Stevens Street, Camden. The house, a narrow three-storied one, stood in one of those broad tree-planted streets which are common in the States; and Whitman was staying there, boarding with his brother Colonel George Whitman and wife—making the establishment at any rate his headquarters, though frequently absent from it. I waited a few minutes in a sitting-room of the usual type—one or two ornamental tables, with photograph books, things under glass shades, etc.—while "Walt" was called upstairs. He soon came down, slowly, leaning heavily on the banisters, always dragging somewhat his paralysed leg—at first sight quite an old man with long grey, almost white, beard, and shaggy head and neck, grey dress too; but tall, erect, and at closer sight not so old—a florid fresh complexion, pure grey-blue eye (no sign of age there), and full, strong, well-formed hands.

At the foot of the staircase he took me by the hand, and said, "I was afraid we should miss after all"—this in reference to a previous unsuccessful call I had made. There was no hurry in his manner; having found me a seat, and then only leaving hold of my hand, he sat down himself and asked me "what news I brought from Britain." War had just been declared between Russia and Turkey. Like other Americans, his sympathies lay with Russia. His idea was that Russia stood *in need* of a southern outlet (Constantinople) for her people and growing energies, that Turkey was falling in pieces, and that England was beginning to pursue "the wise policy of absolute non-intervention." Conversation then turned on England. He asked about friends there; also about myself some questions.

Meanwhile in that first ten minutes I was becoming conscious of an impression which subsequently grew even more marked—the impression, namely, of immense vista or background in his personality. If I had thought before (and I do not know that I had) that Whitman was eccentric, unbalanced, violent, my first interview certainly produced a contrary effect. No one could be more considerate, I may almost say courteous; no one could have more simplicity of manner and freedom from egotistic wrigglings; and I never met anyone who gave me more the impression of *knowing what he was doing* than he did. Yet away and beyond all this I was aware of a certain radiant power in him, a large benign effluence and inclusiveness, as of the sun, which filled out the place where he was—yet with something of reserve and sadness in it too, and a sense of remoteness and inaccessibility.

Some such impressions, at any rate, I gathered in the first interview. I remember how I was most struck, in his face, by the high arch of the eyebrows, giving a touch of child-like wonder and contemplation to his expression; yet his eyes, though full of a kind of wistful tenderness, were essentially not contemplative but perceptive—active rather than receptive—lying far back, steady, clear, with small definite pupils and heavy lids of passion and experience. A face of majestic simple proportion, like a Greek temple as some one has said; the nose Greek in outline, straight (but not at all thin or narrow, rather the contrary), broad between the brows, and meeting the line of the forehead without any great change of direction; the forehead high, with horizontal furrows, but not excessively high; the head domed, and rising to a great height in the middle, above the ears—not projecting behind; ears large and finely formed; mouth full, but almost quite concealed by hair. A head altogether impressing one by its height, and by a certain untamed "wild hawk" look, not uncommon among the Americans.

After some conversation Whitman proposed a walk across to Philadelphia. Putting on his grey slouch hat he sallied forth with evident pleasure, and taking my arm as a support walked slowly the best part of a mile to the ferry. Crossing the ferry was always a great pleasure to him. His "Brooklyn Ferry" and the section entitled "Delaware River—Days and Nights" in "Specimen Days," sufficiently prove this.

Edward Carpenter

The life of the streets and of the people was so near, so dear. The men on the ferry steamer were evidently old friends; and when we landed on the Philadelphia side we were before long quite besieged. The man or woman selling fish at the corner of the street, the tramway conductor, the loafers on the pavement—a word of recognition from Walt, or as often from the other first. Presently a cheery shout from the top of a dray; and before we had gone many yards farther the driver was down and standing in front of us—his horses given to the care of some bystander. He was an old Broadway "stager," "had not seen Walt for three or four years"; and tears were in his eyes as he held his hand. We were now brought to a standstill, and others gathered round; "George" was ill, and Walt must go and see him. There was a message for the children, and in his pocket the poet discovered one or two packets of sweatmeats for absent little ones. But for the most part his words were few. It was the others who spoke, and apparently without reserve.

Thus we rambled through Philadelphia—mostly using the tramcars. The Yankees do not walk; the trams in their large towns are very complete, and are universally used for all but short distances. Whitman *could* not walk far. I was content being with him anyhow. He certainly was restfulness itself. When we reached the Ferry on our return, the last bell was ringing—we might have caught the boat, but Whitman seemed not to think of hurrying. The boat went, and he sat down to enjoy life waiting for the next.

A few days later, Walt having gone into the country to stay with his "dear and valued friends" the Staffords, I paid him a visit there. "White Horse," or Kirkwood, was the third or fourth station from Camden on the Camden and Atlantic line; and consisted at that time of only some half-dozen houses and stores, forming a centre to the scattered and outlying farmsteads of that part. The Staffords' little farm lay a mile and a half or so from the station—a five or six-roomed wooden house, a barn, one or two fruit trees, and a few fields running down 300 or 400 yards to a little stream. The country level, very slightly undulating, wooded here and there, not unlike some parts of Cambridgeshire that I have seen—neither particularly attractive or unattractive. Here on this farm, and working it himself, lived Mr. Stafford with his family; he a loyal Methodist, sometimes acting as local preacher, silent-mannered, dark-skinned, of bilious temperament, subject to illness, hard-working, and faithful; his wife a fine woman of cultured expression and spiritual mind, pretty well absorbed in domestic work; two sons, young fellows, one of whom, Harry, at this time working in a printer's office in Camden, was a great ally and favourite of Walt's; a grown-up daughter, and one or two children. Here Whitman would often stay, weeks or months at a time, boarding and living with the family, and attracting the members of it to him, and himself to them, with the ties of enduring friendship. Mrs. Stafford once said to me: "He *is* a good man; I think he is the best man I ever knew."

It was his delight, and doubtless one of the chief attractions of this favourite resort, to go down and spend a large part of the day by the "creek" I have spoken of—and which figures so largely in "Specimen Days." At a point not a quarter of a mile distant from the house it widened into a kind of little lake surrounded by trees, the haunt of innumerable birds; and here Whitman would sit for hours in an old chair; silent, enjoying the scene, becoming a part of it, almost, himself; or would undress and bathe in the still, deep pool. At this time he was nearly sixty years old, and ten years before had been heavily stricken with paralysis. As is well known, he attributed his partial recovery very largely to the beneficence of this creek, with its water-baths and sun-baths and open-air influences generally.

That day being Sunday I found the family all at home, and Whitman in the midst of them. When the opportunity occurred I told him something of the appreciation of his writings that had grown up in England during those years. After a pause he asked if the Rossetti edition was out of print. I said I thought so. W.: "I hope it is; I approved of Rossetti's plan for the time being, but now would rather appear without alteration." [I am here simply transcribing my notes made a day or two after; these are not his exact words, but as good as I could remember.] "I had hardly realised that there was so much interest in me in England. I confess I am surprised that America, to whom I have especially addressed myself, is so utterly silent. Lowell, and indeed almost all the critics, say that I am crude, inartistic—do you think that?" I said I had heard such criticisms, but I did not myself think his work crude and hasty; on the contrary much of it seemed to me to have been written very deliberately and carefully; and as to the question of art, I thought he had laid an altogether broader basis of style (instancing some of his poems)—a great foundation; others would build here and there upon it, but he had struck the main lines. W.: "I did, in fact, re-write and destroy much before I published; I cannot think that I have altogether attained, but I have planted the seed; it is for others to continue the work. My original idea was that if I could bring men together by putting before them the heart of man, with all its joys and sorrows and experiences and surrounding, it would be a great thing; up to this time I have had America chiefly in view, but this appreciation of me in England makes me think I might perhaps do the same for the old world also. I have endeavoured from the first to get free as much as possible from all literary attitudinising—to strip off integuments, coverings, bridges—and to speak straight from and to the heart." [In reference to this, he said at another time that it had been a "whim" of his when writing "to discard all conventional poetic phrases, and every touch of or reference to ancient or mediæval images, metaphors, subjects, styles, etc., and to write *de novo* with words and phrases appropriate to his own days."]

When we went in to dinner Mr. Stafford was already seated; I think he was about to say grace. Walt, with greater grace, stood for a moment bending over him from behind, and clasped Stafford's head in his great hands; then passed on in silence. What a large, sweet presence—so benign, yet so determined! The children loved him, and the little boy would lie coiled, lost, on his knees, half-asleep, half-awake, Walt's hand covering and compressing his entire face.

In Philadelphia, the day before, Whitman had introduced me to his English friends, the Gilchrists. Mrs. Gilchrist, widow of Alexander Gilchrist, the biographer of Blake, was a capable and large-minded woman. A year earlier she, with two daughters and a son, had come from England for a two or three year's visit to the States, and had settled in Philadelphia. As is well known, she was the first of English-women to fully and publicly recognise (as she did in some printed letters) the splendid genius of the poet, and that at a time (1868 or '69) when "Leaves of Grass" to most of the literary world was little better than the incoherent ramblings of a maniac. More than once did she relate to me how, on first opening the volume, when her eye fell upon the fine nearly full-length engraving (taken from a daguerrotype) of the author, she exclaimed: "Here at last is the face of Christ, which the painters have so long sought for"; and she always maintained that the reading of the book itself did but confirm and deepen that first impression.

At the Gilchrists's house Whitman would not unfrequently stay. Indeed there was a kind of prophet's chamber for him there, always ready. And as it happened that he was about to pay a visit there, it was arranged that I also should come. They lived at No. 1929, North 22nd Street. If the American method of numbering streets and houses is prosiac, it certainly has the advantage of being practical. Philadelphia is like a chess-board; you find your way by co-ordinate geometry. The streets are straight, parallel, and not far from infinite in length. The address being put in your hands, you know at once the exact spot to which you are destined.

I remember very well arriving, bag in hand, and finding the whole family (a general custom in Philadelphia on those warm evenings) sitting out on the doorsteps—Whitman in the midst, in an armchair, his white beard and hair glistening in the young moonlight,

Walt Whitman, early 1870s (Feinberg Collection, Library of Congress)

looking like some old god—the others grouped around him or at his feet. After this for a week of evenings I made one of the party. How pleasant it was! Whitman had a knack of making ordinary life enjoyable, redeeming it from commonplaceness. Instead of making you feel (as so many do) that the Present is a kind of squalid necessity to be got over as best may be, in view of something always in the future, he gave you that good sense of *nowness*, that faith that the present is enjoyable, which imparts colour and life to the thousand and one dry details of existence. As I have hinted before, he was no great talker, and would generally let the conversation ebb and flow at its own will, without effort, ready apparently for grave or gay alike.

Unlike many highly important people who seem to enjoy holding forth to a general audience, Whitman, as I thought, preferred to let conversation turn on the pivot of personal relationship. Often as not he would have his listener by the hand; and his words too had an attractive force, from their very simplicity and purity from affectation or display. I think he did not really care to have conversational dealings with people except on such a basis of personal affection. To such as he did not like—to all mere gabblers, bores, spying and prying persons—he became a precipice, instantly and utterly inaccessible. Certainly it was one of the pleasures of his society that you always felt he was there in person, *bonâ fide*, not by deputy; and no current notion of politeness could make him do a thing he did not enjoy doing. One evening we were looking over some fine engravings, mostly portraits, Gainsboroughs, Reynolds, Lelys, and others, from Mrs. Gilchrist's collection. He enjoyed them greatly, and very deliberately, dwelling long and long over some of them, criticising style, workmanship, composition, character, etc. But when he had had enough of it all—well, he said so! I have seldom known anyone who, though so cordial and near to others, detached and withdrew himself at times more decisively than he did, or who in the whole spent more time in solitude. Also no rough draft of his character would be complete which did not take into account the strong Quaker element of obstinacy which existed in him—but this might require a separate chapter!

To return to our evenings. I have said something about Walt Whitman's manner in conversation; I cannot attempt to reproduce its effect, but I will just transcribe such notes of some of his remarks as I have by me.

One evening conversation turned upon the Chinese. W.: "I fancy they are like the Germans, only more refined. My notion is that the Germans are simple, true, affectionate folk, but there is a kind of roughness, one may almost say brutishness, about them; the Chinese have the same good qualities, with a certain alertness and grace which the Germans lack." I quoted some accounts of Japan by a man who had lived there for a long time, and who told me that the manners of the old Japenese aristocracy were so elaborately perfect that he himself would go any distance to get *out of their way*, feeling such a boor compared with them! This amused Whitman; seemed to "tally with his own idea." Mrs. Gilchrist wondered, with regard to the natives of India and Orientals generally, that the degradation of the women did not bring about a gradual deterioration of the whole race. W.: "I suppose that among the *masses* of the people the women (and men too) live, after all, much as they do in the West, and as they must do in all times and climes; and that the special treatment of women in the East only applies to the upper classes. The masses in every part of the globe are dominated by the necessities of Nature. Thus also among the Greeks and Romans the peasant-life must have had its races of fine women." And here he cited Juvenal, and his comparison of the effeminate lady of his time with the "stern magnificent mothers" of the early days of Rome.

Going on to Oriental literature, Whitman spoke of "Sakúntala," the Indian drama, its "modernness"—the comic scenes especially being as of the times of Shakespeare; and of the great Hindu epic, the "Ramáyana"; and told the story of Yudísthura, which occurs as an episode in the latter. Conversation got round presently—I think in reference to the cramped life of "high-born" women in the East—to the shoddiness and vulgarity of modern well-to-do life. W.: "It seems a strange thing to me, this love of gilt and upholstery among the Americans—that people leading a free natural open-air life should, directly they make a little money, want to go in for sofas, expensively furnished rooms, dress, and the like; yet it seems to be a law, a kind of necessity, that they should do so. I suppose it is partly that each man wishes to feel himself as good as others, to feel that he can have of the 'best' too; democracy showing itself for a time in that way, reducing the borrowed old-world standard of superiority to an absurdity; and I guess it will not last for ever."

We did not generally sit up later than eleven. Breakfast was at 7.30 or 8. Walt's arrival in the morning was as exhilarating as a fine sunrise. After breakfast and a chat we would separate to our respective occupations. In the afternoon, almost every day I was there, the poet went off to Camden to visit his sister-in-law, who was at that time confined to the house, and to whom, I believe, he was much attached. As I have said, Walt was very simple and domestic in his ways; and would quite enjoy, on a rainy afternoon, having a game of twenty questions such as he had "often played in camp with the soldiers during the war," or would take pleasure in preparing some little dish of his own devising for the evening meal. One evening we pressed him to read. He would not recite anything of his own; but he read out Tennyson's "Ulysses"—in a clear, strong, and rugged tone. The subtle harmonies of the Tennysonian verse effloresced under the treatment, but the sterner qualities of the poem stood out finely. We expressed admiration. He said: "I guess it is about the best Tennysonian poem." Another evening, I remember, he told us how, when living in New York, he had had a "fancy" to visit Sing-sing prison, the great penal establishment up the Hudson river. He obtained permission to do so, got to know one or two of the warders, and for some time went there pretty frequently. He wrote letters for the prisoners, etc. "It was a whim."

We had a long talk on manual labour. Most of us agreed it would be a good thing for all classes to take part in—not to be left to one class only. Walt maintained with regard to reforms and the like, that it was no good trying to *benefit* people (labouring people for instance) who did not feel the need of any change. "Many people came to me at one time about slavery, and 'wondered' that I was so quiet about it; but, in truth, I felt that abolitionists were making quite noise enough, and that there were other things just as important which had to be attended to." We got talking of Abraham Lincoln—I suppose in reference to slavery—and I mentioned the story that Lincoln went out of his mind and nearly committed suicide over a love affair. Walt, who always was a great admirer of Lincoln, and who knew a good deal about him and his history, gave this a most emphatic denial, saying that Lincoln was "never even near being crazy."

One of the most amusing incidents of my stay occurred one morning shortly after breakfast, when a visiting card was handed in bearing the ominous inscription "Madame Dorbiney D'Aubigné," and was quickly followed by the appearance of an elderly and loquacious little lady. She was one of those detached women with a reticule who travel about the world in quest of anything "interesting." She had been, she told us, all over the States and seen many celebrities, but could not return to Europe without visiting Whitman—and it was only by a piece of luck that she found out where he was staying. However, it soon began to appear that her interest in Walt was not so great, naturally, as in herself; for after a few preliminary compliments she settled down to tell us all about the wonderful D'Aubigné family to which she belonged. It ramified all over the civilised world, she said; and the name was spelt in ever so many different ways, but they were all branches of the same family, they were all related to each other—as her own name indeed showed. Walt listened in an amused manner, and for about ten minutes was quite decently courteous and patient. Then I suddenly perceived that his face was becoming "precipitous"; the little woman of course was addressing him, no one else being of any importance; but he seemed to be becoming deaf, there was no speculation in his eyes; it *was* rather awful; for a minute or two she tried vainly to effect a lodgment for her words, to get any kind of handhold on the sheer surface, and then gathering up her tackle, she made the best of a bad job, bade a hasty goodbye, and disappeared.

I told Walt about a visit I paid to Oliver Wendell Holmes, and the criticisms of "Leaves of Grass" which I heard on that occasion. I saw the "Autocrat of the Breakfast table" at his house in Boston. He was then about 70 years of age—a dapper active little man, full of life and go, rather enjoying the visits of strangers—"Oh yes, I have a large 'parish'—people write to me and come and call from all parts of the world—we authors are rather vain, you know, and quite enjoy a little homage; but *my* parish is not as big as Longfellow's—not as big as Longfellow's. But this is not a good time for you to see Boston. Boston is very empty now—(getting up and glancing through the window) very empty; you might almost see a fox run down the street; etc., etc.". I said something about American literature and "Leaves of Grass." "Oh! Whitman," he said, "well—well—well—Whitman is all very well—he has capacity, but it won't do—it won't do. I tell you what, it's something like this: You know skilful cooks say that the faintest odour, the merest whiff, of *assafœtida*, will give a piquant flavour to a dish—and I can believe that; but to *drench* it in *assafœtida*, no, that won't do. The poets *coquette* with Nature and weave garlands of roses for her; but Whitman *goes at her* like a great hirsute man—no, it won't do. Now," he continued, "the other day Lowell and Longfellow and I were chatting together, and the subject of Whitman turned up. Said Lowell, 'I can't think why there is all this stir about Whitman; I have read a good deal of his poetry, but I can't see anything in it—*I can't see anything in it.*' Well,' said Longfellow, 'I believe the man might have done something if he had only had a decent training and education.' As to my own opinion, why," said Holmes, "I have already given you that. So you see what we think of him in America." Whitman was a good deal amused, and took it all in good part, saying he knew pretty well already what they thought.

As the days went by I began to see more clearly the depths which lay behind the poet's simple and unconcerned exterior. Literary persons, as a rule, write over their own heads; they talk a little bigger than themselves. But Whitman seemed to fill out "Leaves of Grass," and form an interpretation of it. I began to see that all he had written there was a matter of absolute personal experience—that you might be sure that what was said was meant. There was the

Walt Whitman, early 1870s

same deliberate suggestiveness about his actions and manners that you find in his writings—only, of course, with the added force of bodily presence; and far down too there were clearly enough visible the same strong and contrary moods, the same strange omnivorous egotism, controlled and restrained by that wonderful genius of his for human affection and love. "Who has the most enamoured body?" were words which somehow his presence often suggested. It was with real reluctance that, a week after my arrival, I bade adieu to all that friendly household; and the next morning but one, from the stern of the "Siberia," watched the flat shores of New England, and the lighthouse that marks the entrance to Boston Harbour, recede and dip below the broadening waters of the Atlantic.

Progressive Review, 1 (February 1897): 407-417; reprinted in Carpenter's *Days with Walt Whitman* (1906).

REMINISCENT OF WHITMAN

Franklin Benjamin Sanborn

It is always useful to print two selections by Sanborn because they often differ from each other. This article stands on its own, though, for its account of Whitman's impact of the Concord writers, especially Emerson and Thoreau.

I have brought in with me to-night, and perhaps I will hand it around before I begin to speak, a copy of the first editon of "Leaves of Grass" which belonged to Henry Thoreau, and was given to me by his sister, Sophia, a few years before her death. I do not know the history of the volume further than that; but I imagine it was either given to Thoreau by Whitman himself, or by Emerson. It may be that Thoreau received this from Whitman himself. The fly leaf, which the ignorant binder took out, contains Thoreau's autograph, and there is also a little matter that came to me in it, which contains a line in Thoreau's handwriting: "Please give this to Mrs. Thoreau." The reading of these letters which Mr. Maynard has brought to you to-night has revived in my memory several facts which were lying there concealed. The first letter—the one written from Boston in March, 1860—was dated by a few days before I first met Whitman. I will speak presently of my acquaintance with his book, which was five years earlier. But the first time of my seeing Whitman was during that visit to Boston, when he was printing his Boston edition of "Leaves of Grass." I knew his publishers, Thayer & Eldridge, very well. They were young anti-slavery men who had started publishing in this neighborhood, and such was the success of their "Life of Brown" (Redpath's) that they launched out as publishers with a good deal of confidence and with a result, pretty speedily, of failure. But at this time they were in active business, and were very ready to take up any book which Mr. Redpath recommended. It is perhaps known to some of this company, though probably not to many, that on the third or fourth of April, 1860—about five days after this letter of Whitman's was written—I was arrested in Concord, taken out

142

of my house, handcuffed by a party of men from Boston, headed by a United States marshal, who wished to carry me to Washington to testify in the case of John Brown. I was taken out of the hands of these United States officers by the sheriff or deputy and brought before the court here. The district attorney, their counsel at that time, was Charles Levi Woodbury. My counsel were the late Governor Andrew, Mr. Samuel Sewall, and my classmate, Robert Treat Paine. I sat in the old court house listening to their arguments, and as I sat there saw an extraordinary man sitting near the door, wearing a carpenter's jacket, gray or blue—a very striking looking person. Many friends of mine had gathered there under the impression that if the court refused to discharge me they would themselves take a hand in the business. By three or four o'clock in the afternoon (the first time I had ever been subjected to any process in court) the Chief Justice, old Judge Shaw, pronounced the decision of the court, which was, that this warrrant on which I was arrested to McNair and was served by Carlton, and that under the law laid down by Broome in his "Legal Maxims" delegated power could not be delegated again. I forget exactly how the Chief Justice expressed his opinion. It signified little to me. I said, "All right. That sounds very well," and just sat there. Wendell Phillips came over to me and said, "You are discharged. It is time for you to go." I got up, bowed to the court, and left the room. My friends took me over to Cambridge and put me on the train for Concord.

A few days after I was in Boston and went round to the publishing office of Thayer & Eldridge, and there, sitting on the counter, was this extraordinary person I had seen in the court house. I was introduced to him. He was Walt Whitman. My personal acquaintance began at that time. I had known a great deal about his book and about himself before, from my neighbors, Mr. Emerson, Mr. Thoreau and Mr. Alcott.

It was in the summer of 1855, I should suppose not later than the first of September (I think the book was published in July or August), that I was walking one day with Mr. Emerson. We were crossing a bridge over the Concord river, about a mile from Mr. Emerson's house, when he began to tell me about this book, "Leaves of Grass," which had been published in New York. He asked me if I had seen it. I said, "No!" "Well," he said, "you shall see it." I went home with him and he gave me a copy of this first edition, bound in paper, and in our walk he gave me some description of it, saying:

143

Walt Whitman, 1872

"It is a remarkable mixture of the Bhagvat Ghita and the *New York Herald*." I then, of course, took the book and read it, and was astonished, as everybody was, at the remarkable power it displayed, and also at the remarkable incongruities in it; it was unlike anything. Mr. Emerson soon after that went to New York, and when he got back home, told me about his acquaintance with Whitman. He said he went to New York and sought out Whitman, and Whitman came and dined with him at the hotel which he then frequented, the Astor House, and after dinner Whitman took him round to one or two of the engine houses; for his particular friends then were the firemen, and he wanted to show Mr. Emerson what the firemen did at that time for their leisure. He also told me about Whitman's spending so much time riding on the omnibuses in New York, up and down Broadway, sitting with the drivers and observing the city from that point of view.

144

My friend Ellery Channing, who is living with me, the other night, speaking of Whitman, said to me: "I was present when Mr. Emerson first saw his own letter of praise printed by Whitman." I asked, "What did Mr. Emerson say?" He replied, "Nothing; but he was as angry as I ever saw him in my life." That was the occasion of a certain change of mind in Mr. Emerson, not, however, with regard to the genius of Mr. Whitman. His letter was a private letter and it had not business with the public, and Emerson should have been asked if there had been any wish to publish it or any part of it. Instead of asking consent Whitman rushed into print with the letter. That shocked Mr. Emerson's sense of propriety, which was very acute, so he probably very seldom thought of Whitman after that without thinking, "That is the man who printed my private letter." His opinion of Whitman's genius never changed, but he lost interest in the later poems. When "Drum Taps" came out, or soon after, I was very much struck with them and took the book down to Mr. Emerson's house, where I was in the habit of going frequently, and asked him if he had seen it. I think he said he had seen it but took no particular interest in it. I asked, "Have you seen this poem?" and called his attention to the Lincoln poem, and to that very extraordinary poem in which the old colored woman appears, surveying Sherman's army. I either read them to him, or he read them; but he said, "I like the 'Leaves of Grass,' but I do not see in these later poems what I saw in them." He never spoke with the slightest disrespect of Whitman.

You may remember that after Thoreau's death (he died in 1862) Mr. Emerson edited a collection of Thoreau's letters and poems (I have since edited a more complete edition of the letters). Soon after it appeared I was walking with him one day and he said to me: "When, in eulogizing Thoreau, I made that remark about three persons (the three persons, as you probably know, were John Brown, Joe Polis and Walt Whitman), and Sophia Thoreau heard what I said, she told me she did not think that her brother was so much interested in Whitman as I thought, and, in deference to her, in printing I left out that passage. But I have lately been looking over the journals of Thoreau, and I am satisfied that I was right. He did make that impression on Thoreau which I thought he made."

That introduces another little circumstance: During the first visit of Whitman in Boston, in 1860, it was the wish of Emerson and

Thoreau to invite him to Concord. The ladies of these houses, Mrs. Emerson, Sophia Thoreau, and Mrs. Alcott, declared they would not have him in the house. Afterwards Louisa Alcott was so much interested in Whitman, that when I went to see him in Philadelphia in 1876 (while visiting the exposition there), she desired me to purchase for her a copy of his last edition. Mrs. Alcott was not living when Whitman finally visited Concord, though I think she had overcome her prejudices on the subject; and Sophia Thoreau was not living; but Louisa Alcott was present at my house on the occasion that Whitman speaks of in his "Specimen Days," when we discussed Thoreau, and we were invited the next day to Emerson's house, where, as he says, he had a very pleasant conversation with Mrs. Emerson. But still, there was a great feeling of prejudice in regard to Whitman. When I invited my neighbors to be present at this conference there was considerable censure on the part of the people in the town. They advised their friends, especially the young ladies, not to come. Emerson came and Mr. Alcott and Louisa Alcott, as Whitman mentions in his account of the matter.

I have printed in my edition of Thoreau's "Familiar Letters" the same passages that Emerson printed with regard to Whitman, and perhaps some that Emerson omitted, and you will find there in that volume, either in the letters or in my notes, some passages showing how strong was the impression Whitman produced upon Thoreau and Alcott. They went together to see him in Brooklyn.

Whitman was certainly a striking looking man, and would attract the attention of people in any city of the world. I think Whitman was a little too well aware of his fine appearance. There was a strong element of individuality mixed up with his personality, and he did not have occasion to experience what the Arkansas colonel did in walking up and down Broadway. The colonel put on his military cloak with red facing, and walked up and down, and when he met his friend the major, in the evening, he said: "I am going to leave this town. I walked up and down Broadway this morning and not a man looked at me, but when I am at home I am hell on Pea Ridge."

When Whitman came to visit me in Concord, in 1881, he wore, as always in his later years, some white, soft colors and that long, white beard. His hair was perfectly white. He had a singular resemblance to Gerrit Smith, which I attributed to his Dutch ancestry, Smith being almost wholly Dutch.

Then Whitman's manners were interesting. I fancy in his younger days, when he dined with Mr. Emerson at the Astor House and insisted on having a tin cup at table, that his manners were not so distinguished; but after he had been through the war and had seen more of life he certainly had very distinguished manners, so that anybody accustomed to the circles of the great would have been struck with them. As Thomas Cholmondeley said of Bronson Alcott, Whitman "had the manners of *a very great peer*." He was independent in bearing and had the composure of manner which always produces an impression on the people of Europe. He was extremely friendly to all persons. In Concord, on the morning of the Sunday spent with me, he drove with Miss Prestonia Mann, who was living in Concord for the summer, and had a fine pair of Arabian-looking horses. She took him in her carriage, driving herself. In the afternoon I took a carriage, and with Whitman, Mrs. Sanborn and some friend—Mr. Alcott, I think—we also took a drive around the town, and we were out an hour or two; and, finally, towards sunset (this was in September), we drove to my house. We had been driven by a coachman because I wished to leave the carriage and show Whitman those places which I thought he had not seen in the morning, and it was more convenient to have some one drive this pair of horses. We were helping Whitman out; his movements were slow, and we were about going into the house. The rest of us had not thought about the driver. I was in the habit of seeing him every day. Whitman turned to him, with his magnificent manner, and said: "My friend, I suppose I shall not see you again," giving him his hand, and bidding him good-bye, which is, I suppose, what "a very great peer" would do, though it is not customary in this part of the world.

In the call which Thoreau and Alcott made upon Whitman they found him living with his mother and sister, in great simplicity. They were taken up to his bedroom, which was a small room and there had their conversation with him. They were struck with the simple, affectionate relations which he seemed to have with everybody, and how proud his mother was of him! Mr. Alcott called in the morning, and found he was not at home; but his mother was there, and Mr. Alcott stayed as long as he had time, for Mrs. Whitman, the mother, occupied a good deal of that time in telling Mr. Alcott what a remarkable boy Walt had been, what a good son, etc., things that mothers generally say concerning such sons.

Caricature of Whitman, 1872

My own relations with Whitman, though always friendly, were not very close. I corresponded with him but little. When there was occasion to mention him or render any service to him, I did so, but I think I only saw him on those three occasions, possibly four: in Boston, in 1860, at the Court House, afterwards at the publishers'; in 1876, at Camden, and in 1881, when he came to my house. I had seen him in Boston at another time, and may have heard him read his account of the assassination of Lincoln, in Boston. Although I read his "Leaves of Grass," I cannot say I have read very carefully his prose writings. I have read them more or less. The extraordinary impression that his first book produced on a few persons was repeated when the English people came to know about him. I printed some years ago, in the *Atlantic Monthly*, some letters of an English friend, Thomas Cholmondeley, and in one letter he speaks of having received from Thoreau a copy of "Leaves of Grass." He says: "I fail to find the *gentleman* in it." In 1859-60, before I had ever seen Whitman, a friend of mine, Edwin Morton, who was in England, and knew Cholmondeley, went down to Cholmondeley's home in the town of Shrewsbury. Mrs. Cholmondeley, his mother, living at Hodnet, had married again, and Cholmondeley's step-father was the Rev. Zachary Macaulay, a cousin of Lord Macaulay. Cholmondeley told Morton: "Thoreau sent over to me your Walt Whitman's 'Leaves of Grass,' and I was greatly interested in it. One day, after dinner, I undertook to read some pages of it to the Rev. Mr. Macaulay, and he said he would not listen to it, and if I went on reading he would throw it into the fire."

As you well know, Whitman's genius has received more full recognition in England than in this country, partly because the English do not well understand the conditions in which it was written. The most striking personal tribute to Whitman's influence that I have read, I think, is by that remarkable writer, J. A. Symonds. I have only recently read it; but he seems to ascribe to Whitman an effect on his own life and character and hopes, such as we commonly ascribe to the process called "regeneration." I do not know that any Americans have taken precisely that view. Some of the younger generation may. What was particularly impressive, I think, to Emerson, was the enormous reach of Whitman's thought. That shocking conception of poetical form which Whitman had, but which he sometimes departed from, *always* to the advantage of what he was saying, produced no favorable impression upon Emerson, who had a very accurate ear for verse or prose. He was willing to regard Whitman as a prose writer, but did not take him seriously as a poet, and I am inclined to think the absence in "Drum Taps" of that wide-reaching imagination of earlier poems in "Leaves of Grass" accounted for his failure to regard "Drum Taps" with the same interest, though they came nearer to conformity to accepted poetical forms. The curious fact that Whitman was wholly unlike most American writers was what Emerson saw. Whitman did not impress Thoreau exactly so.

I find a great deal of affectation in Whitman's poetry; a great deal that he borrowed; and a certain kind of egoism, as if he identified the universe with himself, and considered the course of the stars more important because they had passed through the mind of Whitman.

I showed these notes in *The Conservator* about Julian Hawthorne to a friend who was a great friend to the elder Hawthorne and knew Julian as a boy. I asked him: "What do you think of this?" He replied: "In that speech at the Camden dinner Julian presented what may be called the opinion of courtesy, but he has now presented the critic's opinion." Julian Hawthorne, however, knows a great deal too much to say what he has lately said about Whitman.

I was much struck in the "Drum Taps" with the rythmical movement of some of Whitman's lines as resembling those in the choruses of Greek tragedies. I happened to meet one day in the train a gentleman that I never saw afterwards, old Uncle Sam Taylor of Andover. I had just been reading Whitman, and I said, "I want you to observe what a similarity there is in some of these lines of Whitman to the Greek in such and such a tragedy." He was a great deal impressed by it. He said, "I will look that up." Whitman's r[h]ythmical faculty is very peculiar. It is sometimes of the most perfect description and then it seems to fail entirely. He might have a strophe; he never had the antistrophe.

Conservator, 8 (May 1897): 37-40.

CHATS WITH WALT WHITMAN

Grace Gilchrist

Grace was the daughter of Anne Gilchrist of England, who arrived in America in 1876 to press her suit for Whitman's affections. She was unsuccessful, but Grace evidently endeared herself to the old man.

> That glorious man Whitman will one day be known as one of the greatest sons of earth, a few steps below Shakespeare on the throne of immortality.—*Wm. Rossetti*

Walt Whitman, whose "Leaves of Grass" evoked such a storm of literary and moral condemnation in the now remote and Philistine fifties and sixties—in two great countries, America and England—it was the present writer's privilege often to see and to hear converse amid a knot of intimate friends, during a period of two years spent in the quiet Quaker city of Philadelphia, toward the close of the Poet's life.

Time has not yet passed its verdict on this athlete of Democracy. A hundred years scarcely adds one name to the rank of the Immortals, thus his literary reputation may safely be left for "the amplitude of Time to ripen," while I offer my little appreciation from the human, and not the literary point of view, and perhaps to have been so remembered is what this great humanist would have best desired.

For those readers who wish for a critical and literary estimate of him there are many, both by friend and critic. "Walt Whitman," by his personal friend Mr. John Burroughs; "A Study of Walt Whitman," by the late Mr. Addington Symonds; Mr. Havelock Ellis's paper upon him, contained in his essays entitled the "New Spirit," and Robert Louis Stevenson's rather faint-hearted one in his book of "Memories and Portraits"; and the still older, and more exhaustive study of him, by his warm personal friend and admirer—Mr. Maurice Bucke.

151

Thus relieved of all literary responsibility, my mind travels back to formal, prim, Quaker Philadelphia, and the long, hot dewless evenings of an American summer, to a street planted with long rows of plane trees, "one of those long straight streets, running at right angles to each other, and long enough to present that always pleasing effect of vista—converging lines that stretch out indefinitely." These pleasing effects being further enhanced by the clear, cloudless skies, from which no canopy of smoke ever hovered to blacken buildings or trees.

Walt Whitman lived in the somewhat dreary and ugly suburb of Camden, New Jersey, across the Delaware river, and he would on many a fine afternoon cross by the five o'clock ferry to Philadelphia, and taking the car, reach our house in time for tea-supper. After that was over, we would all take our chairs out, American fashion, beside the "stoop,"—that is, on to the pavement, below the front steps of the house. The poet sat in our midst, in a large bamboo rocking-chair, and we listened as he talked on many subjects—human and literary. Walt Whitman was at this time fifty-eight, but he looked seventy. His beard and hair were snow-white, his complexion a fine color, and unwrinkled. He had still, though stricken in 1873 by paralysis, a most majestic presence. He was over six feet, but he walked lame, dragging the left leg, and leaning heavily on a stick. He was dressed always in a complete suit of grey clothes with a large and spotless white linen collar, his flowing white beard filling in the gap at his strong sunburnt throat. He possessed a full-toned, rather high, baritone voice, a little harsh and lacking in the finer modulations for sustained recitation; having an excellent memory, he declaimed many scenes from Shakespeare, poems by Tennyson, and occasionally his own. The "Mystic Trumpeter" was a favorite with him, because he had often recited to his soldiers in the hospitals the opening lines beginning—

Hark! some wild trumpeter: Some strange musician,
Hovering unseen in air, vibrates capricious tunes to-night.
I hear thee, trumpeter—listening, alert, I catch thy notes,
Now pouring, whirling like a tempest round me,
Now low, subdued—now in the distance lost.

About the house, and while bathing and dressing before breakfast, he might be heard singing opening bars of many songs—some

Whitman's draft manuscript for an introduction to Leaves of Grass

culled from operas, some from popular street airs; perhaps a bar from the "Star-Spangled Banner." I never remember to have heard him sing a song completely through, only bars and snatches, here and there—reminiscences lingering in his memory, from his opera and concert going days. He said of his turn for reciting, that he entered into it more from the side of pure physical enjoyment in the free exercise of his lungs than from mere intellectual appreciation of the poem or play he recited. Perhaps it was thus with his singing: he had no preconceived idea of rendering any set harmony or musical *motif*—it was rather, with him, an outburst of pure emotional and physical *abandon* to the delight of living. In a sense, this was an element in his personality—it was a very grand one, magnetic, and charged with the great elemental forces, which drew in great and small natures to minister to his omnivorous humanity. Yet those not under the spell of his large personality felt him to be rather like a great mountain basking in the full glare of the noonday sun—they longed, in looking up, for the shade of the valley; all was too defined, too open; they feared to approach nearer—there was no shelter from the fierce rays beating on the rough crags of his robust individuality. Mr. Havelock Ellis has aptly described him as a huge "Titanic Undine," for, devoid of all religious experiences, he was never troubled by those painful searchings of the heart for moral and religious certainties which beset more sensitively poised souls.

His talk was often of the actors and singers of his prime, of the books from which he had received the highest pleasure. His greatest enjoyment in music was derived from the Italian operas, from those of Rossini, Verdi, Donizetti. Alboni had been his favorite primadonna; Jenny Lind, who came to New York in her prime, he cared little for—her singing, sweet and bird-like as it was, lacked the fire or the passion to move him.

The authors he talked most of were Homer, Shakespeare, Scott, George Sand, and Bulwer Lytton; Scott he loved even better than Shakespeare. One quaint method of reading which he indulged in would have driven the devout book-lover wild. He would tear a book to pieces—literally shed its leaves, putting the loose sheets into the breast pocket of his coat—that he might pursue his reading in less weighty fashion under the branches of his favorite trees at Timber Creek. Many have averred that they never heard him laugh—he laughed rarely, but when he did, it was a deep, hearty melodious laugh. He laughed at very simple things—homely jests, and episodes in daily life. One exceedingly simple story illustrative of this he would jokingly relate, to emphasize his own love of notice.

An old fellow in a drunken fit, having returned home and thrown himself down on his bed, is awakened by the noise of several people in his room gossiping about their affairs—where they have been, and whom they have seen. The old fellow raises his head and asks: "Did any one inquire after me?" On joining a group of friends Walt would often laughingly ask: "Did any one inquire after me?" And after recounting this story, laugh in his slow leisurely way, with a twinkle of amusement in his blue eyes, their blueness intensified by their overhanging, bushy, snow-white brows.

He was quite indifferent, however, to any form of persiflage, repartee, chaffing, or any form of "smart" talk—remaining always perfectly grave and silent amid that kind of by-play; or, as with an importunate questioner, generally withdrawing himself altogether from the group of talkers, and finally leaving the room. In his large, serene, sane personality there was no room for trifling or the display of "intellectual fireworks"; with him existed no *arrière-pensée*. His phraseology was direct and simple, free from all bookishness or studied grace of expression. He stuck to homely Yankee idioms, with a fair percentage of slang.

He had in extreme the American trait of sympathy and of deference to the young. He loved very young men, and boys and girls, and if there was one present at the social board, or among a group of older talkers, he never rested till he had drawn such a one into the conversation; while some animated discussion was in full swing, he would turn to the callow listener with the query, "And what does G—— say?" though probably the opinion thus solicited was not to the smallest importance to any rational being present. If any quaint character whom he encountered in his jaunts on car or ferry struck him as an oddity, he would say that he or she was quite "Dickensee."

Dickens, however, was not with him such a favorite novelist as Scott, or Bulwer Lytton. George Sand's heroines he preferred to Shakespeare's. He dwelt much upon "Consuelo," the most beautiful of George Sand's novels. One scene he once laughingly enacted. It was that in which old Porpora, the musician, is trying to teach his frivolous fine lady pupils to declaim their songs with intelligence. Among them is Consuelo, Porpora's one earnest pupil.

155

Porpora says, "There is one among you who sings well." "Is it I?" exclaim half a dozen—and as the old man rises they push him down. (Here Walt would rise and imitate them.)

"How often," said Walt, "have I dwelt upon that passage?" Some one here asked him if George Sand's heroines did not equal Shakespeare's. He answered: "I don't know why, but Shakespeare's heroines give me very little satisfaction. I think it is partly owing to the fact that women never actually acted in Shakespeare's time; boys were dressed up, and I think that Shakespeare must have had these boys in his mind. I always compare Shakespeare's plays to large, rich, splendid tapestry—like Raphael's historical cartoons, where everything is broad and colossal. Royal kings and queens did not really talk like that, but ought to if they did not; it is redeemed in that way. Now you can't say that of nature—a tree is what it is, and you can't make it out better than it is."

Asked if he did not admire Rosalind, Portia, and other favorite heroines—

"No, I think Consuelo far superior to any of Shakespeare's heroines." He added that he relied upon translations, for he could not read French with any enjoyment.

Did he think the worse of George Sand for the latitude she took in the relation of marriage?

"No," he replied unhesitatingly, "the finest teachers in life, the most artistic, are the darkest; it is necessary for an artist to see everything—to go to the depths of life. I don't regret anything about George Sand; her very frailties were the result of her good qualities. She was impatient of the goody-good; she wanted something freer."

Yet another favorite chapter of his in "Consuelo" was the one where Haydn and Consuelo, having set forth on their travels, she disguised as a boy, come to the canon's garden by moonlight, and there, beneath his window among the flowers and the cool dew, pour forth sweet music—Consuelo singing in her rich pure contralto voice, and Haydn skilfully accompanying her with his violin. They are both tired and belated; it is with them a question of no song, no supper. They hope by the former to touch the heart of the canon, and in this they succeed, for he invites them in; giving them supper and a night's lodging.

One evening in October, one of those lovely, warm, still evenings of the American fall, the conversation turned on beauty. Walt

Walt Whitman, 1878

doubted if extreme beauty was well for a woman.

"But," queried one, "how could the Greeks have got on without it?"

"Now arises the almost terrific question," answered Walt: "is there not something artificial and fictitious in what we call beauty? Should we appreciate the severe beauty of the Greeks? The wholesome outdoor life of the Greeks begets something so different from ours, which is the result of books, picture galleries, and bred in the drawing-room." The grace of the Venus of Milo is here instanced. Another talker (a woman) suggests that her face lacks intellect. Walt rejoined energetically, "So much the better. Intellect is a *fiend*. It is a curse that all our American boys and girls are taught so much.

157

There's a boy I take a great interest in; he is sent to a school in Camden, his people want him to be taught shorthand, and three languages; why, it's like putting jewels on a person before he has got shoes. The boy is sharp enough of wit. I suggested that he should study literature, and soon. But no, this learning is helpful.

"Education, what is meant by the grammar, I think the study of that fatuous—filling growing boys with a lot of dead matter, perfectly useless. For my part when I meet any one of erudition I want to get away, it terrifies me. Among the young boys and girls there is a tendency to dyspepsia, to wear glasses, and look interesting.

"They don't know how to handle a gun, or ride, or run.

"I would have a boy taught ciphering, reading, writing, and give him plenty of literature. I would be very particular about the company he should associate with; he should be athletic, and learn to express himself."

"Was Consuelo too intellectual?"

"Why, no, she was bred in a rich and sunny land, and she cultivated the fine voice she had."

Did he like Boston?

"Not very much."

"You don't like its people?"

Here his friend noted that he never forgot the poet's sweet and human smile, as he said—

"People are much the same everywhere"; but he added, "there is not enough *abandon* about the Bostonians."

Did he not think Shakespeare must have been a very jolly fellow to know?

"I think so," said Walt. "I think one can see and understand him without knowing all about the little facts of his life. There are a great many fellows here who would like to be Shakespeare scholars. I remember an old general, a very noble old fellow. He had a belief that Shakespeare's sonnets were theological discussions. He gave me his book, very dull I remember. I think I shall give Mr. T. a copy of it.

"Have you seen Tennyson's new poem, 'Harold'? Tennyson's treatment of these old subjects is like beautifully wrought china, nothing more."

Upon another occasion, my brother—with whom most of the conversations here cited were held, and by whose care in transcribing them and kind permission I am now enabled to put them to their present use—visited Walt at his brother George Whitman's house at Camden.

Walt was led to describe some of the beginnings of his older friendships— of his meeting with John Burroughs, the American naturalist.

"I have known him about fourteen years; his health failed before he went into the army, and he went in to be either killed or cured. I fell in with him there. He is just the same as when I first saw him, always the same. Not, like some of my friends, very thick at first, then falling off."

Professor Dowden was an English admirer whose letters Walt greatly prized. One passage in one of Professor Dowden's essays especially appealed to him.

"I was much moved—unspeakably so, by that quotation Dowden gives from Hugo—'Fine genius is like a promontory stretching out into the infinite.' "

Late in the same year (1876) his friend again visited Walt at Camden. He found him musing alone in a twilight of a December afternoon.

"This is one of the few evenings in which we have twilight."

The talk turned on poets.

"The poetry that appears in the various magazines, with its cheap sentiment, is like small change—a certain amount of it is wanted. How good is that article in the January number of *Appleton's Journal* on Heine! I have read it twice. I should almost call it Shakesperian in its deep reflectiveness. He is not at all blinded or led away by his subject—such a true portrayal of Heine."

"What an unhappy nature Heine's was!" rejoined his friend.

"Well—no, I should hardly say that. He bore his sufferings—bore up through it all; there was something bouyant and cheerful in him. Poor fellow! I often think of him lying on that couch, so patient through it all. . . . I suppose it is impossible in a translation to get a notion of his power of language, and dashing brilliant wit."

Of Hugo, Walt Whitman remarked—

"I can't swallow his exaggeration and bombast. There are some who defend all that, but I can't stomach it. I have tried to, because there is so much that I like about him, sympathetical withal. I think 'Les Miserables' about the best thing he has written. Jean Valjean is fine, also Cosette.

"I like his 'La Légende des Siècles' best. I have heard it read aloud and translated at the same time, by an old Frenchman. I know there is something in personal magnetism. All that I know about ships and whalers has been picked up through the medium of close personal narration. I remember how gratified I was when in the presence of whalers or fishermen my poems were read descriptive of these events, and when the fishermen or whaleman were moved and excited, I felt it a triumph."

He reverts to Bostonians and their ways.

"They are supercilious to everybody; there is Emerson, the only sweet one among them, and he has been spoilt by them."

"Yes, it is a stultifying atmosphere for him."

"That is just what I should say. There are certain recognized parlor laws of propriety which we allow. But to carry their notions of drawing-room properties into poetry is too absurd."

Would he like to go to California?

"No, if the world were before me, instead of behind me—I might; but it is not by going to fresh countries that you see new things and faces and fresh experiences of people, it's the same old round, all the world over. Literature can't express everything. There is an effervescence—an atmosphere that can't be caught. Literature, with all its proud haughtiness, must come down. I have often tried to write what I have said."

To all forms of personal criticism Walt Whitman was adverse, and leaned ever on the side of charity and of tolerance.

It was a point very strongly insisted upon by him, that all the mock gentility and homage of society detracted from the true dignity and freedom of the individual, and I never heard him employ the term "lady" or "gentleman" to any one. He was fond of children, retailing their quaint ways in many an amusing anecdote.

"I have quite a circle of acquaintance amongst the *gamins* in Camden. I was walking there the other day when a little boy, whom I suppose I had spoken to and taken some notice of, said to his father, 'There goes a good man.' I turned round and said, 'Don't you be so sure of that,'—the child looked quite abashed."

Perhaps the child was nearer the truth than the poet guessed, if humanity at large is destined to gain moral health and strength from his poems, just as the wounded soldiers of the Secession War revived in his invigorating presence, so full of "the august beauty of the strong."

Of the ordinary forms of social amusements Walt Whitman fought very shy. Strawberry teas, of which the Americans are very fond, he described as "very stupid things"; "I don't care," he said, "about that kind of thing at all. I like being with those I love, I never get tired of that."

On physical perfection and the systematic cultivation of the body he laid great stress—as much so as in his poems. When asked if he had cultivated his body as much when he was a boy as in middle life, he answered—

"More so, oh! I used to be more proud when I went to the bath and some one would say that I was the finest-shaped youngster in the bath, than I have been of all my literary admiration since."

A favorite summer haunt of the poet's was a farm in New Jersey named Timber Creek. Here he led a perfectly *al fresco* life, and was more completely in his element than at any other time of the year. He distinguished the note of every bird, and noted any rarer warbler which chanced to build his nest at the White Horse, a lovely spot near Timber Creek. In the Spring of the year of which I write he stayed at Timber Creek, and dilated on these pleasures:—

"The birds at the White Horse—oh! how beautiful they are now. They have burst upon me all at once. I am studying them anew, and there is one little bird that lurks in the background, and sings by himself. Then all the birds strike in together. I can't find his nest; the boys, who have all a farmer's lore, have described him to me, but I am not satisfied."

"Was your favorite buzzard among them?"

"Yes."

He liked reading critiques on himself. In one of these chats by the creek, his friend asked him how he liked one which had appeared in the *Gentleman's Magazine* for that year (1877).

"I like it," said Walt; "I was a good deal tickled by the title ('Walt Whitman the Poet of Joy')—the dashing off kind. I was so pleased with it that I wrote to the office of the *Gentleman's Magazine*, for Clive's address, sending a portrait of myself, but received no answer." [The real name of the author of this appreciative article was Arthur O'Shaughnessy.]

"I sometimes wonder," he mused, "that I am not more ostracized than I am on account of my free opinions."

"Yes," replied his friend, "we are almost completely so. In Philadelphia the question is—what church do you go to?"

Walt Whitman, 1878

"Good, you don't know what you escape by it. It is well to go to church sometimes to see what people are like. For my part, I am so out of these things, that I am quite surprised when I go, to find myself living in such a different world. The people round here have been warned by the school director of my poems, and that I am an improper person, and bad character for the young men and maidens to associate with. The time of my boyhood was a very restless and unhappy one; I did not know what to do."

Still under the trees at Timber Creek, the following conversation, half earnest, half jest, took place between Walt Whitman and his young English friend.

"I think," said Walt, "I shall have to leave these parts. Do you have that old expression of having your nose put out of joint when a new lover comes? I used to be a great King Pin down here; I daresay you have noticed something of the same sort yourself?"

"No, indeed, I have not; I think you are laboring under an hallucination. I hope you will stick down here a good time, and not take any kinks into your head."

"Well, it does me good to hear anything like that; when a wise man sees anything that other people can't the people call it a kink."

He once more reverted to Shakespeare—

"It is not dwelt upon, but what a great deal of superfluous matter there is in Shakespeare—a great deal might be left out. Unlike the Greeks, they would not have anything in but what was absolutely necessary, and that is why the moderns are so inferior in art. We want pretty verbiage, part of a poem or a picture, without reference to the whole."

"I don't see that it is any use trying to refine Shakespeare into Greek—he is essentially Gothic."

"Yes, you have hit it—hit the bull's eye; Shakespeare is distinctly Gothic."

Sometimes Walt Whitman described his more stirring life in New York in his prime:—

"At one time," he said, "nothing was so exhilarating to me, not even books or picture galleries, as a walk down Broadway. There was something so stirring in the scene—the brilliancy, the contact with crowds of new faces. The gaily dressed people, the crowds of foreigners in Spring. Then the fine vista of buildings, some four and five stories high. In July I used to seek the sea; the *débris* and the atmosphere in parts of the City became unpleasant to me. The sea is so soothing, so sympathetic. Oh! I used to spend hours by the sea."

Did he like companionship in walking?

He laughingly quoted Emerson—the sun seems to look down, and say, "Why so hot, my little man?"

He constrasted him didactically with George Sand.

"Emerson has not George Sand's art of preaching without appearing to be sermonizing, which is the art of arts. One does not like to be told one must not laugh or smile. . . . Emerson conforms in small conventional things; he says himself that, as he does not give up in all the large important things in life, he can afford to in the small affairs of life."

He described Carlyle as "kinky"—a word he often made use of, meaning crotchety.

"Carlyle has terrible deficiencies and gaps; he is not amorous like the Greeks."

Of the late Mr. Addington Symonds, Walt spoke with very warm regard, and of his literary admiration he was justly proud.

"What Mr. Symonds admires in my books is the comradeship; he says that he had often felt it, and wanted to express it, but dared not! He thinks that the Englishman has it in him, but puts on gruffness, and is ashamed to show it."

Mr. Symonds generously acknowledges his debt to Walt Whitman in his last book, which appeared after his death.

"I came across a saying by Bacon, that bad-tempered and ill-natured people are the vermin of humanity, but," he added indulgently, "you can't say what these things are—how much of it is not stomachic. Literature, with all its uses, has had pernicious influences. It has marred that story-telling faculty—the memory. I have known laborers who have recited poems to me with wonderful clearness. My dear mother possessed the story-telling faculty; whenever she had been anywhere she could describe it, tell me all about it.

"If I had to choose, were I looking about for a profession, I should choose that of a doctor. Yes; widely opposite as science and the emotional element are, they might be joined in the medical profession, and there would be great opportunities for developing them. Nowhere is there such call for them."

"Doctors seem rather to hold back from that."

"Oh, a doctor should be a superb fellow. He does not approach at present to what he should be."

Once his friend asked him if he would really care to visit England, or if the atmosphere, physically and morally, might not prove oppressive.

"Oh, no," he answered; "you don't know me. No, I should be glad to get away; I could spend the rest of my time in England, though it does not do to say so to Americans."

"You would miss the democratic atmosphere?"

"Oh! I should have my friends there, as I have here."

"Yes; I don't see why one can't be as democratic in England as in America."

"More so, I think."

In the summer of 1877 Walt read some of his poems to the students of Swarthmore College.

Afterward he said of this occasion—

"They did not see what I was driving at—it was not to be expected that they should. After it was over, the boys took me round to have some refreshments that I liked. I felt a good deal flattered. . . ."

Walt Whitman was not a full or copious letter-writer; his letters were, in the main, more like telegraphic despatches than letters, the postcard being his favorite mode of written communication; but I give these one or two letters addressed to his friend because they serve to picture the mode and surroundings of his daily life.

The letters were written in the summer of 1877 and the winter of 1878. The first two are written from Camden, after his return from Timber Creek; the last from his friend's house in Philadelphia, when that friend was staying away from home:—

431, Stevens Street, Camden.
"*Sunday morn, July 22nd* (1877).

"Dear Herb,—Here I am, at my room and haunts in Camden, so different from the Creek, and bathing and exercising in the open air, yet I keep myself busy, at one thing and another. I am feeling pretty well so far (Yet I attribute my feeling pretty well now to my visit for the last year and a half, to the Creek and farm, and being with my dear friends the S---'s). We had a nice healthy ride up from Kirkwood, Mrs. S. and I, Friday morning, and I enjoyed it much. I am glad I came up that way, instead of the railway. I went over to your Mother's yesterday afternoon, about 5 1/2 and stayed till 8. Nothing especially new with them. Mother and Bee and Giddy are all well and in good spirits. We had a good tea, I punished a fearful quantity of good oatmeal, and mush and stewed blackberries—then we sat and talked for an hour and a half in the cool of the evening on the front stoop. Then a delightful jaunt home to Camden, a most lovely evening (the moon and Jupiter in conjunction, and I 'speering' them all the way home especially on the river.'

"I am particularly busy at some writing, feel *most first rate for me*, to-day. Herb you will see by the enclosed that Bucke is in Camden (or *en route* thither). Write to me,
Your old Walt.
"I have written to-day to Mrs. Stafford."

To the same—

"1929, North 22nd Street,
Saturday, 6 P.M.

"Dear Herbert,—I will just write a line to put in your mother's letter. I

165

am well as usual. We have had three awful hot days and nights (but I have stood 'em capitally) up to last evening when it rained hard and though warm enough again yet it is now quite tolerable. I have been here 24 hours (go back to Camden this evening). Your mother and Bee and Giddy are very well. I am writing this up in the bow window room—it is jolly up here—I slept like a top last night. We all sat in the big room in the dark, till 10 (had to put down the windows it was so coolish and windy).

"Herb, your Creek picture looks steadily good. Don't give out the more you are acquainted with it and examine it—seems to me indeed a true bit of Nature.

"I miss the Creek and Spring—miss my dear friends at the house. Shall write to Mrs. S. probably same mail with this—rec'd your letter—and thank you for it, as I close it is 6 o'clock a real fine evening.
    "Love to you from
        "Your old Walt."

"Six o'clock, and a real fine evening"—thus do we take our last look at Walt Whitman, leaving him in the mellow glow of his life's evening. Pencilled on the flyleaf of a favorite book were those beautiful lines Michael Angelo addressed to Dante—

Gladly would I to be such as he
With his exile and all his persecutions and his anguish
Forego the happiest fortunes of mankind.

Might these lines not serve this free, strong poet for his own epitaph? He rests three miles from Camden. His monument a huge stone banked against a hill, a design he himself chose from Blake's fine engraving of Death's Door.—*Temple Bar.*

Eclectic Magazine, 67 (April 1898): 451-459.

From LITERARY FRIENDS AND ACQUAINTANCE

William Dean Howells

William Dean Howells became an important novelist and a major spokesman for the realistic school of American fiction. In 1860, he was an Ohio journalist making a literary tour of New England and New York, including a visit to Whitman and the bohemian crowd at Pfaff's restaurant on Bleecker Street.

He was often at Pfaff's with them, and the night of my visit he was the chief fact of my experience. I did not know he was there till I was on my way out, for he did not sit at the table under the pavement, but at the head of one farther into the room. There, as I passed, some amiable fellow stopped me and named me to him, and I remember how he leaned back in his chair, and reached out his great hand to me, as if he were going to give it me for good and all. He had a fine head, with a cloud of Jovian hair upon it, and a branching beard and mustache, and gentle eyes that looked most kindly into mine, and seemed to wish the liking which I instantly gave him, though we hardly passed a word, and our acquaintance was summed up in that glance and the grasp of his mighty fist upon my hand. I doubt if he had any notion who or what I was beyond the fact that I was a young poet of some sort, but he may possibly have remembered seeing my name printed after some very Heinesque verses in the *Press*. I did not meet him again for twenty years, and then I had only a moment with him when he was reading the proofs of his poems in Boston. Some years later I saw him for the last time, one day after his lecture on Lincoln, in that city, when he came down from the platform to speak with some hand-shaking friends who gathered about him. Then and always he gave me the sense of a sweet and true soul, and I felt in him a spiritual dignity which I will not try to reconcile with his printing in the forefront of his book a passage from a private letter of Emerson's, though I believe he would not have seen such a thing as most other men would, or thought ill of it in another. The spiritual purity which I felt in him no less than the dignity is something that I will no more try to reconcile with what denies it in his page; but such things we may well leave to the adjustment of finer balances than we have at hand. I will make sure only of the greatest benignity in the presence of the man. The apostle of the rough, the uncouth, was the gentlest person; his barbaric yawp, translated into the terms of social encounter, was an address of singular quiet, delivered in a voice of winning and endearing friendliness.

From *Literary Friends and Acquaintance*, (New York: Harper, 1900), pp. 74-75.

REMINISCENCES OF WALT WHITMAN

John Townsend Trowbridge

John Townsend Trowbridge's friendship with Whitman, a fellow journalist, began in 1860. The article below is the source for what is the most well-known comment on Emerson attributed to Whitman: "I was simmering, simmering; Emerson brought me to a boil."

I first made acquaintance with Whitman's writings when a newspaper notice of the earliest edition of Leaves of Grass reached me, in Paris, in the autumn of 1855. It was the most exhilarating piece of news I had received from America during the six months of my absence abroad. Such vigor, such graphic force, such human sympathy, such scope and audacity in the choice and treatment of themes, found in me an eagerly interested reader of the copious extracts which the notice contained. When I came to see the volume itself,— the thin, small quarto of 1855,—I found in it much that impressed me as formless and needlessly offensive; and these faults were carried to extremes in the second and enlarged edition of 1856. Yet the tremendous original power of this new bard, and the freshness, as of nature itself, which breathed through the best of his songs or sayings, continued to hold their spell over me, and inspired me with intense curiosity as to the man himself. But I had no opportunity of meeting him till he came to Boston in the spring of 1860, to put his third edition through the press.

Then, one day, I was stopped on Washington Street by a friend who made this startling announcement: "Walt Whitman is in town; I have just seen him!" When I asked where, he replied: "At the stereotype foundry, just around the corner. Come along! I'll take you to him." The author of Leaves of Grass had loomed so large in my imagination as to seem almost superhuman; and I was filled with some such feeling of wonder and astonishment as if I had been invited to meet Socrates or King Solomon.

We found a large, gray-haired and gray-bearded, plainly dressed man, reading proof-sheets at a desk in a little dingy office, with a lank, unwholesome-looking lad at his elbow, listlessly watching him. The man was Whitman, and the proofs were those of his new edition. There was a scarcity of chairs, and Whitman, rising to receive us, offered me his; but we all remained standing except the sickly looking lad, who kept his seat until Whitman turned to him and said, "You'd better go now; I'll see you this evening." After he had gone out, Whitman explained: "He is a friendless boy I found at my boarding place. I am trying to cheer him up and strengthen him with my magnetism." My readers may think this a practical but curiously prosaic illustration of these powerful lines in the early poems:—

To any one dying, thither I speed and twist the knob of the door.

.   .   .   .

I seize the descending man, I raise him with resistless will.

.   .   .   .

Every room of the house do I fill with an armed force, lovers of me, bafflers of graves.

The difference between the prosaic fact and the poetic expression was not greater than the contrast between Whitman as I had imagined him and the simple, well-mannered man who stood and talked with us. From his own descriptions of himself, and from the swing and impetus of his lines, I had pictured him proud, alert, grandiose, defiant of the usages of society; and I found him the quietest of men. I really remember but one thing he said, after sending away the boy. The talk turning on his proof-sheets, I asked how the first poems impressed him, at this re-reading; to which he replied, "I am astonished to find myself capable of feeling so much." The conversation was all very quiet, pitched in a low key, and I went away somewhat disappointed that he did not say or do something extraordinary and admirable; one of the noticeable things about him being an absence of all effort to make a good impression.

I got on vastly better with him when, the next Sunday morning, he came out to see me on Prospect Hill, in Somerville, where I was then living. The weather was perfect,—it was early May; the few

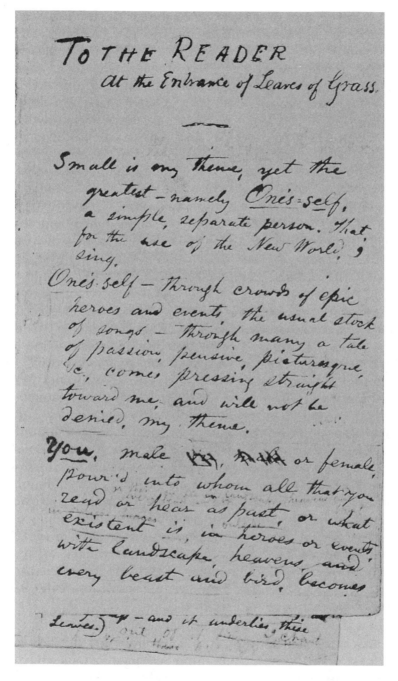

Whitman's draft manuscript poetic introduction to Leaves of Grass

friends I introduced to him were congenial spirits; he was happy and animated, and we spent the day together in such hearty and familiar intercourse that when I parted with him in the evening, on East Cambridge bridge, having walked to Boston, I felt that a large, new friendship had shed a glow on my life. Of much of that day's talk I have a vivid recollection,—even of its trivialities. He was not a loud laugher, and rarely made a joke, but he greatly enjoyed the pleasantries of others. He liked especially any allusion, serious or jocular, to his poems. When, at dinner, preparing my dish of salad, I remarked that I was employed as his critics would be when his new edition was out, he queried, "Devouring Leaves of Grass?" "No," I said, "cutting up Leaves of Grass,"—which amused him more, I fancy, than the cutting up did which came later. As the afternoon waned, and he spoke of leaving us, somebody placed a book before the face of the clock. I said: "Put Leaves of Grass there. Nobody can see through that." "Not even the author?" he said, with a whimsical lifting of the brows.

Much of the talk was about himself and his poems, in every particular of which I was profoundly interested. He told me of his boyhood in Brooklyn; going to work in a printing office at the age of fourteen; teaching school at seventeen and eighteen; writing stories and sketches for periodicals under his full name, Walter Whitman (his first Leaves of Grass was copyrighted by Walter Whitman, after which he discarded "Walter" for "Walt"); editing newspapers and making political speeches, on the Democratic side; leading an impulsive, irregular sort of life, and absorbing, as probably no other man ever did, the common aspects of the cities he was so proud of, Brooklyn and New York. His friendships were mostly with the common people, —pilots, drivers, mechanics; and his favorite diversions, crossing the ferries, riding on the top of the omnibuses, and attending operas. He liked to get off alone by the seashore, read Homer and Ossian with the salt air on his cheeks, and shout their winged words to the winds and waves. The book he knew best was the Bible, the prophetical parts of which stirred in him a vague desire to be the bard or prophet of his own time and country.

Then, at the right moment, he read Emerson.

I was extremely interested to know how far the influence of our greatest writer had been felt in the making of a book which, without being at all imitative, was pitched in the very highest key of self-reliance. In his letter to Emerson, printed in the second edition of

Leaves of Grass, speaking of "Individuality, the new moral American continent," Whitman had averred: "Those shores you found; I say, you led the States there,—have led me there." And it seemed hardly possible that the first determined attempt to cast into literature a complete man, with all his pride and passions, should have been made by one whose feet were not already firmly planted on "those shores." Then there was the significant fact of his having mailed a copy of his first edition to Emerson.

Whitman talked frankly on the subject, that day on Prospect Hill, and told how he became acquainted with Emerson's writings. He was at work as a carpenter (his father's trade before him) in Brooklyn, building with his own hands and on his own account small and very plain houses for laboring men; as soon as one was finished and sold, beginning another,—houses of two or three rooms. This was in 1854; he was then thirty-five years old. He lived at home with his mother; going off to his work in the morning and returning at night, carrying his dinner pail like any common laborer. Along with his pail he usually carried a book, between which and his solitary meal he would divide his nooning. Once the book chanced to be a volume of Emerson; and from that time he took with him no other writer. His half-formed purpose, his vague aspirations, all that had lain smoldering so long within him, waiting to be fired, rushed into flame at the touch of those electric words,—the words that burn in the prose-poem Nature, and in the essays on Spiritual Laws, The Over-Soul, Self-Reliance. The sturdy carpenter in his working-day garb, seated on his pile of boards; a poet in that rude disguise, as yet but dimly conscious of his powers; in one hand the sandwich put up for him by his good mother; his other hand holding open the volume that revealed to him his greatness and his destiny,—this is the picture which his simple narrative called up, that Sunday so long ago, and which has never faded from my memory.

He freely admitted that he could never have written his poems if he had not first "come to himself," and that Emerson helped him to "find himself." I asked if he thought he would have come to himself without that help. He said, "Yes, but it would have taken longer." And he used his characteristic expression: "I was simmering, simmering; Emerson brought me to a boil."

It was in that summer of 1854, while he was still at work upon his houses, that he began the Leaves of Grass, which he wrote, rewrote, and re-rewrote (to quote again his own words), and afterward set in type with his own hand.

I make this statement thus explicit because a question of profound personal and literary interest is involved, and becaused it is claimed by some of the later friends of Whitman that he wrote his first Leaves of Grass before he had read Emerson. When they urge his own authority for their contention, I can only reply that he told me distinctly the contrary, when his memory was fresher.

The Emersonian influence is often clearly traceable in Whitman's early poems; seldom in the later. It is in the first line of the very first poem in which he struck the keynote of his defiant chant: "I celebrate myself." Yet the form Whitman chose for his message was as independent of Emerson's as of all other literary forms whatsoever. Outwardly, his unrhymed and unmeasured lines resemble those of Tupper's Proverbial Philosophy; but in no other way are they akin to those colorless platitudes. To the music of the opera, for which he had a passion, more than to anything else, was due his emancipation from what he called the "ballad style" of poetry, by which he meant poetry hampered by rhyme and metre. "But for the opera," he declared that day on Prospect Hill, "I could never have written Leaves of Grass."

Whitman was at that time a man of striking personal appearance, as indeed he always was: fully six feet tall, and large proportionally; slow of movement, and inclined to walk with a lounging gait, which somebody has likened to an "elephantine roll." He wore his shirt collar open at the throat, exposing his hairy chest, in decidedly unconventional fashion. His necktie was drawn into a loose knot, or hung free, with serpentine ends coiled away somewhere in his clothing. He was scrupulously neat in person,—"never dressed in black, always dressed freely and clean in strong clothes," according to his own description of himself; head massive, complexion florid-tawny, forehead seamed with wrinkles, which, along with his premature grayness, made him look much older than he was. Mr. Howells, in his First Impressions of Literary New York, describes a meeting with him a few months later, that same year (1860), and calls him "the benign old man." Whitman was at that time forty-one.

I did not see him again for three years and a half: meanwhile the Civil War was raging, and in 1862 he went to the front, to nurse his brother, Lieutenant Colonel George W. Whitman, who had been wounded at Fredericksburg. This was the beginning of his hospital work, which became so important an episode in his life.

In the latter part of November, 1863, a fortunate circumstance placed me in friendly relations with Salmon P. Chase, then at the summit of his fame as Secretary of the Treasury in Lincoln's Cabinet, and I became a guest in his house.

I had at that time few acquaintances in Washington. One of the most prized of these was William Douglas O'Connor. He had turned aside from literature, in which we who knew him in the flower of his youthful promise had believed him destined to excel, and entered a department of the government,—one of those vast mausoleums in which so many talents, small and great, have been buried, and brave ambitions have turned quietly to dust. His first employment was in the Treasury; in the Treasury, also, when I first knew him, was that other valiant friend of Whitman's, John Burroughs, who, fortunately for himself and his readers, escaped O'Connor's fate. When O'Connor left the Treasury it was to enter the Lighthouse Board, where he became head clerk, and sat like a spider in the midst of his web, a coast light at the end of each invisible line, hundreds of thousands of miles away. In those useful radiations the beams of his genius became too deeply immersed to shine otherwise than fitfully in what I always deemed his proper sphere.

I knew of his intimacy with Whitman, and when one day I found him at his office, and had answered his many questions, telling him where I was domiciled, one of the first I asked in return was, "Where's Walt?"—the familiar name by which Whitman was known to his friends.

"What a chance!" said O'Connor, in his ardent way. "Walt is here in Washington, living close by you, within a stone's throw of the Secretary's door. Come to my house on Sunday evening, and I will have him there to meet you."

On seeing him again at O'Connor's, I found Whitman but little changed, except that he was more trimly attired, wearing a loosely fitting but quite elegant suit of black,—yes, black at last! He was in the best of spirits; and I remember with what a superb and joyous pace he swung along the street, between O'Connor and me, as we walked home with him, after ten o'clock.

Diagonally opposite to Chase's great house, on the corner of E and 6th streets, stood one of those old wooden buildings which then and for some years afterwards lingered among the new and hand-

Walt Whitman, 1878

some blocks rising around them, and made the "city of magnificent distances" also a city of astonishing architectural contrasts. In the fine, large mansion, sumptuously furnished, cared for by sleek and silent colored servants, and thronged by distinguished guests, dwelt the great statesman; in the old tenement opposite, in a bare and desolate back room, up three flights of stairs, quite alone, lived the poet. Walt led the way up those dreary stairs, partly in darkness, found the keyhole of a door which he unlocked and opened, scratched a match, and welcomed us to his garret.

Garret it literally was, containing hardly any more furniture than a bed, a cheap pine table, and a little sheet-iron stove in which there was no fire. A window was open, and it was a December night.

But Walt, clearing a chair or two of their litter of newspapers, invited us to sit down and stop awhile, with as simple and sweet hospitality as if he had been offering us the luxuries of the great mansion across the square.

Sit down we did (O'Connor on the bed, as I remember), and "drank delight of battle" over books, the principal subjects being Shakespeare and Walt's own Leaves of Grass. Over Shakespeare it was a sort of triangular combat,—O'Connor maintaining the Baconian theory of the authorship of the plays, and Walt joining with me in attacking that chimera. On the other hand, I agreed with O'Connor in his estimate of Lear and Hamlet and Othello, which Walt belittled, preferring the historical plays, and placing Richard II foremost; although he thought all the plays preposterously overrated. Of his own poems ("pomes" he called them) he spoke modestly, listening with interest to frank criticism of them (which he always had from me), and disclaiming the profound hidden meanings which O'Connor was inclined to read into some of them. Ordinarily inert and slow of speech, on occasions like this his large and generous nature became suffused with a magnificent glow, which gave one some idea of the heat and momentum that went to the making of his truly great poems; just as his sluggish moods seemed to account for so much of his labored, unleavened work.

O'Connor was a man of unfailing eloquence, whom it was always delightful to listen to, even when the rush of his enthusiasm carried him beyond the bounds of discretion, as it did in the Bacon-Shakespeare business. Whitman's reasoning powers were not remarkable; he did not impress me, then or at any time, as a great intellect; but he was original, intuitive, a seer, and his immense and genial personality gave an interest to everything he said. In my enjoyment of such high discourse, I forgot the cheerless garret, the stove in which there was no fire, the window that remained open (Walt was a "fresh-air fiend"), and my own freezing feet (we all kept on our overcoats). I also forget that I was a guest at the great house across the quadrangle, and that I was unprovided with a latch key, —a fact of which I was reminded with rather startling unpleasantness, when I left O'Connor at the foot of Walt's stairs, hurried to the Secretary's door, I know not how long after midnight, and found myself locked out. All was still and dark within, except that I could see a light left burning low for me in my own chamber, a tantalizing reminder of the comfort I had exchanged for the bleak, deserted streets. My embarrassment was relieved when I reflected that in those wild war times the Secretary was prepared to receive dispatches at any hour of the night. I rang boldly, as if I had been a messenger bearing tidings of a nation's fate. The vestibule gas was quickly turned up and a sleepy-looking colored boy let me in.

Two mornings after this I went by appointment to call on Whitman in his garret. "Don't come before ten o'clock," he had warned me; and it was after ten when I mounted his three flights and knocked at the door of his room,—his terrible room, as I termed it in notes taken at the time.

I found him partly dressed, and preparing his own breakfast. There was a fire in the sheet-iron stove,—the open door showed a few coals,—and he was cutting slices of bread from a baker's loaf with his jackknife, getting them ready for toasting. The smallest of tin teakettles simmering on the stove, a bowl and spoon, and a covered tin cup used as a teapot comprised, with the aforesaid useful jackknife, his entire outfit of visible housekeeping utensils. His sugar bowl was a brown paper bag. His butter plate was another piece of brown paper, the same coarse wrapping in which he had brought home his modest lump from the corner grocery. His cupboard was an oblong pine box, set up a few feet from the floor, opening outward, with the bottom against the wall; the two sides one above the other, made very good shelves.

I toasted his bread for him on the end of a sharpened stick; he buttered the slices with his jackknife, and poured his tea at a corner of the table cleared for that purpose of its litter of books and newspapers; and while he breakfasted we talked.

His last slice buttered and eaten, he burned his butter plate (showing the advantage of having no dishes to wash), and set his bag of sugar in the cupboard, along with his small parcel of tea; then he brought out from his trunk a package of manuscript poems, which he read to me, and which we discussed, for the next hour.

These were his war pieces, the Drum Taps, then nearly ready for publication. He read them unaffectedly, with force and feeling, and in a voice of rich but not resonant tones. I was interested not alone in the poems, but also in his own interpretation of the irregular yet often not unrhythmical lines. I did not find in them anything comparable with the great moving passages in the earlier Leaves: they were more literary in their tone, showing here and there lapses into the conventional poetic diction, which he had flung off so haughtily in the surge of early impulse. They contained, however, some fine, effective, patriotic, and pathetic chants; and were, moreover, entirely free from the old offenses against propriety. I hoped to be able to persuade some good Boston house to publish the volume, but found, when I came to make the attempt, that no firm would undertake it; and it remained in manuscipt until 1865, when Whitman issued it at his own expense.

From that morning, I saw him almost every day or evening as long as I remained in Washington. He was then engaged in his missionary work in the hospitals; talking to the sick and wounded soldiers, reading to them, writing letters for them, cheering and comforting them sometimes by merely sitting silent beside their cots, and perhaps soothing a pallid brow with his sympathetic hand.

He took me two or three times to the great Amory Square Hospital, where I observed his methods of work. I was surprised to learn that he never read to the patients any of his own compositions, and that not one of those I talked with knew him for a poet, or for anybody but plain "Mr. Whitman." I cannot help speaking of one poor fellow, who had asked to see me because Whitman had told him I was the author of one of the pieces he liked to hear read, and who talked to me with tears in his eyes of the comfort Whitman's visits had given him. The pathos of the situation was impressed upon me by the circumstance that his foot was to be amputated within an hour.

Whitman always carried into the wards a few fruits and delicacies, which he distributed with the approval of the surgeons and nurses. He also circulated, among those who were well enough to read, books and periodicals sent to him for that purpose by friends in the North. Sometimes he gave paper and envelopes and postage stamps, and he was never without some good tobacco, to be dispensed in special cases. He never used tobacco himself, but he had compassion for those who had been deprived of that solace, as he had for all forms of suffering. He wrote Washington letters that winter for the New York Times, the income from which, together with contributions from Northern friends, enabled him to carry on his hospital work.

Whitman and Chase were the two men I saw most of, at that time, in Washington. I saw Chase daily, at his own table, with his friends and distinguished guests, and had many long walks and talks with him, when we took our morning exercise together before break-

Walt Whitman, 1880

fast. That I should know them both familiarly, passing often from the stately residence of the one to the humble lodging of the other, seemed to me a simple and natural thing at the time; it appears much less simple to me now. Great men both, each nobly proportioned in body and stalwart in character, and each invincibly true to his own ideals and purposes; near neighbors, and yet very antipodes in their widely contrasted lives. One princely in position, dispensing an enormous patronage, the slenderest rill of which would have made life green for the other, struggling along the arid ways of an honorable poverty. Both greatly ambitious: Chase devoutly believing it his right and likewise his destiny, to succeed Lincoln in the presidency; Whitman aspiring to be for all the poet of democracy and emancipated manhood,—his simple prayer being, "Give me to speak beautiful words; take all the rest!" One a conscientious High Churchman, reverencing tradition, and finding ceremonious worship so helpful and solacing that (as he once said to me earnestly) he would have become a Roman Catholic, if he could have brought himself to accept the Romish dogmas; the other believing in the immanent spirit and an ever living inspiration, and as free from all forms and doctrines as Abraham alone with Deity in the desert. For the statesman I had a very great admiration and respect; for the poet I felt a powerful attraction, something like a younger brother's love; and I confess a sweet and secret joy in sometimes stealing away from the company of polished and eminent people in the great house, and crossing over to Walt in his garret, or going to meet him at O'Connor's.

I thought no man more than Whitman merited recognition and assistance from the government, and I once asked him if he would accept a position in one of the departments. He answered frankly that he would. But he believed it improbable that he could get an appointment, although (as he mentioned casually) he had letters of recommendation from Emerson.

There were two of these, and they were especially interesting to me, as I knew something of the disturbed relations existing between the two men, on account of Whitman's indiscreet use of Emerson's famous letter to him, acknowledging the gift copy of the first Leaves of Grass. Whitman not only published that letter without the writer's authority, but printed an extract from it, in conspicuous gold, on the back of his second edition,—"I greet you at the beginning of a great career"; thus making Emerson in some sense an indorser not only of the first poems, but of others he had never seen, and which he would have preferred never to see in print. This was an instance of bad taste, but not of intentional bad faith, on the part of Whitman. Talking of it once, he said, in his grand way: "I supposed the letter was meant to be blazoned; I regarded it as the chart of an emperor." But Emerson had no thought of acting the imperial part toward so adventurous a voyager. I remember hearing him allude to the incident shortly after that second edition appeared. Speaking of the attention the new poet was attracting, he mentioned an Englishman who had come to this country bringing a letter to Whitman from Monckton Milnes (afterward Lord Houghton). "But," said Emerson, "hearing that Whitman had not used me well in the matter of letters, he did not deliver it." He had afterwards made a strenuous effort to induce Whitman to omit certain objectionable passages from his edition of 1860, and failed. And I knew that the later writings of Whitman interested him less and less. "No more evidence of getting into form," he once remarked,—a singular comment, it may be thought, from one whose own chief defect as a writer seemed to be an imperfect mastery of form.

With these things in mind, I read eagerly the two letters from Emerson recommending Whitman for a government appointment. One was addressed to Senator Sumner; the other, I was surprised and pleased to find, to Secretary Chase. I had but a slight acquaintance with Sumner, and the letter to him I handed back. The one written to Chase I wished to retain, in order to deliver it to the Secretary with my own hands, and with such furthering words as I could summon in so good a cause. Whitman expressed small hope in the venture, and stipulated that in case of the failure he anticipated I should bring back the letter.

As we left the breakfast table, the next morning, I followed the Secretary into his private office, where, after some pleasant talk, I remarked that I was about to overstep a rule I had laid down for myself on entering his house. He said, "What rule?" I replied, "Never to repay your hospitality by asking of you any official favor." He said I needn't have thought it necessary to make that rule, for he was always glad to do for his friends such things as he was constantly called upon to do for strangers. Then I laid before the Whitman business. He was evidently impressed by Emerson's letter, and he listened with interest to what I had to say of the man and his patriotic work. But he was troubled. "I am placed," he said, "in a very embarrassing position. It would give me great pleasure to grant this request, out of my regard to Mr. Emerson"; and he was gracious enough to extend the courtesy of this "regard" to me, also. But then he went on to speak of Leaves of Grass as a book that had made the author notorious; and I found that he judged it, as all but a very few persons then did, not independently, on its own epoch-making merits, but by conventional standards of taste and propriety. He had understood that the writer was a rowdy,—"one of the roughs,"—according to his descriptions of himself.

I said, "He is as quiet a gentleman in his manners and conversation as any guest who enters your door."

He replied: "I am bound to believe what you say; but his writings have given him a bad repute, and I should not know what sort of place to give to such a man,"—with more to the same purpose.

I respected his decision, much as I regretted it; and, persuaded that nothing I could urge would induce him to change it, I said I would relieve him of all embarrassment in the business by withdrawing the letter. He glanced again at the signature, hesitated, and made this surprising response:—

"I have nothing of Emerson's in his handwriting, and I shall be glad to keep this."

I thought it hardly fair, but as the letter was addressed to him, and had passed into his hands, I couldn't well reclaim it against his wishes.

Whitman seemed really to have formed some hopes of the success of my mission, after I had undertaken it, as he showed when I went to give him an account of my interview with the Secretary. He took the disappointment philosophically, but indulged in some sardonic remarks regarding Chase and his department. "He is right," he said, "in preserving his saints from contamination by a man like me!" But I stood up for the Secretary, as, with the Secretary, I had stood up for Whitman. Could any one be blamed for taking the writer of Leaves of Grass at his word when, in his defiance of conventionality, he had described himself as "rowdyish," "disorderly," and worse? " 'I cock my hat as I please, indoors and out,' " I quoted. Walt laughed, and said, "I don't blame him; it's about what I expected." He asked for the letter, and showed his amused disgust when I explained how it had been pocketed by the Secretary.

I should probably have had no difficulty in securing the appointment if I had withheld Emerson's letter, and called my friend simply Mr. Whitman, or Mr. Walter Whitman, without mentioning Leaves of Grass. But I felt that the Secretary, if he was to appoint him, should know just whom he was appointing; and Whitman was the last person in the world to shirk the responsibility of having written an audacious book.

Whether the same candor was used in procuring for him a clerkship in the Interior Department, I do not know. He had been for some time performing the duties of that position, without exciting any other comment than that he performed them well, when a new Secretary, coming in under Johnson, and discovering that the grave and silent man at a certain desk was the author of a reprehensible book, dismissed him uncermoniously.

It was this incident that called out from O'Connor his brilliant monograph, The Good Gray Poet, in which Whitman was so eloquently vindicated, and the Secretary received so terrible a scourging. What seemed for a time unmitigated ill fortune proved to be a very good thing for Whitman. He was soon after appointed to a better place in the office of the Attorney-General, and he himself used to say that it was O'Connor's defense that turned the tide in his favor; meaning the tide of criticism and public opinion, which had until then set so tremendously against him. O'Connor's pamphlet was followed, two years later (1867), by John Burroughs's Walt Whitman as Poet and Person. Countless other publications on the same inexhaustible theme have appeared since,—reviews, biographies, personal recollections, studies of Walt Whitman; a recent Study by Burroughs himself; volumes of eulogy and exegesis, commentary and controversy, wise and foolish; a whole library of Whitman literature, in English, French, German, and other languages. There are Walt Whitman Societies and Fellowships, and at least one periodical is devoted mainly to Whitmanana.

I saw Whitman many times in Washington, after that memorable season of 1863; again when he came to Boston to deliver his lecture on Lincoln; and lastly in his Camden home, where the feet of many pilgrims mounted the steps that led to his door, and where an infirm but serene old age closed the "great career" Emerson had been the first to acclaim.

All this time I have watched with deep interest the growth of his influence and the change in public opinion regarding him. To me, now almost the sole survivor among his earliest friends and adherents, wonderful indeed seems that change since the first thin quarto edition of the Leaves appeared, in 1855. If noticed at all by the critics, it was, with rare exceptions, to be ridiculed and reviled; and Emerson himself suffered abuse for pronouncing it "the most extraordinary piece of wit and wisdom America had yet contributed." Even so accomplished a man of letters as James Russell Lowell saw in it nothing but commonplace tricked out with eccentricity. I remember walking with him once in Cambridge, when he pointed out a doorway sign, "Groceries," with the letters set zigzag, to produce a bizarre effect. "That," said he, "is Walt Whitman,—with very common goods inside." It was not until his writings became less prophetical, and more

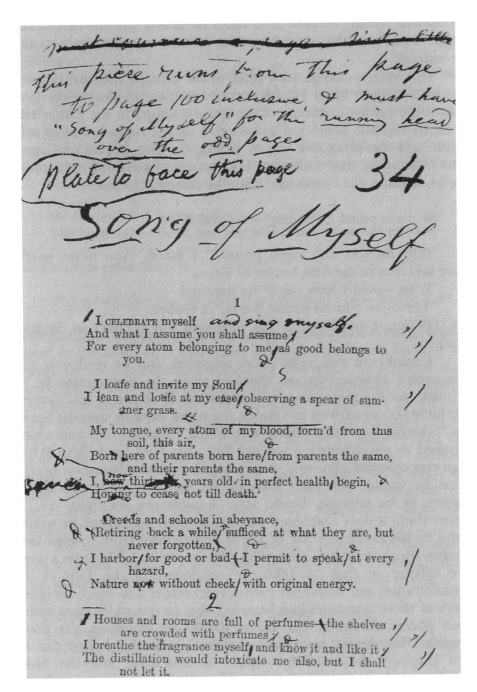

Whitman's manuscript revision of "Song of Myself"

consciously literary in their aim, that Lowell and scholars of his class began to see something besides oddity in Whitman, and his popularity widened.

That such a change took place in his writings Whitman himself was aware. Once when I confessed to him that nothing in the later poems moved me like some of the great passages in the earlier editions, he replied: "I am not surprised. I do not suppose I shall ever again have the afflatus I had in writing the first Leaves of Grass." One evening he was reading to O'Connor and me some manuscript pieces, inviting our comments, when he came to the line,—

No poem proud I, chanting, bring to thee.

"Why do you say 'poem proud'?" I asked. "You never would have said that in the first Leaves of Grass."

"What would I have said?" he inquired.

"'I bring to you no proud poem,'" I replied.

O'Connor cried out, in his vehement way, "That's so, Walt,— that's so!"

"I think you are right," Walt admitted, and he read over the line, which I looked to see changed when the poem came to be printed; but it appeared without alteration. It occurs in Lo, Victress on the Peaks, an address to Liberty, for which word he uses the Spanish "Libertad,"—another thing with which I found fault, and which I hoped to see changed. I will say here that I do not believe Whitman ever changed a line or a word to please anybody. In answer to criticism, he would sometimes maintain his point; at others, he would answer, in his tolerant, candid way, "I guess you are right," or, "I rather think it is so"; but even when apparently convinced, he would stand by his faults. His use of words and phrases from foreign languages, which he began in his 1856 edition, and which became a positive offense in that of 1860, he continued in the face of all remonstrance, and would not even correct errors into which his ignorance of those languages had betrayed him. In one of his most ambitious poems, Chanting the Square Deific, he translates our good English "Holy Spirit" into "Santa Spirita," meant for Italian; but in that language the word for "spirit" is masculine, and the form should have been "Spirito Santo," with the adjective correspondingly masculine. William Rossetti, who edited a volume of selections from Leaves of Grass for the British public, pointed this out in a letter to

186

Whitman, who, in talking of it with me, acknowledged the blunder; yet through some perversity he allowed it to pass on into subsequent editions.

In these editions Whitman showed that he was not averse to making changes; he was always rearranging the contents, mixing up the early with the later poems, and altering titles, to the confusion of the faithful. Now and then he would interject into some familiar passage of the old pieces a phrase or a line in his later manner, strangely discordant to an ear of any discrimination. A good example is this, where to the original lines,—

> My rendezvous is appointed, it is certain,
> The Lord will be there, and wait till I come, on perfect terms,—

he adds this third line,—

> The great Camerado, the lover true for whom I pine, will be there,—

a tawdry patch on the strong original homespun. The French "rendezvous" in the first line is legitimate, having been adopted into our language because it expresses something for which we have no other single word, and Whitman would be a benefactor had he enriched our vernacular in that way. But "camerado"—of which he seems to have become very fond, using it wherever he had a chance—is neither French (camarade) nor Spanish (camarada), nor anything else, to my mind, but a malformed substitute for our good and sufficient word "comrade." "Lover true," like "poem proud," is a piece with those "stock poetical touches" which he used to say he had great trouble in leaving out of his first Leaves, but which here, as in other places, he went back and deliberately wrote into them.

For another set of changes to which I objected he was able to give a reason, though a poor one. In the Poem of Faces, "the old face of the mother of many children" has this beautiful setting:—

> Lulled and late is the smoke of the Sabbath morning,
> It hangs low over the rows of trees by the fences,
> It hangs thin by the sassafras, the wild cherry, and the cat-brier under
>   them.

"Smoke of the Sabbath morning" he altered, after the first two editions, to "smoke of the First Day morning." In like manner, elsewhere, "the field-sprouts of April and May" was changed to "the field-sprouts of Fourth Month and Fifth Month;" "the short last daylight of December" to "the short last daylight of Twelfth Month," and so on, —all our good old pagan names for the months and days, wherever they occurred in the original Leaves, being reduced to numbers, in plain Quaker fashion, or got rid of in some other way. "I mind how we lay in June" became "I mind how we once lay"; and

The exquisite, delicate-thin curve of the new moon in May—

a most exquisite and most delicate line, it may be observed in passing— was made to read, not "new moon in Fifth Month" (that would have been a little too bad) but "new moon in spring." I thought all of these alterations unfortunate, except perhaps the last; nearly all involving a sacrifice of euphony or of atmosphere in the lines. When I remonstrated against what seemed an affectation, he told me that he was brought up among Quakers; but I considered that too narrow a ground for the throwing out of words in common use among all English-speaking peoples except a single sect. To my mind, it was another proof that in matters of taste and judgment he was extremely fallible, and capable of doing unwise and wayward things for the sake of a theory or of a caprice.

In one important particular he changed, if not his theory, at least his practice. After the edition of 1860 he became reserved upon the one subject tabooed in polite society, the free treatment of which he had declared essential to his scheme of exhibiting in his poems humanity entire and undraped. For just six years, from 1855 to 1860 only, he illustrated that theory with arrogant defiance; then no further exemplifications of it appeared in all his prose and verse for more than thirty years, or as long as he continued to write. It was a sudden and significant change, which was, however, covered from observation in the reshuffling of the Leaves. In thus reediting the earlier poems, he quietly dropped out a few of the most startling lines, and would, I believe, have canceled many more, but his pride was adamant to anything that seemed a concession.

No doubt Whitman suffered some impairment of his mental faculties in the long years of his invalidism. He is said to have gone over to the Bacon side of the Bacon-Shakespeare controversy, and even to have accepted the Donnelly cipher. How confused his memory became on one subject of a paramount interest is evinced by a passage in his Backward Glance o'er Travel'd Roads, where he says of the beginnings of Leaves of Grass that, although he had "made a start before," all might have come to naught—"almost positively would have come to naught"—but for the stimulus he received from the "sights and scenes" of the secession war. To make this more emphatic, he adds the astounding assertion, "Without those three or four years [1862 to 1865], and the experiences they gave, Leaves of Grass would not now be existing." Whereas he had only to look at his title-pages to see that not his first, nor his second, but his *third* edition, comprising the larger and by far the most important part of his poetic work, was published in 1860, months before the first gun of the war was fired or a single state had seceded. After this, we need not wonder that he forgot he had read Emerson before writing his first Leaves.

When Whitman's genius flows, his unhampered lines suit his purpose as no other form of verse could do. The thought is sometimes elusive, hiding in metaphor and suggestion, but the language is direct, idiomatic, swift, its torrent force and copiousness justifying his disregard of rhyme and metre; indeed, it has often a wild, swinging rhythm of its own. But when no longer impelled by the stress of meaning and emotion, it becomes strained and flavorless, and, at its worst, involved, parenthetical, enfeebled by weak inversions.

There are the same disturbing inequalities in his prose as in his verse. The preface to his edition exhibits the masterful characteristics of his great poems; indeed, much of that preface made very good Leaves, when he afterwards rewrote it in lines and printed it as poetry. At its worst, his prose is lax and slovenly, or it takes on ruggedness to simulate strength, and jars and jolts like a farm wagon on stony roads. Some of his published letters are slipshod in their composition, and in their disregard of capitalization and punctuation, almost to the verge of illiteracy. Had William Shakespeare left any authentic writings as empty of thought and imagination, and void of literary value, as some of the Calamus letters, they would have afforded a better argument than any we now have against his authorship of the plays. Perhaps some future tilter at windmills will attempt to prove that the man we know as Walt Whitman was an uncultured impostor, who had obtained possession of a mass of powerful but fragmentary writings by some unknown man of genius, which he exploited, pieced together, and mixed up with compositions of his own.

Walt Whitman, 1880

But after all deductions it remains to be unequivocally affirmed that Whitman stands as a great original force in our literature; perhaps one of the greatest. Art, as exemplified by such poets as Longfellow and Tennyson, he has little or none; but in the free play of his power he produces the effect of an art beyond art. His words are often steeped in the very sentiment of the themes they touch, and suggest more than they express. He has largeness of view, an all-including optimism, boundless love and faith. To sum all in a sentence, I should say that his main purpose was to bring into his poems Nature, with unflinching realism,—especially Nature's divine masterpiece, May; and to demonstrate that everything in Nature and in Man, all that he is, feels, and observes, is worthy of celebration by the poet; not in the old, selective, artificial poetic forms, but with a freedom of method commensurate with Nature's own amplitude and unconstraint. It was a grand conception, an intrepid revolt against the established canons of taste and art, a challenge and a menace to the greatest and most venerated names. That the attempt was not so foolhardy as at first appeared, and that it has not been altogether a failure, the growing interest in the man and his work sufficiently attests; and who can say how greatly it might have succeeded, if adequate judgment had reinforced his genius, and if his inspiration had continued as long as he continued to write?

Atlantic Monthly Magazine, 89 (February 1902): 163-175.

From AUTOBIOGRAPHY, MEMORIES AND EXPERIENCES

Moncure Daniel Conway

Moncure Daniel Conway, a Concord resident and friend of Emerson, visited Whitman in New York soon after the 1855 Leaves of Grass *was published and sent the following description of him back to Emerson.*

Washington, September 17, 1855.

My dear Mr. Emerson,—I immediately procured the *Leaves of Grass* after hearing you speak of it. I read it on board the steamer Metropolis on my way to New York the evening after seeing you, and resolved to see its author if I could while I was in the city. As you seemed much interested in him and his work, I have taken the earliest moment which I could command since my return to give you some account of my visit.

I found by the director that one Walter Whitman lived fearfully far (out of Brooklyn, nearly), on Ryerton Street a short way from Myrtle Avenue. The way to reach the house is to go down to Fulton Street Ferry, after crossing take the Fulton and Myrtle Avenue car, and get out at Ryerton Street. It is one of a row of small wooden houses with porches, which all seem occupied by mechanics. I didn't find him there, however. His mother directed me to Rome's Printing Office (corner Fulton and Cranberry Streets), which is much nearer, and where he often is.

I found him revising some proof. A man you would not have marked in a thousand; blue striped shirt, opening from a red throat, sitting on a chair without a back, which, being the only one, he offered me, and sat down on a round of the printer's desk himself. His manner was blunt enough also, without being disagreeably so.

I told him that I had spent the evening before with you, and that what you had said of him, and the perusal of his book had resulted in my call. He seemed very eager to hear from you and about you, and what you thought of his book. He had once seen you and

192

heard you in the lecture-room, and was anxious to know all he could of your life, yet not with any vulgar curiosity but entire frankness. I told him of the occasions in which Mr. Bartol and others had attempted to read it in company and failed, at which he seemed much amused.

The likeness in the book is fair. His beard and hair are greyer than is usual with a man of thirty-six. His face and eye are interesting, and his head rather narrow behind the eyes; but a thick brow looks as if it might have absorbed much. He walked with me and crossed the Ferry; he seemed 'hail fellow' with every man he met, all apparently in the labouring class. He says he is one of that class by choice; that he is personally dear to some thousands of such in New York, who 'love him but cannot make head or tail of his book.' He rides on the stage with the driver. Stops to talk with the old man or woman selling at the street corner. And his dress, etc., is consistent with that.

I am quite sure after talking with him that there is much in all this of what you might call 'playing Providence a little with the baser sort' (so much to the distress of the Rev. Vaughan's nerves). . . . I could see that he had some books if only a bottle-stick like Alton Locke to read them by; though he told me I thought too much of books. But I came off delighted with him. His eye can kindle strangely; and his words are ruddy with health. He is clearly his Book, —and I went off impressed with the sense of a new city on my map, viz., Brooklyn, just as if it had suddenly risen through the boiling sea.

From *Autobiography, Memories and Experiences*, 2 vols. (Boston: Houghton, Mifflin, 1904), 1:215-216.

PERSONAL RECOLLECTIONS
OF WALT WHITMAN

Ellen M. Calder

Ellen M. Calder was married to William Douglas O'Connor and both were among Whitman's closest friends during his time in Washington. O'Connor published The Good Gray Poet: A Vindication *(1866) in defense of Whitman following his dismissal from government service, a book on which Whitman assisted in the writing.*

It was on Sunday, the 28th day of December, 1862, that I first saw Walt Whitman in person. We were then living in Washington. As we sat at table, a knock at the door of our room—which served both as dining and sitting room—was answered by my husband, William Douglas O'Connor, with a hearty "Come in," and there stood the man whom Mr. O'Connor afterwards christened "The Good Gray Poet." He was immediately made known to me by name, but I could not have had a moment's doubt, for he looked as his pictures at that time represented him.

He had just returned from the "front," where he had gone to look up his brother George, who was wounded by a spent ball in the battle of Fredericksburg. He had remained some days in camp, and found some of his Brooklyn "boys," and brought with him the names of others whom he wished to see, some of them his friends of the omnibus, horse-car, ferry-boat, and so on, in Brooklyn and New York, soldier boys who were then in hosptials in and around Washington. He thought he might like to remain in Washington perhaps ten days, or two weeks, and had a memorandum of some possible boarding-places that he wanted to see. Mr. O'Connor offered to go out on the search with him; but before they started my husband asked me, aside, if I would not like to have Walt for our guest at table during his stay in Washington, as there was a vacant hall bed-room on the floor where we were keeping house—in two rooms of

194

the upper story of a house on L street. I was delighted at the proposal, and hailed the opportunity of becoming personally acquainted with the poet. Mr. O'Connor had already made his acquaintance in Boston in 1860, when Thayer and Eldridge were printing Whitman's third edition of *Leaves of Grass*, and O'Connor's *Harrington* at the same time. The landlord was consulted, the room could be rented, and on the return of Walt and William from the inspection of the places visited, they not having proved desirable, the room was engaged, our invitation accepted, and Walt became our most welcome guest for months.

Visiting one sick boy in hospital led to his finding another, there or elsewhere, and soon his occupation was the daily visiting of the soldier "boys," as they nearly all were to him,—not only the Brooklyn boys, but any and all who needed ministrations of any kind. These visits led him to Carver Hospital out on Seventh Street, to Columbia Hospital on Fourteenth Street, and to many others, as we had at that time and later twenty-one hospitals and convalescent camps in and around Washington, full of boys and men sick of fevers, and of all the diseases that are incurred by the hardships and exposures of war, aside from the wounded and those dying of disease and exhaustion caused by wounds. And this was the beginning of Whitman's service in behalf of the stricken, a service in which he found himself enlisted not for weeks, but for months and years. After making visits to many hospitals, and ministering to our soldiers in several of them, Walt largely confined his work to the Armory Square Hospital,—that being the nearest to the boat landing, and where many of the worst cases were necessarily detained, the soldiers being too badly wounded to be carried farther. Soon Dr. Bliss, the surgeon in charge discovered that there was a man who could be trusted to go about the wards and give an apple, an orange, or tobacco, or whatever, to the patients, as his intuition might prompt him, and not give the wrong thing. Walt told me one day that he found soldiers from the West who had never seen an orange till he carried them to the hospital. And he said the aroma of a lemon held in the hand was often most grateful to a fever patient.

On his way to the front in that search for his brother, Walt had reached Washington almost penniless, having had his pocked picked of all the money which had been gathered together by the family. He was, however, soon able to find Mr. C. W. Eldridge, his former publisher, now clerk to Major L. S. Hapgood of Massachusetts, Pay-

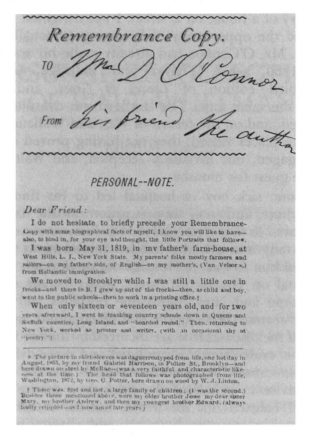

Whitman's inscription to William Douglas O'Connor in Memoranda During the War *(1876)*

master United States Volunteers. When Whitman had made his situation known, Mr. Eldridge and Mr. O'Connor were glad to relieve it at once. I had not met him then, being on a visit in Massachusetts. Serious as the situation was, Mr. Eldridge could not repress the facetious comment that any pickpocket who failed to avail himself of such an opportunity as Walt offered, with his loose baggy trousers, and no suspenders, would have been a disgrace to his profession. Through Major Hapgood Mr. Eldridge secured passes to the front for himself and Whitman. Walt had left his "carpet bag" with my husband, on his way down, wishing to be burdened with as little luggage as possible. Thus I was hoping and almost expecting to see him on his return from the seat of war. I was still, however, somewhat skeptical as to whether he would actually appear, as I had already learned of his elusive disposition, and of his dislike to be bound in any way. We had been promised by our friend Hector Tyndale of Philadelphia that we should meet him in that city, where he had often been looked for, on the strength of his vague assurances.

He was seldom betrayed into making appointments, as I had learned. When I expressed my doubts about his coming to us on his return from camp,—my husband's answer was, "Yes, he surely will, for there is his carpet bag," which was plainly in evidence.

It was soon after this that Whitman's old friend, William Swinton, who was war correspondent for one of the great New York papers, met him on Pennsylvania Avenue, and asked him where he was to be found in the evening. Being told that he was staying at our house, Swinton said he would come up. Great was his surprise to find Walt actually there. Swinton exclaimed, "Well, Walt, I have known you dozens of years, and made hundreds of appointments with you, but this is the first time that I ever knew you to keep one. I *thought* I saw signs of decay!"

At this time, Whitman's fine physique was impressive; measuring, as he said, only a half inch less than six feet in height, and weighing about two hundred pounds, with no ailment but those occasional intense headaches, caused by exposure to the fierce midday sun upon one of the hottest of summer days, after having had his hair cut at the shortest, and strolling along Broadway with head uncovered. He barely escaped sunstroke at the time, and now had to use the protection of an umbrella, as did most persons in our fierce summer weather in Washington.

He told us that the physician also held that the unusual combination which existed in his case, of a rapidly moving brain in a slow-moving, rather lethargic body, was unfavorable. The discrepancy was unfortunate. Even the ability to stop thinking at will, and to make his brain "negative," as he described a gift of his at that time of almost perfect health, did not insure him against these attacks of headache.

Whitman's evenings were usually spent with us at home, and with such friends as came to see us. I wish I had some record of the talks, discussions, arguments, that were nightly indulged in. No notes were taken, for all were engaged more or less in the mêlée, and no one could dream how valuable such notes might have been as future reminders. Dr. Bucke, a later friend and biographer of Whitman, groaned in spirit when he learned that no record had been preserved of anything, for in those early days of intimate acquaintance no subject, whether under the heavens above or in the earth beneath, was ignored. Philosophy, history, religion, literature,—authors, ancient and modern,—language, music, and every possible question as the conduct of the Civil War,—everything was discussed, and every side was heard.

Soon the friends living in Washington and those visiting the city knew where to find Whitman, and besides the regular, constant group, there were many others who were with us more or less.

The desk which Major Hapgood gave Walt for his daily use was in the Major's own room in the Corcoran Building, and there very often the soldiers who were able to climb up the four flights of stairs—for the office was on the fifth floor—used to call on him for such service as he was always glad to give,—writing letters for one, going to the train to see another properly started on his way home for his furlough, long or short as the case might be, and seeing to it that the funds for the trip were sufficient for all needs.

Soon after Whitman began his work in the hospitals, friends from Massachusetts and elsewhere, who learned of his good offices, sent him money to use according to his own discretion, and this was continued more or less to the end of the war. He earned a little money himself by corresponding for the New York papers.

In the matter of writing letters Walt found plenty of employment, for he soon discovered the fact that it is next to impossible for persons of limited education, unaccustomed to the use of the pen, to write readily, and many soldiers told him that they had not written home since leaving. He found boys, too,—and some of them literally *boys*, for they were under seventeen,—who had run away from home to enter the army, and whose parents had no knowledge of the whereabouts of their sons. Very often Walt used to remark that he thought "the institution of the father a failure." Mothers were loving, affectionate, indulgent, and sympathetic, but he did not find it so with fathers, and in many cases that came under his own observation undue severity at home had driven the boys to enlist in the army, when not of age.

The consciousness that the Walt Whitman whom I knew so intimately in the sixties is not the man whom later comers are familiar with, has been a large factor in the reluctance which I have hitherto felt in giving these recollections to the world. The man who came to

Washington in 1862 was in the vigor of health, and remained in that condition for years. He had a pleasant habit of singing in his room while making his morning toilet, and also of quoting his favorite authors, and bits of poems and verses, when with us in the evening. One verse that he liked to repeat I well remember. It was called "The Greatest Pain."

> A mighty *pain* to love it is,
> And yet a pain that love to miss;
> But of all pains, the greatest pain
> It is to love, but love in vain!

Unlike some of his later admirers, who thought his elocution admirable, we did not flatter him much on his recitations, as he had a somewhat theatrical, artificial manner, and a habit of using his voice as if his throat were stiffened, instead of the clear flexible voice that he used in conversation. Among the plays of Shakespeare, *King Richard the Second* was a great favorite of Whitman's, and he had a copy of it unbound, in pamphlet form, which was well worn from constant reading and use. Scott's *Quentin Durward* was a book that he especially liked, and he gave a copy of it to Mr. O'Connor and told our little Jeannie that she must read it when she was older.

In the innumerable talks and discussions about books, many times Walt said that he wished competent persons would give brief but careful and accurate digests of new books without interjecting any opinons, so that a busy man need not read all of the author, but could get the *gist* of the book, scientific, historical, philosophical, or whatever,—and that the reviewer in every case should be a man who was capable of doing the whole work well, some one who was "up" in that department.

In those early days before Whitman obtained a position in the Interior Department, he spent much time in wandering about Washington and its vicinity; visiting the public buildings and straying into all kinds of out-of-the-way places. The broad avenues and streets had a great charm for him; the Capitol, too, was a never-ending source of pleasure; and with him I explored the older part of Washington, the Navy Yard district, and over the Eastern Branch, into Anacostia. Sometimes we all went after dinner when the days were longer, into the woods of Georgetown, and spent hours watching the rising moon, and the attractive landscape.

William Douglas O'Connor

The splendid health and vigor of Walt at this time was refreshing to see. It impressed me in many little ways. As I have said, Mr. O'Connor and I were living in two rooms, and I was doing much of the housework, attending to the breakfast, and so forth. At that time Washington had no general system of water supply or drainage, and a pump at the corner of our street was reputed to be of very pure water and fed from a spring at Rock Creek. To this pump every morning Walt would go for a pitcher of fresh cold water for our table, and he was especially fond of taking a long draught of the same at the pump. I remember how his warm, strong hands impressed me then, as they grasped the pitcher and communicated their genial temperature to the handle of it.

It is a matter of constant and increasing regret that no record was made of the talks of those days when at breakfast we lingered long over Emerson, Wordsworth, Tennyson, or any poet or author who was suggested at the moment. The talk about Emerson's "Snow Storm" was a memorable one, both Walt and Mr. O'Connor regarding it as one of his most beautiful and finished poems, full of suggestions of home and seclusion. When Whitman first came to us on his return from the seat of war, he was, he said, continually thinking: How would all this have looked to Emerson,—how would he be affected by such scenes, how would he act, feel, seem, under these conditions? Would he keep that calm and sweet exterior?

We lingered long over those pleasant breakfast-table chats,— much past the allotted time, I suspect; for the office rules were not then as strict as they are now. As we saw day after day the punctual Mr. Evans, him of the "meteor beard," go past to his office, it was suggested that O'Connor write a story called, "The Faithful Clerk, A Tale of the Treasury,—Dedicated to the Nine O'Clockers, by a Half-past Tener." Our friend Mr. Evans was one of Walt's admirers, but not a constant visitor at our house. He was dubbed the "Meteor Beard," because of his very long and fiery red beard, which I think had never been either "shaven or shorn." He was English by birth, and was somewhat attracted by Walt and his writings.

The stimulating mental society of a man like Mr. O'Connor was no doubt requisite to the full arousing of Whitman's nature. Here was a man who loved and understood Walt so well that he dared to disagree with him on any and all questions, and whose opposition was couched in no uncertain words. Many a time the mild and pleasant morning breakfast-table chats were continued as heated discussions in the evening, after Walt's return from the hospitals.

As the circle of friends enlarged, and the gatherings were constant, we fell into the habit of immediately taking up certain pet subjects. The discussion upon all topics was always open and ready, and the fun and good-natured banter always free. No subject under the sun was neglected. As new conditions arose there was no lack of material, and the debates were often fierce and furious. Then, too, certain stock subjects were always at hand. We were somewhat divided in our pet beliefs. Free Trade, I recall, was at one time a favorite, and one ingenious guest proposed ballooning as a method of evading the customs. Sometimes the talks and arguments were upon mat-

201

ters of deepest moment,—the war, the freedom of the slave, the Mormon question, the so-called "Free Love" doctrine. The Mormon question was treated with tolerance by one or more of the group, impressed by the great material benefit which had been accomplished, more than by the moral degradation consequent upon the practice of polygamy. The fiercest denunciations that were ever heard from Whitman were against that which was called "Free Love." He gave it no quarter, said that its chief exponent and disciple—Stephen Pearl Andrews—was of the type of Mephistopheles, a man of intellect without heart, and there were no terms too strong in which to express his opinion of its "damnable" teaching and practices.

To the later comers and newer friends of Whitman, who aver that he never raised his voice, and that argument was distasteful to him, I commend the following account given by Laurence Franklin, of the meeting of the famous "Four" Frenchman, as a not much over-colored picture of some of our gatherings and discussions, which frequently lasted into the small hours of the morning, and during which Walt, with his strong lungs and loud voice, did his full share of the roaring, and by no means as gently as the sucking dove. "The four friends, Flaubert and Edmond de Goncourt as the older members, and Zola and Daudet as the younger ones, remained inseparable from 1872 to 1880, the date of Flaubert's death. Three times a week they dined together at some tavern or restaurant; and with the first mouthful began the discussion of literature. By midnight the debate had grown so hot that the other habitúes of the inn often rushed upstairs in the belief that a murder was being committed."

Not fear of murder, perhaps, but intense curiosity as to *what* on earth was going on, led a policeman to stop and investigate the cause of the clamor one hot Sunday afternoon when we were gathered in the back dooryard, after we had moved into more ample quarters and were near the street. He went on his way smiling when he learned that the exciting topic was the currency question, which was then being discussed in Congress and before the country. Our landlady said that the neighbors were convinced that a furious quarrel was going on.

Notwithstanding Whitman's fondness for coining words, and using many in uncommon fashions, he was, in a way, a great stickler for the correct use of certain words,—one of which was "paraphernalia," which he insisted could be correctly used only in reference to a bride's belongings or trousseau. We had many amusing discussions about words, and the best dictionary for final settlement of any vexed question, whether it should be Webster or Worcester. He used generally to say, "We will see what Booby says,"—his pet name for either dictionary; but he did not readily allow either one to *settle* any point.

Many times in the course of our numerous talks the marriage question was discussed. And invariably Whitman upheld the modern theory of marriage as being the true and ideal relation between the sexes. He staunchly and strongly adhered to that. In speaking of marriage the idea which he conveyed was that he did not think it would have been well for him to have formed that closest of ties. He was so fond of his freedom, he so reacted from any restraint; that it seemed that it would have been a mistake if he had ever married. He added, however, "True if I had been caught young, I might have done certain things, or formed certain habits." He often said he "did not envy men their wives, but he did envy them their children." As we were passing along the street one day a little girl said in her smiling way, "I know you." He answered, "I wish I knew you."

The game of "Twenty Questions," as a relaxation after hospital work, was one that sometimes entertained Walt and the rest of us, and the wit and quickness that it brought out were very amusing. A half-dozen of us, playing the game frequently together, became able easily to discover the thing thought of, in much less than the twenty questions. Even so remote and unheard-of a subject as the white beard of Secretary Welles—then Secretary of the Navy—was once the subject of thought.

On one occasion the object was done up in a neat package, and deposited by Walt, as he came into the supper-room, upon the mantel, hinting that it was to be won by the twenty-question method. It took no more than half that number of questions and answers to guess the contents of the package, which proved to be a good-sized, large-type Bible, one member of the family having expressed a desire for such a copy, for frequent use, and having none at hand that answered the want. It was inscribed inside with the names of the giver and the friends to whom given, with the request that it pass on to "Little Jeannie," who, alas! passed out of this life before any one of the company then present.

It was not unusual for the group to watch the old year out and the new year in. On one occasion, when the snow was falling in large flakes, Walt appeared at the door, a veritable Santa Claus, with his thin, shaggy white beard and straggling hair falling below his coat collar; the coat and hat all covered with snow,—for he never used an umbrella,—his cheeks ruddy, and his whole appearance one that any child would have gazed at with wondering eyes. After entering, and shaking and stamping off the soft snow from his garments, he began to unload his pockets,—those ample pockets on the outside of his coat, where he was so often in the habit of burying his hands as he sauntered down the streets. Out of those capacious receptacles he brought forth a small bottle of Scotch whiskey, a lemon, and some lump sugar, and he said we would welcome in the New Year. Some fresh cold water must be brought in, in a little kettle,—for a very important part of the proceeding was proper attention to the boiling, which must be *à la Delmonico*,—to be removed from the fire at the exact moment of boiling. Into each tumbler was poured the quantity of the liquid that would be required, a careful paring of the rind of the lemon,—not too much, but just enough,—a sufficient quantity of sugar, and last the hot water; and then came the gay and merry discussion of any and everything under the sun and stars, while the punch so carefully concocted was slowly sipped till the midnight bells pealed out the hour of twelve, and the guests departed, wishing each other all sorts of piquant and jolly good wishes.

It was about this time that, one evening, as Walt was slowly sauntering down Seventh Street, from a visit to Carver Hospital, he was accosted by a policeman and ordered to remove that "false face," his name for a mask. Walt quietly assured him that the only face he wore was his very own, but added, "Do we not all wear 'false faces'?" The incident amused him, but we thought it a very happy Christmas compliment, his being mistaken for Old Santa Claus.

One chilly, disagreeable morning, Walt was sauntering along to his breakfast, to a restaurant kept by a man named Evans, on F Street. Snow had fallen, and the rain followed, and then snow again, which was still falling, till the walks were covered with the mixture of soft snow and rain that makes a combination perfectly described by Whitman's word "*posh*." Slowly sauntering, with his hands in his ample coat pockets, the wrists bent down, which gave his arms the suggestion of the fins of a fish, he was overtaken by his friend Mr.

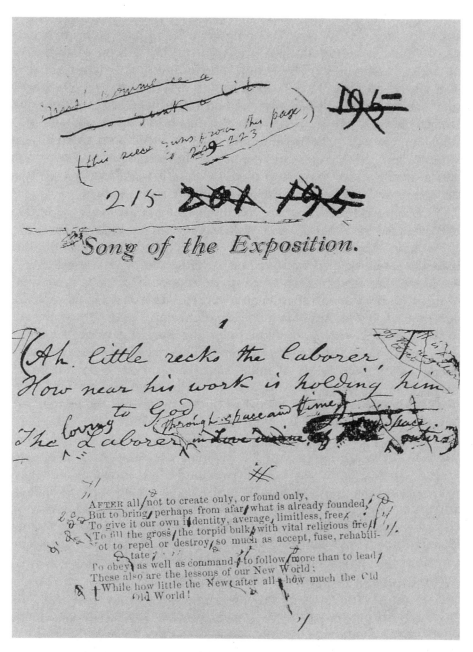

Whitman's manuscript revision of "Song of the Exposition"

Eldridge, who took his meals at the same place. After walking a short distance Eldridge said, "Come Walt, let's hurry along to breakfast." "You can hurry along if you want to, but I want to enjoy the morning," was Walt's reply. I think no condition of weather but dust ever disturbed him. That he thoroughly disliked, and he laughingly said that he believed that, after he had taken his bath, and gone out for a stroll, with a fresh, clean shirt, the dust hunted him out, and pursued him. At that time Washington was not paved with asphalt, as it is today, and the heavy army wagons ploughed deeply into the mud, which soon became dust; and in those days it was literally true that the streets of Washington were always either mud or dust.

In some of the various experiments of getting his own breakfast, after we had moved, and Walt was no longer with us, he spoke of cooking beefsteak and chops. When asked who washed the dishes, he said he had none to wash. "How then did you manage?" was asked. He ate his steak or chop, he replied, from a "clean chip." Wooden plates had not then been invented. He had no cups and saucers to wash, as his tea was made in a "tin cup," and he put the tea in the tin cup, with cold water, over the gas, and went out for a short stroll while the tea was steeping! This delicious beverage, with "white sugar" and plenty of milk, was taken directly from the vessel in which it was steeped. And this from the same person who gave most minute directions in regard to boiling water for the punch! No fear of tannin disturbed his enjoyment of the decoction.

A friend and near neighbor, who had conceived a great disgust for Walt Whitman because of his writings, who thought him coarse, vulgar, and obscene, was nevertheless much impressed by his daily work among the soldiers. Seeing him pass her door with his haversack slung across his shoulder,—with oranges, or perhaps apples, tobacco, paper, or whatever he happened to be carrying to his hospital boys,—she said to me one day, "Why did he write those dreadful, shocking things, which so offend the sense of decency which we are all supposed to have?"

To which I replied, "I don't know, but I will ask him." His answer was, "It always pains me to be misunderstood by good women, mothers especially,"—whom he regarded as the best of the earth;—"but," he added, "*I had to do it.*" Then, enlarging a little, he said that, when a boy, he was struck with the *pretense* of respect which he observed in a class of men such as he used to see congregated at the country grocery store, entertaining themselves with vile, obscene stories

206

and jokes. Upon the approach of a woman, he noticed that there was a sudden change, and that a show of respect was assumed. This made so deep an impression that he felt it was for him, as he expressed it, "to tear off the mask, to lay bare the truth,—to proclaim that all in nature is good and pure." And I have sometimes questioned if he did not use the very coarseness which shocks, to confront the vile in their hypocrisy. But again and again the old question has come up, why did he do it?

No man ever lived who loathed coarseness and vulgarity in speech more than he, and I am witness that on two occasions he reproved men, supposed to be gentlemen, for their license in that respect.

So deep and instinctive was Walt's veneration for the mother that he did not relish any fun at her expense. We had an illustration of this one evening when O'Connor was reading aloud the "Students' Song" in Longfellow's *Hyperion*, and came to the stanza where the "Frau Mamma" is celebrated, as the "leathery Frau Mamma." Walt objected to that, and said, "No, no,—that will not do; the mamma is not to be lightly treated, even in the way of a joke." All through the song, the refrain is "the leathery," and even the Herr Rector is so sung; but it was only at the "mamma" that Walt winced in the least.

In answer to the question so often asked me, "Do you like Mr. Whitman as much as Mr. O'Connor does?" I could always say, "Yes, personally I am as fond of him, but I do not consider that I am a judge of his literary work, and am not competent to say what rank he will take as a writer. I cannot compare him with all the great, not having read all myself. My own first impression after reading the quarto edition of *Leaves of Grass*, recommended by Emerson to the friend who gave it to me, was that the writer must be a pure man, or he would never have dared to speak so plainly of forbidden subjects." In discussing the manner in which this book was written, Whitman said that very much of it was written under great pressure,— pressure from within. He felt that he *must* do it.

When asked, as he sometimes was, why he did that hospital work, which brought him into contact with such painful and horrible revelations, he said again and again, that he loved it, that he should not do it if he did not like it. Humanity in all conditions and exhibitions was profoundly dear to him. A human being was an object of love, and it gratified him that these men and boys loved him, and depended on him, and the consciousness that his sympathy and affection saved a life sometimes, made him deeply happy.

Regarding his own personality Walt said that some persons were strongly repelled by him as others were attracted to him. Once when I was walking with him down Fifteenth Street, as we turned into Pennsylvania Avenue, a woman passing drew herself far away, as if afraid of contamination by even a touch of his garment. No doubt I looked the astonishment which I felt; and seeing my look, Walt said, "Oh, yes some persons feel that way towards me, and do not hide it."

In those days of wandering and of taking in all sights and sounds, of which I have spoken, he once went over to Georgetown, where coal barges were being unloaded at the Canal, and he told us that he watched for hours a negro at work, who was naked to the waist, and the play of his muscles, as he loaded and unloaded the buckets of coal, was most fascinating; "No Greek statue could have been more superb," he said.

I have been asked how Walt felt about the war, and if he was affected by it. On one occasion he was persuaded to go to see two elderly ladies at whose home Rev. William Henry Channing was living. They had often asked us to bring Whitman, and he and Mr. Channing had a long and warm talk. Mr. Channing's church—Unitarian— was the first one in Washington to be used as a hospital. The burden of Walt's remarks was,—"I say stop this war, this horrible massacre of men." He became excited and walked the floor, as he talked. To all of this Mr. Channing's reply was, "You are sick; the daily contact with these poor maimed and suffering men has made you sick; don't you see that the war cannot be stopped now? Some issue must be made and met." But Walt could only reiterate that thought. This was in the early part of the conflict, as early perhaps as the spring of 1863.

I never again saw Walt in that mood of mind,—however horrible the condition of our men. He saw the struggle had to go on till some conclusion was reached; and when the end came he felt that the thing was justified, if war ever can be justified.

Once when speaking of the pain of longing for loved ones absent, and perhaps forever separated, he said, "Yes, I have felt and suffered that too, but have outgrown it."

He spoke often of his life in New Orleans. I think that our old market sheds—this was before we had the brick market—and the appearance of things there reminded him of certain conditions in New Orleans. Often we went to market before breakfast to get fruit for our breakfast, and for him to take to the hospital. On one or two occasions we met Count Gurowski, the Russian refugee, who greatly approved, in his original way, of our errand, and magnified it much, I learned.

In his *Hospital Notes* Whitman has given an interesting account of the paying of the first regiment of colored troops on Mason's Island, near Washington, by Major Hapgood, assisted by his clerk, Mr. Eldridge. Major Hapgood kindly invited Whitman, O'Connor, and me, with our little Jeannie, to witness the historic event. The colored troops had always done themselves credit, and we were often amused by one of the cries of the newspaper boys, who used to shout, after any battle in which the colored men were engaged, "the colored troops fought nobly."

A thousand touching and almost heart-breaking incidents have never been, nor ever can be repeated, but one I well recall that came home very close to us. General Casey's Division had long been stationed out on Fourteenth Street, but the day came when they marched down that street to join the military forces in the field. As the men passed the house where we were then living, on the corner of Fourteenth and L streets, little Jeannie and a friend of hers, of about her age, both stood on chairs waving to the men their little flags. Instantly, on seeing them, the officers half halted and saluted the tiny flags, which spoke of intense loyalty to those men who were, many of them, on the way to their death.

Loyalty to our government was not the invariable rule in Washington at the time. I heard one woman say that she had both a "Secesh" flag and a Union flag in her house, and was ready to wave to whichever army was successful, her argument being that all of her property and that of her family was in Washington, and she "should go with the winning side."

The rush of persons to Washington from North and South was much greater than the accommodations of the city could house comfortably,—for until there was some hope of the North winning in the end, capitalists were very cautious as to expending any money there. This being the case; the clan O'Connor made several moves; not indeed for pleasure, as at least one member of the family had the inborn New England deep-rooted love of a stationary abiding-place; but at the time of which this is written one was fortunate to

Walt Whitman, 1881 (Feinberg Collection, Library of Congress)

be able to find any sort of a decent refuge. At last, however, a kind friend in one of his early morning walks stumbled on a small house in process of building, and immediately made report of it. At once the builder was seen; the little house was engaged, and occupied when finished; and there the family remained until Mr. O'Connor's death, something over twenty years.

It was June 30, 1865, that James Harlan, Secretary of the Interior, dismissed Whitman for the offense of having written *Leaves of Grass*, an obscene book, as he styled it. At once Walt came to us to make known the fact. At first O'Connor could not realize the enormity of the proceeding, and Walt said he was surprised at the almost speechless manner in which the news was received; but the longer it was dwelt upon, the more Mr. O'Connor realized the full extent and meaning of it, and nine weeks from that time his vindication of the Good Gray Poet was ready for the printer.

In the mean time, Mr. O'Connor had interested many persons in the transaction. J. Hubley Ashton, whose death has occurred while these pages were being written, was then Assistant Attorney-General. He was an old and warm friend of both Whitman and O'Connor, and now came to Whitman's relief by offering him a position in the Attorney-General's office, which Whitman retained until his failing health obliged him to resign. For some time before the final resignation, he had employed a young man to do his work, and they shared the pay.

Some of the many subjects of debate among us have been mentioned, but when the Fifteenth Amendment came before the Senate, and was up for discussion in 1871, it proved a topic that provoked the most vehement battle, and at that point we separated,—Walt taking the ground that the negroes were wholly unfit for the ballot, and Mr. O'Connor and others believing that the measure was the only one to adopt.

As soon however as the Osgood edition of *Leaves of Grass* was challenged by the Attorney-General of Massachusetts, as being unfit for household reading unless expurgated, all past differences of opinion were forgotten, and Mr. O'Connor, though no longer a well man, came to the rescue with the same energy and devotion that he had given to the cause of his Good Gray Poet in 1865, and the old-time love, now chastened by years and sorrow, and deepened and strengthened too, was reëstablished and continued unabated to the end,—in the death of O'Connor in 1889.

Those of us who knew the Good Gray Poet in his best days of health, who saw him day and night, before and after his watches with his sick and maimed soldier boys, feel that a great privilege was ours. To live with one who was, and could be, as has been said of another, an "incorrigible optimist" in the midst of slaughter and all the horrors of war, a man who felt that after all, the world was pretty good, and men and women not so bad as they were pictured, was uplifiting and helpful in those awful days, and all other days, and the last word that must be said of Walt Whitman, was that he was first and last and forever an Optimist. His was an intense and abiding faith in the triumph of right and justice; he felt no doubt as to results, he had absolute confidence that the men and women of "these States," and of all the world, would finally solve the problem of the unification of all races and peoples.

Atlantic Monthly Magazine, 99 (June 1907): 825-834.

WALT WHITMAN: THE LAST PHASE

Elizabeth Leavitt Keller

Elizabeth Leavitt Keller served as Whitman's nurse during the last few months of his life. Her detailed account of Whitman's approaching death was revised as Walt Whitman in Mickle Street *(1921).*

When questioning me about my patient, the late Walt Whitman, people have usually asked first, "What was his religious belief?" The following poem from his pen, entitled "The Soul," has enlightened me more upon this subject than any words I ever heard him utter.

The Soul,

Forever and forever—longer than soil is brown and solid—longer than water ebbs and flows.

Each is not for its own sake,
I say the whole earth and all the stars in the sky are for religion's sake.

In this broad earth of ours,
Amid the measureless grossness and the slag,
Enclosed and safe within its central heart,
Nestles the seed perfection.

By every life a share, or more or less,—
None born but is born, conceal'd or unconceal'd the seed is waiting.

Do you not see, O my brothers and sisters?
It is not chaos or death—it is form, union, plan—it is eternal life—it is happiness.

The song is to the singer, and comes back most to him,

213

The love is to the lover, and comes back most to him—it cannot fail.

I see Hermes, unsuspected, dying, well belov'd, saying to the people,
    Do not weep for me;
This is not my true country; I have lived banish'd from my true coun-
    try, I now go back there,—
I return to the celestial sphere where every one goes in his turn.

During my attendance upon Mr. Whitman he was too near his "true country" to be able to explain or communicate his views regarding that, or the alien land which he felt that he was leaving.

To question, or encourage him to talk, was impossible; and especially for me, whose only wish was to secure to him all the rest and quiet that I could.

On December 17th, 1891, Walt Whitman was stricken with pneumonia, and from that date until the second week in the new year, each and every day was full of anxiety; then came a rally of the vital powers, followed by slow sinking. He lingered until March 26th; sometimes bright and talkative, and sometimes lying in a state bordering upon collapse.

It was evident that he had no dread of death and even looked forward to it with fearless expectancy. He always spoke of this as his last illness, and once, in referring to those earlier, anxious days, he said: "My life was going out. I said 'Let it go', but doctors and nurses made a strong pull for it; fought for it like royal tigers, and prevailed. I am here."

He was dying in his own slow way; the certainty of death, calmly accepted by him, was in the atmosphere of the sick-room.

To the query often put to me, "Who was his favorite author?" I must plead ignorance. The only lines I ever heard him quote were these:

Not heaven itself upon the past has power;
But what has been, has been, and I have had my hour.

This quotation (from Dryden's "Imitation of Horace") he used when anyone suggested to him the possibility of recovery. "No, 'I have had my hour'; *I have had my hour*; only let me rest in peace until its close."

In the volume "*In re* Walt Whitman," on page 414, are these words:

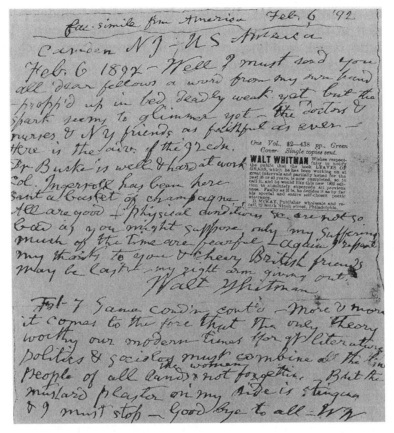

Facsimile of Whitman's letter of 6 and 7 February 1892 to Dr. Johnston

Dec. 29th. A dead, inarticulate day; unchanged from yesterday's condition. As he requires constant attendance night and day, we yesterday introduced a trained nurse, Mrs. K—, who will share with Warren the burdens and duties of the watch.

The late Dr. Maurice Bucke of London, Canada, one of Mr. Whitman's most intimate friends, afterward his biographer, and one of his literary executors, met me at the Nurses' Directory of Philadelphia, and in a measure prepared me for the scenes and the people I was to encounter. He believed that my services would be required for a few days only, and said that he wished particularly that the sick room should be put into some kind of order.

For twenty years Mr. Whitman had lived in Camden—for the last seven in the only house he had ever called his own.[1] To this poor little frame building, crowded in between two much larger ones, Dr. Bucke accompanied me.

Our ring was answered by Mrs. Davis, Mr. Whitman's good housekeeper, so well known to all the friends of his later years. I saw a tall, sweet-faced, middle-aged woman of quiet, modest demeanor, and when she spoke I noticed that her voice was remarkably pleasant and well modulated. I confess that I met her with a prejudice which further acquaintance wholly dissipated. She had been lying down to rest, and had a small quilt pinned about her shoulders. She looked weary, and her eyes were red with weeping.

I laid aside my wraps, and still in company with Dr. Bucke groped my way up the dark staircase, and passing through a closet-like anteroom entered the chamber of the dying poet. The small room was crowded with objects which the dusk of a winter's afternoon did not fully reveal. The only things that stood out vividly were the white pillow, and the placid face encircled with snowy hair. Motionless he lay, but when I was presented to him, he raised his eyelids, extended his hand, and welcomed me kindly. His brother, his literary executors, and certain other friends, grouped together, were speaking in low tones. A handsome, boyish-looking man, who seemed to be at everyone's beck and call, greeted me pleasantly, and although he was seemingly tired to exhaustion, there was a merry gleam in his eyes as we shook hands. This was Warren Fritzinger,[2] his nurse, and my constant associate in taking care of the patient. Some etchings of the poet, recently completed, had just been sent to him. One of these he gave to Dr. Bucke, who was about to return home; by request he added his autograph. He was held up in bed for this purpose, which he accomplished with much difficulty. Dr. Bucke took an affectionate leave of his friend, and bidding all good-bye, hastened away; the others soon followed, and I was summoned to tea.

On entering the dining-room I was impressed—as I have since learned that others have been—by its remarkable likeness to the cabin of a ship. The table, with but one leaf up and just large enough for two places, was placed against the wall. The stove stood near enough to serve as side table when needed; and in line with this was a small sink, over which were some closed shelves for dishes. In order to reach these dishes it was necessary to stand upon a stool. This was at hand under a rear extension of the stove. Then came a passage from the hall to the back door. In the hall was the flour barrel, opposite which was the cellar door. The cellarway I found had a wide shelf for food, and was hung around with tins, rolling pin, and other kitchen utensils. Elsewhere in this room—which might properly be called the living-room, being dining-room, kitchen and sitting-room combined—were a lounge, a sewing-machine and some chairs. Every inch of wall-space was covered. There were small shelves, brackets, wall-pockets, a clock, a calendar and some pictures. The ceiling was hung with cages, in two of which were turtle doves; in the others were a robin and a canary. The plaintive cooing of the doves and the shrill notes of the canary were deafening. In a wooden case, behind a glass, were the stuffed remains of a parroquet, which formerly had added his voice to the din. On the lounge a coach-dog, carefully covered with a shawl, was serenely sleeping; two cats were sitting near the stove. They showed every disposition to friendliness, by coming at once to the table and rubbing against me. Everything was homelike and the table was well supplied. When I returned to the anteroom, Warren gave me some instructions, and insisted that I should call him if needed; then I was left alone.

As I sat in that little dimly lighted den and peered into the still dimmer apartment beyond, or stood upon the heaps of rubbish in the doorway—over which I occasionally stumbled,—either to minister to my patient or to replenish the fire, I was more and more struck with the disorder on all sides. My first glance had been one of bewilderment; I now looked with deliberation and amazement at my surroundings. Confusion, dust and litter—it seemed the accumulation of ages. I afterwards learned that for over two years no books, magazines or manuscripts had been removed from this, Walt Whitman's peculiar sanctum.

There were no bookcases, large shelves or writing-desk; there was no receptacle for newspapers, and apart from the two overloaded tables, the floor had received all of them. Upon this general table the daily papers had been dropped when read; the weeklies had followed, and in their turn the monthly magazines. An immense number of periodicals and pamphlets had been received in the course of two years, and all were still there. Almost everything was yellow with age and soiled with the constant tramping of feet.

The mass, which was nearly solid, was two feet in depth, and had many transverse ridges. Mr. Whitman had never bought stationery; he utilized wrapping papers, old letters and envelopes, and as he was in the habit of making his poems over and over, afterwards tearing up rejected bits, I found, on clearing up, bushels of fine litter, evenly dispersed. Upon the stove was a large earthen dish. One author, to emphasize the neglect in which he thought Mr. Whitman lived, has declared that contained his soup; but the dish never held anything but clean water, designed to keep the air of the room moist by evaporation. On the right side of the bed was an antiquated chest, on top of which were two bottles, one of eau-de-cologne and the other brandy, an old-fashioned candlestick with candle and matches, a wine-glass and tumbler, and a covered stone mug for drinking water. Within reach was his cane, which he was accustomed to use to summon attendance. On the left of the bed the mass of rubbish had reached a height of at least four feet. On investigation, however, there proved to be a lounge underneath. The tables stood like cows in a meadow with the grass up to their bodies; and the legs of the bed also were buried out of sight. The only thing that had gone up with time was the imposing easy chair. This, with its white wolfskin, surmounted the pile like a throne. The wolfskin was sadly eaten, as were the old and poor garments that hung upon the walls. At one of the tables a bent metal drop-light held a chipped argand burner at a dangerous angle, and within this dingy glass shone a feeble ray of light just making visible the pallid face and hoary hair of the dying man. As I stood on the mass and looked down, the sight was beyond description.

The owner was but a few inches above his worldly possessions; he seemed a part of them, and the picture would have been incomplete without him. Would that it could be reproduced upon canvas with the vividness with which it is stamped upon my memory! And that strange feeling which comes over patient and nurse when they are learning to know each other without speech, was with us both.

By daylight and with companionship, things seemed less unnatural. Fortunately Mr. Whitman took kindly to me, and our intercourse was of the pleasantest. Mrs. Davis, inured to his eccentricity, and extremely indulgent to his wishes, was grieved that anything in his room should be disturbed while he lived. No one then thought that his life was to be spared for weeks instead of days. The litter had invaded the second room, and I began by picking up the newspa-

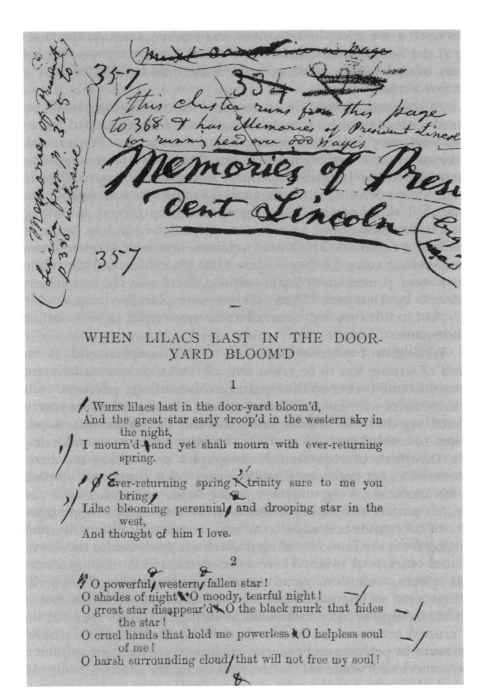

Whitman's manuscript revision of "When Lilacs Last in the Door-Yard Bloom'd"

pers nearest the door, folding them, and stacking them on the landing at the head of the stairs. Little by little I made my way into his room, but it was slow work, and not much could be effected during the first week.

At the expiration of this time, Mr. Whitman had gradually regained something of his former strength, and things assumed a routine, with only incidental changes from day to day. Warren volunteered to take the night work, but there were many occasions when both of us remained on duty. I continued to put things in order, always desisting when my patient showed the least sign of annoyance. I would often go into the room on the pretext of putting wood in the stove, and I soon learned to perceive just how much or how little I could do. The bound volumes, invariably thrown downward into the mass, I arrayed upon some shelves in the little room. Many were presentation copies—among them one by Longfellow, and one by Tennyson. These shelves were already doing double duty, but in this crowded house there always seemed to be room for a little more.

Periodicals I piled outside with the newspapers, and as no shred of writing was to be taken out, all the script was made into a mound in one corner of the room. In this confused pile were rolls of manuscript written on different colored bits of paper; many were pinned together. No wonder some one said that Whitman's manuscripts resembled Joseph's coat! In the litter were innumerable letters; thousands of requests for autographs; poems that had been submitted to his criticism; friendly letters from home and abroad; all his business correspondence; postal cards, notes of congratulation, invitations, envelopes unnumbered, visiting-cards, wrapping papers of all brands and sizes, a variety of string of all lengths, and ranging from the fine colored cord which druggists use, to the heaviest and coarsest of twine. There were several pieces of rope, coins, pins galore, countless pictures, many photographs of himself. Strings were so interwoven through the accumulated layers that it would take days to come to the ends of them. And under all, some little crusted brown worms had made their home. Moths flew around the room in perfect security, and industrious spiders had curtained the corners and windows. On the door hung the old hat, and on a table a plaster bust of the poet stood sentinel.

As a patient, Mr. Whitman was easily satisfied and uncomplaining; when no one was present he was exceedingly quiet. But callers came at all hours, even up to midnight, and not a few were deeply offended at not being admitted even at this unseasonable time.

He always saw his friends when he could, often when he really should not have seen them; and as it was then that the vital spark would brighten with pleasure, most of his visitors were deceived as to his true condition. When they had gone, it was left to his three attendants to see how the oil in the lamp of life had been consumed; and repeatedly the flicking light seemed on the point of vanishing. Mrs. Davis usually answered the door-bell, and Warren always responded to the nightly rap of the reporters.

Many people, even strangers, insisted on seeing Mr. Whitman. One very persistent lady told me she would not leave the house without a personal interview—an interview with that dying man, who so often pleaded pathetically to be unmolested! Mrs. Davis came to the rescue, and afterwards told me that had I lived there as long as she, I should be used to such scenes. She herself had a strong character and much tact. She never offended any one, and throughout Mr. Whitman's protracted illness, which really lasted from a second stroke of paralysis in 1888 to his death, many were admitted to his presence through her intercession.

When the immediate danger had subsided Mr. Whitman ceased to take medicine—that is, to take it with regularity. He objected, and the doctors would not insist. His temperature was never taken; his pulse and respiration were noted without his knowledge. No clinical chart was needed, but by request of his literary executors I kept a daily—almost an hourly—journal, which was taken away each morning. This covered scores of pages, and although it seldom contained anything of importance was a minute record of everything that occurred. It was difficult to follow Mr. Whitman in conversation, for in this he seldom took the leading part; and as it was wished above all things that all he said should be set down as spoken, no wonder the daily report was disappointing. He spoke in short, concise sentences, with many ejaculations and interjections, and his broken utterances were often hardly intelligible without knowing the words to which they replied.

When alone he was spoken to only when speech was unavoidable and then in as few words as possible. He never talked to himself or muttered, as sick people often do. He took but two meals a day; one in the forenoon, and the other about four P.M., his only additional nourishment being milk-punch, or a little champagne, with

221

which his friend Colonel Robert Ingersoll kept him bountifully supplied.

He could not sit upright in bed, no matter how carefully he was propped; he could not raise his head from the pillow; this was done for him when he drank. He ate lying down. I always fed him sitting by his side, holding the tray in my lap. His favorite food was mutton-broth with rice in it. Once when I was giving him some terrapin that had been sent him and asked, "How does it taste?" he replied, in his characteristic way, "*Almost* as good as Mary's mutton-broth."

He ate with quite an appetite when at his best, but there would be days when milk-punch and champagne were all he could take. I was brought into closest contact with my patient at meal time, and it was then that we had our many little confabs. But, alas! then I could not use pencil and paper, and one might as well attempt to repeat a page of "Leaves of Grass" after one reading, as recall what had been said. Our subjects, however, were commonplace enough, seldom soaring above that little home. Once I asked him what he would think of me when I told him that I had never heard of his book until I came there. He chuckled a little and said: "I guess there are plenty of people who can say the same—thousands of them. 'Leaves of Grass' was the aim of my life—I lived for it, worked for it. In these days and nights it is different; my mutton-broth, my little brandy, to be 'turned' promptly and be kept clean—these are much more to me."

His bed was none too comfortable and the large mattress protruded over one side, making it a hard task to turn him. A few weeks before he died, a new bedstead and firm, level mattress were purchased with the fund that some New York City association had subscribed to keep his room supplied with flowers. When these admirers learned that the fragrance of flowers had a suffocating effect upon the poet, they willingly appropriated the money to this more practical purpose.

Twenty-four hours before he died, a water bed was brought to the poet. What a blessing this would have been to all had it come months before! Mr. Whitman was a large man, and of heavy frame; he was totally unable to move himself while lying down, and he required almost constant turning, which he called shifting. His last words were the often repeated request to his faithful attendant, "Shift, Warry."

As a rule visitors were admitted in the afternoon or early evening. Many wrote first and came at an appointed time. In the forenoon we did the work in the sick room and around the house, one assisting the others. My only difficulty with Mrs. Davis and Warren was in getting them to let me do my full share. Warren sawed, split and brought up all the wood. Sometimes Mrs. Davis would come upstairs, where she was always welcome; and when Mr. Whitman was at his best we would pass a pleasant hour together.

I look back upon one morning in particular. Mr. Whitman was feeling unusually well and was in good spirits. Warren handed him an old ambrotype that had long been missing. He took it, and laughed and chatted about the original in a lively strain. He was genial and talkative; he referred to his life in Washington, spoke of the Civil War, and mentioned Abraham Lincoln, for whom he had the highest regard and admiration. Warren said: "Now you have seen a little of 'Old Walt.' This is more like his old self than he has been since he was sick." We hoped that it might be a permanent improvement, but it was the same old story: extra exertion and subsequent relapse.

While Mr. Whitman would have some comparatively easy days, he was never entirely free from pain.

He had a great liking for the two young physicians who attended him, Dr. Alexander McAlister of Camden, who made daily calls, and Dr. Daniel Longaker of Philadelphia, who came whenever he could, or when he was sent for. Both gave their services cheerfully and without price.

Dr. McAlister's standing order was: "Do not disturb him in any way, nor ask him to do anything if he shows the least unwillingness." Sometimes his call would be but a quiet moment by his patient's side, and a single clasp of hands.

By Janurary 10th Mr. Whitman had improved sufficiently to write his name on two of the etchings; one for each young physician. He always found it difficult to write in bed. He did this by having a pillow and a book placed before him. One of us would usually sit behind to support him, and one would hold the inkstand. From this time to the 27th he wrote a few notes to friends, and to his sister in Burlington, Vermont. He also signed a number of photographs and the three remaining etchings, one of which he gave to his faithful housekeeper. On this date he wrote a few lines to his sister; then followed a period wherein he was so low that it was deemed by all that Walt Whitman had written his name for the last time.

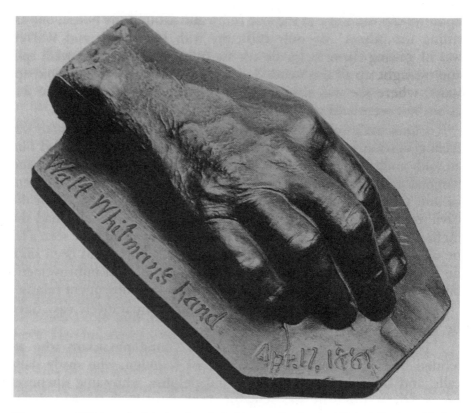

Plaster cast of Whitman's right hand made by Truman Bartlett in 1881 (Collection of Robert O. Harris, Jr.)

This was a mistake; an unlooked for reaction occurred, and on February 5th he again asked for writing materials. He could no longer hold the book, and it looked as though his attempt would fail. Failure was a word Mrs. Davis had never learned, and grasping the situation at once, she went to a teacher of painting who lived next door, and procured a drawing-board, and had legs attached by its hinges, thereby making it adjustable to Mr. Whitman's position in writing. He was delighted with this impromptu desk when it was placed before him the next day. "Ah!" he exclaimed, "that's *Mary*—that's *Mary*. Just the right thing at the right time."

Upon this board, and in the presence of no one but Mrs. Davis and myself, his last message to his friends was written. The weary old man was two days in completing the message—or greeting, as it is sometimes called—and but for Mary Davis's foresight and prompt action, the task would never have been accomplished.

The message was written on post-office paper, and inscribed upon two separate pieces which he pasted together. This testimonial of his remembrance and regard for others was sent over to England, where a facsimile was made, about fifty copies being sent back to him. These he distributed among his friends and acquaintances; and in nothing did he ever forget his nurses.

After this Walt Whitman wrote very little. One of his executors says under date of Feb. 11th: "I got him to write his signature for the use of a paper, and the job completely exhausted him." At this time Mr. Whitman was totally unfit to do anything except at his own pleasure.

He could always take his own part, and fortunately was capable of doing so still; had it been otherwise, there is no telling how soon he would have been hustled out of the world by a number of his enthusiastic admirers. On the 22d he signed some contracts, and kindly put his signature to a picture for me. At this time he had discarded ink, and used a blue pencil only. He wrote his name but once again, and that was for some business purpose. His last communication—a feeble attempt to write to his sister, on March 17th—was signed "W. W." only.

I hoped and expected to be with my patient to the end. The following—again quoting from "*In re* Walt Whitman"—will explain why I was not:

> Mrs. K. leaves to-morrow, and Mrs. Davis and Warry will assume the watching between them, some one being engaged to relieve Mrs. Davis in the kitchen. Walt takes the change very hard, and we all regret it, but Mrs. K had made an advance contract with another person some months ago.

Thinking it improbable that Mr. Whitman would outlive the time for which I could remain with him, we all thought it best not to inform him of my impending departure, and agreed that he should be told of it only at the last moment. At breakfast in the morning before I left, by a great effort I summoned resolution to inform him of the coming change. He was wholly unprepared for it, and said, "You cannot go. You cannot go." When I told him the circumstances, and how much against my own wishes it was to leave him, he said: "Well, it cannot be helped."

He was reconciled when he learned that no other nurse was to follow me, and I promised to return as soon as possible should he need me, to which he said "Do, do, do."

When the doctor mentioned my leaving, the poor old man replied: "Yes, that is the worst news that I have heard in a long time." I do not mean to boast that I was so much to Mr. Whitman; hundreds of nurses would have done as well, and no doubt better; but I am thankful that it was my good fortune to be the one chosen, and more thankful that my services were always acceptable and never repugnant to him. The next morning I entered the room, ostensibly to put wood in the stove, and seeing that he wished to speak, I went to the bedside. I sat there for the last time—without the little tray,— and took his proffered hand. He held mine a few moments in silence, then bade me good-bye. His fingers relaxed, and I arose to go. Stooping down, I kissed his forehead. A single tear ran down his furrowed check, and my own eyes were dim as I took my last look at the dying Walt Whitman. He lived but seventeen days longer.

Putnam's Magazine, 6 (June 1909): 331-337.

1. Late number, 328 Mickle Street

2. Died in October 1899.

A VISIT TO WALT WHITMAN

William Hawley Smith

During the late 1880s, people could walk in off the street and buy Whitman's books from the author himself. William Hawley Smith's account is evidence of one such visit.

On a hot August afternoon, in 1889, wife and I went to call on Walt. We had no letters of introduction, or credentials of any kind. We were just "anybody." We knocked at his door, and a stout and hearty young man, in his shirtsleeves, came to find out who was there. We asked him if we could meet Mr. Whitman, and he said: "Come in, and I'll see." He showed us into the front room, at the left of the hall, and then went to make inquiry for us. He immediately came back and said: "Mr. Whitman will be in in a few minutes." Then he went away. We sat down on a lounge that was at the rear of the room, and put in our brief wait in looking at the thousand-and-one things of interest that were everywhere about us. These so absorbed us that we did not hear the footsteps of the old man as he came down the hall. As it happened, our backs were toward the door when he reached it, and the first we knew of his presence was when he said, in the sweetest and most engaging voice I ever heard: "Well, friends!"

We turned, and there stood Walt, "framed," as it were, by the door-casings. It was a picture never to be forgotten. He wore a long gray gown that reached the floor. The collar was wide and turned back, and there was fine lace at the ends of the full sleeves. The light from the windows fell on the left side of his face, and illumined his hair and beard against the shadows it formed on the right. Wife has always said he looked like a god. Never having seen a god, I cant say whether she is right or not. But I do know this—that any god might well be proud to look as Walt did as he stood in the door that August afternoon! We moved forward and shook hands with him, and told him who we were and where we came

227

from. Then he entered the room and sat down in his large armchair by the window. We chatted with him for an hour, talking of all sorts of things. He was as genuinely interested in us as if we were old friends. And he would have been the same to anyone else that he was to us. He had no pets.

A good deal that was said, on both sides, was everyday talk. He made no grand-stand play, nor did we. We just "visited," like "lovers and friends." But he said some things that are well worth telling. Wife said to him: "I should not have wondered so much if you had written what you have at your present time of life, but that you should have done it when you were a comparatively young man is a marvel to me." And Walt replied: "Well, my friends who have known me longest have told me, many times, that I always was a kind of old critter!" When we spoke of our home in Illinois he said: "You live in a great State. Indeed, the whole West is wonderful—so full of possibilities, as yet undreamed of." And then he added, after reflecting a moment: "I think my poems are like your West—crude, uncultured, wild in spots; but as the years go by and they are turned over and over, as your prairies are, I believe they will produce bountiful crops!" Could any faith be finer than that.

I asked Walt if he ever intended to compile all he had written, poetry and prose, in one volume, and he told me that he had just done that very thing, and that a special limited edition of six hundred copies of such a revision had just come from the press. I asked again: "Could one of us common folks get a copy of this edition, or are they all spoken for?" To which he replied (and his answer shows the old man just as he was in so many ways): "Why, anybody can have one of the books, if he can stand the price; but they come pretty steep." "How much?" I inquired. "*Six dollars*," he said; and the way he said it implied that he felt it was rank robbery to charge as much as that for any book that he had ever written. I kept on: "Where can I get one of them?" "O, I have some here in the house," he replied. "If you want to take it with you I'll send up stairs and have one brought down." I told him I would be much obliged if he would do so, and handed him the six dollars on the spot. He called in his housekeeper, who was in a room down the hall, and asked her to go up and get a book for me, which she did forthwith. That is how I came into possession of volume number one hundred and sixteen, Ferguson Brothers and Company, Philadelphia, special single volume edition to six hundred copies. The text is identical with that now

Walt Whitman, 1881

printed in two volumes, which I think are from the same plates. But I like this book just a little better, getting it as I did. I rejoice more, though, that the book is not "limited," but that all who will can have a copy as good as the best, at a merely nominal price. That is the democracy in the premises that would suit Walt.

Just after I got the book the young man who had admitted us came into the room. He was a railroad employee, and was just going out for his night run. He had his lantern on his arm and his long-visored cap was drawn well down over his forehead. He came in to say "So long" to Walt before going on duty. Walt gripped his hand heartily, and then gave him a salute as he went out into the street. When we came away Walt sat in his arm-chair, and held wife with his right hand and me with his left, and said: "So long my young

friends! Expecting the main things from you who come after!" That
was his farewell.

I guess life is worth living. Love to all the crowd.

Conservator, 20 (November 1909): 136-137.

ESTIMATES OF
WELL-KNOWN MEN

[Horace Traubel]

From March 1888 until his death, Whitman met almost daily with Horace Traubel as part of what we today would call an oral history project. To date, their conversations have been published in six volumes. Traubel became one of Whitman's literary executors.

[Following are continued extracts from Mr. Traubel's daily record of conversations with Walt Whitman in his later days in Camden, New Jersey, the first instalment of which appeared in THE CENTURY for November, 1905, and the second and third instalments of which appeared in THE CENTURY for September and October, 1907.—The Editor.]

November 7, 1888.—W. said: "Emerson was a most apt, genuine story-teller. His whole face would light up anticipatingly as he spoke; he was serene, quiet, sweet, conciliatory, as a story was coming. Curiously, too, Emerson enjoyed most repeating those stories which told against himself—took off his edge, his own edge. He had a great dread of being egotistic; had a horror of it, if I may say so—a horror, a shrinking from the suspicion or show of it. Indeed, he had a fear of egotism that was almost,—who knows?—quite an egotism itself. Yet Emerson was on the square—always so. Who ever doubted it?" I quoted an anti-Emerson piece, written by a Presbyterian, in which Emerson was charged with being "egotistic and self-sufficient." W. took that up at once. "No, no, no, no; there never lived a sweeter, saner, more modest man—a less tainted man, a man more gently courageous: he was everything but self-sufficient, taking that word the way it was meant in this instance."

November 8, 1888.—Discussed the question, Should we set a

limit upon ourselves to free expression? W. said: "Some one has said what some people regard as a profound bit of wisdom, 'It is important to say nothing to arouse popular resentment.' Have you ever thought of it? I have often asked myself, What does it mean? For myself, I have never had any difficulty in deciding what I should say and not say. First of all comes sincerity—frankness, open-mindedness. That is the preliminary—to talk straight out. It was said of Pericles that each time before he went to speak he would pray (what was called praying then—what was it?) that he might say nothing to excite the wrath, the anger, of the people." W. shook his head. "That is a doubtful prescription; I should not like to recommend it myself. Emerson, for one, was an impeachment of that principle—Emerson, with his clear, transparent soul. He hid nothing, kept nothing back, yet was not offensive. The world's antagonism softened to Emerson's sweetness."

November 8, 1888.—"Emerson never fails; he can't be rejected; even when he falls on stony ground, he somehow eventuates a harvest."

November 9, 1888.—"Emerson always let it be clearly enough understood where he could be found." I said, "Emerson, like you, never would admit the anti-slavery question was the only question." W. replied, "Yes, that's true." Then I asked, "Did Emerson take this view from more or less heart?" W. said, "From more, certainly." I said, "The antislavery men thought the labor question would be settled with the abolition of slavery, but they found"—W. finished the sentence for me—"a bigger question than that at once and ever since upon their hands." After a pause, he added: "Yes, many's the thing liberty has got to do before we have achieved liberty. Some day we'll make that word real—give it universal meanings: even ministers plenipotentiary and extraordinary will thrive under its wings."

November 10, 1888.—"And Darwin, the sweet, the gracious, the sovereign Darwin—Darwin, whose life was, after all, the most significant, the farthest-influencing life of the age."

He drifted back to Carlyle. "Poor Carlyle! poor Carlyle! the good fellow! the good fellow! I always found myself saying that in spite of my reservations. Some years ago Jennie Gilder wrote me in a hurry for some piece about Carlyle. I said then that to speak of

Horace Traubel

the literature of our century with Carlyle left out would be as if we missed our heavy gun; as if we stopped our ears, refused to listen, resenting the one surest signal that the battle is on. We had the Byrons, Tennysons, Shelleys, Wordsworths,—lots of infantry, cavalry, light artillery,—but this last, the most triumphant evidence of all, this master stroke, this gun of guns, for depth, power, reverberation, unspeakably supreme—this was Carlyle. I repeat it now, have made no change of front: to-day, here, to you, I reaffirm that old judgment—affix to it the seal of my present faith."

November 12, 1888.—"How do you regard Keats, on the whole, anyway? You don't refer to him often or familiarly." He replied: "I have of course read Keats—his works; may be said to have read all. He is sweet—oh, very sweet—all sweetness; almost lush—lush, pol-

233

ish, ornateness, elegancy." "Does he suggest the Greek? He is often called Greek." "Oh, no; Shakspere's sonnets, not the Greek. You know, the sonnets are Keats and more—all Keats was, then a vast sum added. For superb finish, style, beauty, I know of nothing in all literature to come up to these sonnets. They have been a great worry to the fellows, and to me, too—a puzzle, the sonnets being of one character, the plays of another. Has the mystery of this difference suggested itself to you? Try to think of the Shakspere plays—think of their movement, their intensity of life, action; everything hell-bent to get along, on, on; energy, the splendid play of force, across fields, mire, creeks. Never mind who is splashed; spare nothing: this thing must be done, said. Let it be done, said, no faltering." He shot this out with the greatest energy of manner and tone, accompanying animated gestures, saying in conclusion: "The sonnets are all that is opposite—perfect of their kind, exquisite, sweet; lush, elegant ed, refined, and refined, then again refined—again—refinement multiplied by refinement." Then he saw no vigor in them? "No; vigor was not called for. They are personal, more or less of small affairs: they do their own work in their own way. That's all we could ask, and more than most of us do, I suppose." He regarded the plays as being "tremendous, with the virility that seemed so totally absent from the sonnets."

November 13, 1888.—W. gave me this John Hay letter, saying: "It properly belongs in your pigeonholes; it helps to show how we come on with the grandees—what we pass for in the upper circles. John don't call himself upper circle or anything of that sort, but he is in the elect pit—he belongs to the saved, to the respectables. John is first rate in his own way, anyhow—has always been simple enough to break love with me on occasions."

Washington, March, 1887
Dear Walt Whitman:
I have received your book and MS. and send, with my hearty thanks, a New York check for $30. It is a little more than your modest charge. You will pardon the liberty; I am not giving you anything like what the writing is worth to me, but trying to give a just compensation for the trouble of copying, simply.

My boy, ten years old, said to me this morning, "Have you got a book with a poem in it called 'O Captain! My Captain!' I want to learn it to speak at school." I stared at him, having you in mind at the moment, as if he were a mind-reader—and asked him where he had heard of the poem. He said a boy had repeated it last year some-where.

I made him happy by showing him the MS. and promising him it should be his, if he deserved it, after I am gone.

With love and good wishes and hope that the spring may bring healing in its wings to you.

I am faithfully yours,

John Hay

November 20, 1888.—He thought Burr "justly should be re-garded as above the ordinary estimate of him—the school-book sto-ries," as he called them. "I thought there had been a reaction from them; yet they crop up again and again, as if to say, 'Burr was a trai-tor, and that's the end of him.' But that is not the end of him. Burr was an able man—one of the great men of that day. He had his bad spots; in the turns and twists of life"—W. indicating by a gesture of his right hand—"now and then a dark spot would appear. That spot has set itself in the public eye—that spot alone, as if there was noth-ing else. Yet the man was mainly good, mostly noble." He did not think Burr "was worse than the average great man of his day: none of them will bear inspection. Franklin, Washington, Hamilton, sub-ject them to the standards of our time, the nice standards; none of them would shine." I asked, "But you justify our standards?"

"Yes, yes; but I mean Burr should be judged by a standard ap-plied to all, not to him alone. A century ago drunkenness was not nec-essarily a dereliction; now it means shame and reproach. Hamilton has come down to us almost deified; but was he exempt from criti-cism? Hamilton was an intellectualist, cold, dispassionate, calculat-ing; yet he was truly a patriot, performed no inconsiderable part in the consummation of the American revolt. But Hamilton was a monar-chist: there was nothing in him to appeal to our democratic instincts, to the ideals we hold so dear to-day."

November 20, 1888.—"Mazzini was the greatest of them all down there in Italy, infinitely the greatest, went deepest, was biggest around."

235

November 23, 1888.—W. himself spoke of Goethe. "I suppose humility should restrain me; it might be said I have no right to an opinion; I know nothing of Goethe first hand—hit upon translations, pick up a poem, a glint, here and there. I have read 'Faust'—looked into it, not with care, not studiously, yet intelligently, in my own way." Now he "had an opinion of Goethe," and, having it, "might as well own up. Goethe impresses me as, above all, to stand for essential literature, art, life—to argue the importance of centering life in self, in perfect persons—perfect you, me: to force the real into the abstract ideal; to make himself, Goethe, the supremest example of personal identity—everything making for it in us, in Goethe; every man repeating the same experience." Goethe would ask: "What are your forty, fifty, hundred, social, national phantasms? This only is real—this person." While W. felt that "all the great teachers, the Greek, the Roman,—Plato, Seneca, Epictetus (I remember Epictetus says a very like thing),—in some respects placed a related emphasis on personality, identity," yet he observed a break in the fact that "all those eminent teachers were superbly moral (I confess they quite satisfy me as being so), while Goethe was not. Goethe seemed to look upon personal development as an end in itself: the old teachers looked for collective results. I do not mean that Goethe was immoral, bad; only that he laid his stress upon another point. Goethe was for beauty, erudition, knowledge, first of all for culture. I doubt if another imaginist of the first order in all literature, all history, so deeply put his stamp there. Goethe asked, 'What do you make out of your patriotism, army, state, people?' It was all nothing to him." Here W. stopped and laughed. "So, you see, I have an opinion while I confess I know nothing about Goethe." Further: "I do not think Burns was bad any more than I think Goethe was bad; but Burns was without morale, morality." Goethe always "looked askant" at patriotism. "Burns was as little a patriot in any large sense as any man that ever lived. You know it is very easy to get up a hurrah, call it freedom, patriotism; but none of that is patriotism in any sense I accept."

November 24, 1888.—He spoke tenderly of Darwin. Darwin is one of his loves that will last. So of Clifford, so of George Eliot; "Darwin, simplest, greatest, however, of all."

November 25, 1888.—W. spoke of Gladstone: "Gladstone is one of the curiosities; his age, vigor, wonderful alertness, put together, ex-

Whitman's inscription in Traubel's copy of Complete Poems and Prose *(1888)*

cite respect." He spoke of Gladstone's "wide-awakeness," called him the "rarest among well-preserved human beings." Reference was made to Webster—Carlyles' impression of him. W. said: "I heard Webster often—heard him deliver some of the greatest of his political speeches. The effect he had on me was more of grandeur of manner, size, importance, power—the breathing forth of these—than of things said,—of anything said." I referred to Theodore Parker; remarked that Parker looked a bit like Webster. W. reflected. "Can that be so? If that is so, it may be an important thing to know, to have said. But the men are no way alike in essentials. Parker is 'way and beyond bigger, more expansive, sincerer; he leaves Webster in the lurch every how. Why, in pure intellectuality, where Webster shone, Parker was a brilliant luminary." I said, "I would rather say the godlike Theodore than the godlike Dan." W., fervently: "So would I. Good! good! So would I rather—a thousand times rather."

November 25, 1888.—[From a letter written July 30, 1865, by A. Van Renssalaer to Walt Whitman.] Mr. Lincoln asked who you [W.] were, or something like that. I spoke up and said, mentioning your name, that you had written "Leaves of Grass," etc. Mr. Lincoln didn't say anything, but took a good long look till you were quite gone by. Then he says (I can't give you his way of saying it, but it was quite emphatic and odd), "Well," he says, "*he* looks like a *man*."

November 26, 1888.—The reference to Heine was followed by W.'s question: "Have you read Arnold's essay on Heine? Matthew Arnold's?" Adding, after some interjected remarks, "It seems to me the best thing Arnold ever wrote; it gives me a vein in which I run companionably with Arnold." W. was surprised that Arnold so "thoroughly appreciated" Heine's "unique genius." "Arnold does not always stick to his point, like O'Connor, takes excursions, seems to get away from his subject; but that is not detriment. We discover that though it may go underground—subterranean—or dip into forests, or take unaccountable turns, it is always the same stream."

November 25, 1888.— . . . "Emerson is great, oh, very great; I have not attempted to decide how great, how vast, how subtle: but very, very. He was a far-reaching force, a star of the first, the very first, magnitude, maybe; without a doubt that." I spoke of the wariness of the writers. W. said: "That I noticed, too. They are too wary.

Dropping out Shakspere, Byron, Shelley, perhaps,—some of them of the very topmost rank,—I am not afraid to say our fellows, the best of them, deserve an equal rank with the rest—I dare even say Milton." Then further: "I could never go Milton; he is turgid, heavy, over-stately." I said: "Take 'Paradise Lost'; doesn't its vogue come mainly from a sort of Christian, theological self-interest rather than from pure delight in its beauty?" He responded at once: "Oh, an immense lot! Besides, it seems to me that Milton is a copy of a copy—not only Homer, but the Æneid; a sort of modern repetition of the same old story: legions of angels, devils; war is declared, waged. Moreover, even as a story it enlists little of my attention. He seems to me like a bird, soaring, yet over-weighted—dragged down, as if burdened, too greatly burdened; a lamb in its beak; its flight not graceful, powerful, beautiful, satisfying, like the gulls we see over the Delaware in midwinter, their simple motion a delight, attracting you when they first break upon your sight, soaring, soaring, irrespective of cold or storm. It is true Milton soars, but with dull, unwieldy motion." Then, after a slight repetition of points accented above: "There's no use talking: he won't go down me. I have sometimes questioned myself, Have I not been too hasty? Have I not rejected unfairly? Was it humor, whim, that stood in the way? Then I would re-examine my premises. Yet each attempt was fruitless. In this way I have gone back to the book repeatedly. Only the other day the same question returned." He pointed to the floor; a pile of books were at his feet; he pulled out a Milton. "I have a volume here containing 'Paradise Lost'; I have had it about me for twenty years, but it never attracts or exalts me."

November 30, 1888.—"When Cleveland was being so sharply taken to task for having sent a present to the pope on his jubilee—I wrote a few lines in effect to this purport: I for one must go on record approving the President's action. More than that, I contended that, rather than having done too much, the President has done too little: my own impulse would have been to send—send to the pope; to send likewise to the queen,—to England's queen,—from whose forethought of those serious years so much of good came to us. I never sympathized with—always resented—the common American criticisms of the queen."

He said the subject of the war had come up while Donaldson was here yesterday. "Tom said John Brown, Lincoln, Grant, Sherman, Sheridan, were the five men out of that period, brought out by that period, assured of immortality." I asked, "Well, do you accept his selection?" He answered: "Some part of it, anyhow, I have no manner of doubt. I never enthused greatly over Brown, yet I know he is a great and precious memory. I don't deny but that he is to be ranked with the best; such devotion, such superb courage, men will not forget—cannot be forgotten." I referred to Lincoln's "balance, poise," arguing, "We can imagine the war without Grant, Sherman, Sheridan, but with Lincoln not there at that time, *what?*" W. responded: "We must not give too much importance to personalism. It is easy to overcharge it. Man moves as man in all the great achievements—man in the great mass; yet I, too, think of Lincoln much in that same way. As you say, his poise, his simple, loftiest ability to make an emergency sacred, meet every occasion, never shrinking, never failing, never hurrying—these are things to be remembered and things 'providential,' if 'providence' ever has a meaning in human affairs."

December 5, 1888.—Said this of Gilder: "Some of the hard-and-fast penny-a-liners on the poetic field affect to despise Gilder: they are a poor lot, most all of them: Gilder has written some poems which will live out the lives of most of the second-class songs of his day: genuine, fine, pretty big stuff; some of it almost free. I sometimes incline to believe that Watson wants to be free, but don't dare to. At any rate, he has my admiration for some things he has done—yes, admiration; and my personal love surely, always, always." He said of *The Century*: "Sometimes I get mad at it: it seems so sort of fussy, extra-nice, pouting; but then I turn about, have another way of explaining its limitations. I say to myself: those very limitations were designed—maybe rightly designed—therefore, it does not belong to me to complain."

December 7, 1888.—[From a letter from John Burroughs to Walt Whitman, July 24, 1879.] "I find I cannot read Whittier and Longfellow and Lowell with any satisfaction. Your poems spoil me for any but the greatest. Coming from them to you is like coming from a hothouse to the shore or the mountain. I know this is so, and is not predetermined partiality of mine."

When I stopped reading, W. said: "Now you probably know what I mean by come-out, unequivocal, as in the last passage, just before closing. He there makes a declaration, is unqualified, wholesale, final: that's what I call come-out. Also back farther, where he speaks of our science—says he has so far not tripped me up, but that tripping me up is his game." I said: "Brinton has said the same thing to me—that he has tried his best to find flaws in your science, but has failed to do so." "Did Brinton say that?" he replied. "Well, Brinton ought to know; with John and with him on my side I am well defended. John's letter appeals to me because of its undemonstrative personal affection,—that first of all,—then because of its uncompromising red-blooded espousal of the book—of my code. I respond to John: I feel the eminent kindliness, love, of his declaration; John never slushes, but is always on the spot."

December 19, 1888.—"William talks about Grant turning back. When did he ever turn back? He was not that sort: he could no more turn back than time. You can turn the clock back, but you can't turn time back. Grant was one of the inevitables: he always arrived; he was as invincible as a law; he never bragged; often seemed about to be defeated when he was in fact on the eve of a tremendous victory."

December 21, 1888.— W. liked what Burroughs said of Emerson: "To me Emerson filled nearly the whole horizon in that direction." W. said: "I guess I enjoy that; I guess I do." He had had me read the line over again. "John was right: Emerson *was* the whole horizon— Ralph Waldo Emerson, the gentle, noble, perfect, radiant, consolatory, Emerson. I think of something Emerson said in one of our talks. He said, 'I agree with you, Mr. Whitman, that a man who does not live according to his lights—who trims his sails to the current breeze—is already dead, is as many times dead as he is untrue.' Emerson lived according to his lights, not according to libraries, books, literature, the traditions. He was unostentatiously loyal: no collegian, overdone with culture: so gifted, so peculiarly tremendous, that, if I may say so, knowing too much did not, as it often does with the scholar, hurt him." "Didn't you tell me that he expressed regrets to you face to face one day, saying some sort of apologetic thing about his book-learning?" I asked. W. nodded. "Yes, more than once: said he felt like athletes—some athletes—overtrained; that a scholar, like an athlete overtrained, is apt to go stale. He said he felt that culture had done all it could do for him—then it had

241

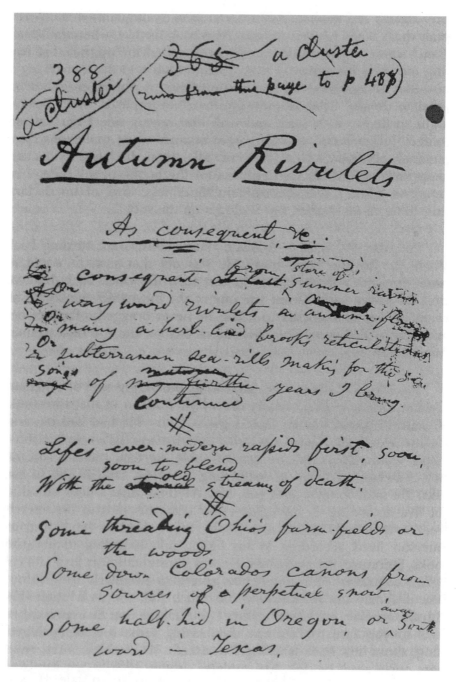

Whitman's manuscript of "Autumn Rivulets"

done something for him which had better been left undone."

December 26, 1888.—Asked about Tolstoi's "My Religion and My Confession." Did not know but he "might read them"; at any rate, would "try." "If they are what they may be, I shall go definitely through them." W. thought "the just word" for Tolstoi to be "vraisemblance." T. is "not surpassed in that Sebastopol book by any of the giants in the history of literature."

December 30, 1888.—"Bryant was very nice to me generally: he seemed to follow my history somewhat—knew about me. He thought I had 'the whole wolf pack' on my heels, and he would say again, 'As you have challenged the whole world, I don't suppose you are surprised or resentful when you find the whole world out against you with its hounds.' It did not seem to me that Bryant was wrong: what else could I have expected? When John Morley came to see me that time he made some remarks of this same tenor. 'Criticism has isolated you here in America,' Morley said, which was true: but it would also have been true to say, 'You have isolated yourself.' I am not a squealer. I don't think that a man has any call to go out breaking heads and expect the people he attacks to bless him for it. In a case like mine it's give and take: after I'm on right foundations, no opposition can upset me; if I am falsely rooted, nothing can save me." No day passes now but W. hands over to me some document which he says is for my "archives." I said to-night to him: "you are giving me some great stuff nowadays. I will find real use for it; I'll make a big story out of it all some day." He nodded. "That's what I want you to do, if the world will stand it. In the final sense they are not records of my life,—of my personal life, of Walt Whitman,—but scripture material applying to a movement in which I am only an episode."

January 2, 1889.—Has at last started reading Tolstoi's "My Confession." He was "curiously interested"—interested "even in things" he "would seem to be naturally driven to protest against." "What does it all mean?" he asked. His cursory, original look into the book had been if anything unfavorable; now he was "alive with interest—in spite of myself," he first said. Then: "It is scarcely fair to use that term, since I have no desire not to like Tolstoi—only the earlier impression of repugnance, now rapidly vanishing. It is hard for me to ex-

plain the book. Is it not morbid? Indeed, may I not say *dreadfully* morbid?" I argued, "It would be morbid for us here in America; it is
not morbid for him there in Russia." W.: "That is a better way to
put it; yet I wonder to myself how a man can get into that state of
mind. It is as though we should sit down to a meal—ask, why do I
eat? Why is this good? Why will it have such and such results? Or,
on a hot day in summer, Why do I feel so good in the glory of the
sun? Or, Why do I strip and souse in the water? Or, Why does the flowing river make me happy? Why? Why? Making that mood the talis-
man for all?" W. raised himself on his elbow as he spoke, then
dropped back again. "Yet I realize that Tolstoi is a big, a genuine
man; a fact, real, a power"—seemingly to reflect in the interval—
"Most of all, a fact—as a fact, adopting Frederick's saying, to be rever-
enced. I do not distrust him: I feel that he is a subject, a bit out of
nature, yet to be grasped, yet to be understood. I am not denying,
only struggling with, him." It was his "first encounter with the Tolstoi mystery." "While baffled still, still I am not all baffled: I must
keep on. For instance, I feel that he is, as a fact, a different fact
from Shakspere; a different order, we may describe it to be." I interrupted. "So are you." W. nodded. "I do not forget; I do not say for
that to be any the less honored." Tolstoi is "strangely removed from
the Shaksperian." How removed he did not seem disposed to de-
fine. "That is what's to come yet." As to being "different" himself, "I
feel that at many points, in essentials, I share the Shaksperian quality—
except," he apologized, "of course"—here again a reflecting moment—"as to the last point, the highest flights, the latest plays, in
which the breadth is so great, so unmistakably phenomenal." But he
must still state his dissent even from Shakspere. "Shakspere, however, is gloomy; looks upon the people with something like despair;
does so especially in these maturer plays; seemed to say: After all,
the human critter is a devil of a poor fellow, full of frailties, evils, poi-
sons, as no doubt he is if you concentrate your light on that side of
him—consent that this, this alone, is the man; are determined to
take the pessimistic view." But his own "deep impressions run
counter to such lack of faith." He recognized Tolstoi's "faith and
call." "Perhaps the strongest point with Tolstoi—this point that most
fastens itself upon men, upon me, is this: that here is a man with a
conviction—a conviction—on which he has planted himself, stakes
all, invites assault, affection, hope. That would be a good deal if
there was nothing more, not a hint more: whereas that there *is* more

to Tolstoi I think no one can doubt." He "clearly perceived, as perhaps not before," that "however little Tolstoi might prove to be *his*, for *him*, his place and purpose, lofty, indeed, for some, perhaps for the modern world, that strange seething European world chiefly, is no longer to be questioned."

January 11, 1889.—In talking of W.'s early adherents, I mentioned Bryant. "Walt, you and Bryant were personal friends. Did he ever care for your work?" "I can't say he did. Bryant was trained in the classics, made no departures. He was a healthy influence, was not a closet man, belonged out-of-doors; but he was afraid of my work. He was interested, but afraid. I remember that he always expressed wonder that with what he called my power and gifts and essential, underlying respect for beauty, I refused to accept and use the only medium which would give me complete expression. I have often tried to think of myself as writing 'Leaves of Grass' in Thanatopsisian verse. Of course I do not intend this as a criticism of Bryant, only as a demurrer to his objection of me. 'Thanatopsis' is all right in Thanatopsisian verse. I suppose Bryant would fare as badly in 'Leaves of Grass' verse as I would fare in 'Thanatopsis' verse. Bryant said to me, 'I will admit that you have power— sometimes great power.' But he would never admit that I had chosen the right vehicle of expression. We never quarreled over such things. I liked Bryant as a man as well as a poet. He, I think, liked me as a man; at least I inferred so from the way he treated me. Bryant belonged to the classics, liked the stately measures prescribed by the old formulas; he handled them marvelously well. Breaking loose is the thing to do—break loose, resenting the bonds, opening new ways. But when a fellow breaks loose, or starts to, or even only thinks he thinks he'll revolt, he should be quite sure he knows what he has undertaken."

Century Magazine, 83 (December 1911): 250-256; this material was incorporated into the third volume of Traubel's *With Walt Whitman in Camden* (1914).

A PERSONAL NOTE ON THE GOOD GRAY POET

Richard Maurice Bucke

Richard Maurice Bucke, superintendent of an insane asylum in London, Ontario, first met Whitman in 1877, became a lifelong friend, and served as one of his literary executors. This article recollects Whitman's visit to Bucke in Canada in 1880.

In the year 1880 Walt Whitman accompanied me from Philadelphia to London and remained with me, in my house, for four months, June, July, August, September. Had it not been for the ample opportunity thus afforded for observing and studying the man it is likely I should never have known (though I might have divined) what sort of personality lived behind the pages of his great book.

The old poet was sixty-one past while with me; he was a large, exceedingly handsome man with very white hair and more than usual color in his face; in manner he was unusually quiet, unassuming and undemonstrative, he wore a white shirt with a large turn down collar open at the throat, and light grey tweed suit. His person and everything about him seemed constantly breathing (as it were) an air of what might be called immaculateness. Every decent individual is clean in person and clothing, but in him there was something beyond that, which though vividly present to my mind this moment I find it difficult if not impossible to put in words. Perhaps the terms purity and freshness best express what I mean—the feeling (for instance) conveyed by a bright breezy spring or summer morning. As you associated more and more with him you perceived that the quality in question was not merely physical, not belonging solely to his person and raiment, but that it inhered, to at least an equal degree, in his mind—that in fact it belonged there and that the external appearances were but the radiation (as it were) of an inner spiritual quality.

246

You found that his speech and thoughts were, if possible, cleaner, purer, freer from taint or stain than were even his body or his linen. Further you noticed that, over and above, the man was singularly free from faults and blemishes that are almost if not quite universal. For instance, I never knew Whitman to speak a word in depreciation of any person, except (and this was only occasional) himself. I never knew him to find fault with the weather, with any of his surroundings, or with anything that might happen, such as "bad luck," sickness, or ill treatment by others. I never knew him to utter a harsh word about or to any one. Very soon after I first knew him I noticed this peculiarity in his every day life and for a long time I used to think: What splendid self control! He will not allow himself to express what he thinks! For it must be remembered he was being constantly attacked, slandered and vilified and it seemed impossible that he should not feel the usual resentment belonging to such circumstances. After a time (seeing no sign of the feeling supposed) I began to doubt whether it was there, and still later I saw (or thought I saw) that it, in fact, had no existence. So with money and usual anxieties and petty annoyances of life—to him they did not exist or at least they did not occupy his mind, and his face showed this. To the last it had no lines of care or worry—he lived in an upper spiritual stratum—above all mean thoughts, sordid feeling, earthly harassments. The fact is, Whitman resembled hardly at all ordinary men, he lived in a different world and was governed by entirely different thoughts, feelings and considerations. What these were I shall not attempt to state here—neither could I state them fully however much I might endeavour to do so. A study of his books and of his life will reveal them in part to the student who is (mentally) near enough to him to enter more or less into his ideas and emotions. The sceptic, the flaneur, the money grubber, the man of low spirituality, of dull imagination will never know anything of him, and will now and always misconceive him and misconstrue his utterances.

The charm of Whitman's presence cannot be conceived by those who have had no experience of it. This charm resided partly in such elements as those mentioned above; but still more in his manner which was courteous, sympathetic and attractive in a very high degree. It would be correct (using the term in its highest and noblest sense) to speak of him as transcendently a gentleman, were it not that the term has been so degraded by ill use that it has become almost impossible to associate it with such a personality as his. I have

Richard Maurice Bucke

met many men in several countries—men of deservedly world wide reputation, such as Tennyson—men of great spriritual force, such as Browning, men of the tenderest heart and most lovable personality, such as Ed. Carpenter, magnificent and magnetic orators, such as Henry Ward Beecher. But I have never met another such man as Whitman and I do not believe there walks the grassy floor of the earth to-day another man so god-like and at the same time so human as the author of Leaves of Grass.

From *Walt Whitman as Man, Poet and Friend,* ed. Charles N. Elliot (Boston: Richard G. Badger, 1915), pp. 45-58.

WITH WALT WHITMAN
IN CAMDEN

Horace Traubel[1]

Unlike the previous selection, which maintains the daily, diarylike order of Traubel's conversations with Whitman, the entries here are grouped by topic.

Humor in Great Men.—W. talked about Garland. "He's greatly interested in the George movement: is strongly impulsive: is maybe a little one-idea'd—though as to that I don't feel quite sure: is wonderfully human: gets at the simple truths—the everyday truths: is not professional." I said: "You speak of one-idea'd men as though you rather discredited them." "Do I? I don't mean to: they certainly have a place—a vast big vital place: they can't be skipped—escaped." I said again: "You may think you're not, but you're a little one-idea'd yourself—and every man is." He nodded. "No doubt: I never heard it put quite in that way: Jesus was one-idea'd, I admit, for instance." I asked him: "Well—have you some objections to Jesus?" "Yes: why not? Emerson had, too: the dear Emerson: he felt that Jesus lacked humor, for one thing: a man who lacks humor is likely to concentrate on one idea." I parried him again. "Why, that's a familiar charge against you, Walt: didn't even Ruskin say that? and I hear it every now and then from somebody or other." He retorted a little hotly: "Well—you've rather got me: I'm not much good in an argument. But on that Jesus matter: take that: I've heard it discussed often: some of the bright fellows have been saying it for a long time: not Emerson alone: others: radical fellows—the strong men: thinkers. Yet I confess I'm not altogether clear in the matter." He used the phrase at one point: "Whether genius needs to be funny"—but caught himself short over it: "I should not say that: that is unjust to Emerson: to all of them: when they say humor they don't mean fun in the narrow sense of that word—they don't mean what we call joking, badinage—anything like that." Spoke of Emerson himself as

249

"not what you would call a funny man: he was something better than that: he would not cut up—make a great noise: but for cheer, quiet, sweet cheer—good humor, a habit of pouring oil on waters—I have never known his equal. Emerson was in no sense priggified—solemnfied: he was not even stately, if that means to be stiff." The word "humor," he said, always "mystified" him. "I think Shakespeare had it—had it to the full: but there have been others—great men, too—who had little or none of it. The question is, was Shakespeare's humor good natured? Good nature is the important equation in humor. Look at Heine, for example: I'm not sure of his place: but look at him—consider him: ask yourself whether he was not a mocker as well as a humorist. They do charge me, as you say, with lacking humor: it never seemed to me it could be true: but I don't dispute it: I only see myself from the inside—with the ordinary prejudice a fellow has in favor of himself: but O'Connor—oh! how he used to boil when he heard me accused of that defect: he'd boil, he'd boil—he'd boil over! The idea that anybody imagines I can't appreciate a joke or even make jokes seems preposterous. Do you find me as infernally impossible as that, Horace? Bryant said to me in one of our chats: 'The most humorous men I have met have been the lightest laughers.' You can't always tell by a man's guffaws whether he is a real humorist or not."

The Future Menace Against Free Speech.—We talked of Bradley's conviction in the Camden courts yesterday. "Yes, I have read the story: Bradley was monstrous—monstrous: but would you not think him abnormal? I see no other way to account for it: certainly he can't be explained by the ordinary process of reasoning. In the present condition of our criminal laws—of crime—as in affairs like this—these extra sex developments—abnormality is the only word that will cover the case. Then we must remember that such individual abnormality comes from the abnormality of society at large. I think any judge would admit that—perhaps express it almost in my words: it seems to me to arise—so much of it, who knows but all of it? —in an absence of simplicity—in a lack of what I may call natural morality. Perhaps that's not the exact word for it, but as I said, any judge would correctly diagnose the case, I have no doubt." "Speaking of judges," said W. the minute after, "would you not like to take the paper along?—Sidney's paper?" Handed me the mail from the table. Had he read it? "Oh yes: every word of it: with great care:

250

Tuesday May 22 '88

To Mr Bennerman
— The bearer of this is Horace
Traubel, a young friend of mine
in whom I have confidence —
I want to have printed & a book stereotyped
of (probably) 160 to 200 page . may be
somewhat less — long primer — exactly same size &
page as the "Specimen Days" you printed
of mine four or five years ago —
Can you & would you like to
do it for me? — Have you some,
good long primer? — The copy is
ready — it is all printed matter
(or nearly all) it all plain sailing you could commence
next Monday — Sh'd want liberal proofs —
— You can talk with Horace
Traubel just the same as you w'd
with me — I am almost entirely
disabled ab't walking or bodily loco
motion — Walt Whitman
328 Mickle Street
Camden. NJ

Whitman's letter of 22 May 1888 introducing Horace Traubel (Feinberg Collection, Library of Congress)

with as much interest as care: I say amen to it all, too: amen, amen: if I find it possible I shall tell him about this feeling in me. If you write to Sidney—to any of the fellows out there—say this—say it for me: in my name if you choose. I feel like thanking the man for myself, for America, for Americans." It had appeared to him "rare among rare decisions." "I know that in regard to these Anarchists there are contending impulses drawing us two ways: but for liberty, abstract, concrete—the broad question of liberty—there is no doubt at all. I look ahead seeing for America a bad day—a dark if not stormy day—in which this policy, this restriction, this attempt to draw a line against free speech, free printing, free assembly, will become a weapon of menace to our future."

Paine.—After continued general talk of Poe W. said: "I have seen Poe—met him: he impressed me very favorably: was dark, quiet, handsome—southern from top to toe: languid, tired out, it is true, but altogether ingratiating." Was that in New York? "Oh, yes: there: we had only a brief visit: he was frankly conciliatory: I left him with no doubts left, if I ever had any." Poe was "curiously a victim of history—like Paine. The disposition to parade, to magnify, his defects has grown into a habit: every literary, every moralistic jackanapes who comes along has to give him an additional kick. His weaknesses were obvious enough to anybody: but what do they amount to, after all? Paine is defamed in the same way: poor Paine: rich Paine: they spare him nothing." I said: "You should write about Paine." He nodded. "So I should: I don't think there's anybody living—anybody at all—(I don't think there ever was anybody, living or dead)—more able than I am to depict, to picture, Paine, in the right way. I have told you of my old friend Colonel Fellows: he was an uncommon man both in what he looked like and in what he was: nobly formed, with thick white hair—white as milk: beard: striking characteristics everyhow." W. asked: "Does this interest you?" I said: "You bet: don't stop." He proceeded: "We had many talks together in the back room of the City Hall. The instant he saw I was interested in Paine he became communicative—frankly unbosomed himself. His Paine story amounted to a resurrection of Paine out of the horrible calumnies, infamies, under which orthodox hatred had buried him. Paine was old, alone, poor: it's that, it's what accrues from that, that his slanderers have made the most of: anything lower, meaner, more contemptible, I cannot imagine: to take an aged man—a man tired to death after a complicated life of toil, struggle, anxiety—weak, dragged down, at death's door: poor: with perhaps habits that may come with such distress: then to pull him into the mud, distort everything he does and says: oh! it's infamous. There seems to be this hyena disposition, some exceptional (thank God, rare) venom, in some men which is never satisfied except it is engaged in some work of vandalism. I can forgive anything but that."

Shakespeare's Feudalism.—Harned said: "Walt, you're hitting a lot of nails on the head today: you almost weaken my faith in Shakespeare." W. said: "Shakespeare stood for the glory of feudalism: Shakespeare, whoever he was, whoever they were: he had his place: I have never doubted his vastness, space: in fact, Homer and Shakespeare are good enough for me—if I can by saying that be understood as not closing out any others. Look at Emerson: he was not only possibly the greatest of our land, our time, but great with the greatness of any land, any time, all worlds: so I could name galaxy after galaxy." Harned asked: "You have decided feelings about the defects of Shakespeare?" "Yes: it is not well for us to forget what Shakespeare stands for: we are over-awed, overfed: it may seem extreme, ungracious, to say so, but Shakespeare appears to me to do much toward effeminacy: toward taking the fiber, the blood, out of our civilization: his gospel was of the medieval—the gospel of the grand, the luxurious: great lords, ladies: plate, hangings, glitter, ostentation, hypocritical chivalry, dress, trimmings"—going on with the strange long catalogue "of social and caste humbuggery" pronounced with the highest contempt. "I can say I am one of the few—unfortunately, of the few—who care nothing for all that, who spit all that out, who reject all that miserable paraphernalia of arrogance, unrighteousness, oppression: who care nothing for your carpets, curtains, uniformed lackeys. I am an animal: I require to eat, to drink, to live: but to put any emphasis whatever on the trapperies, luxuries, that were the stock in trade of the thought of our great grandfathers—oh! that I could never, never, never do!" Then suddenly he fired out with more heat than ever: "And now that I think of it I can say this fact more than any other fact lends weight to the Baconian authorship: I have never written, never said, indeed I have never thought of it as forcibly as at just this moment sitting here with you two fellows: but the emphasis that the author of the Plays places upon these fripperies points an unmistakable finger toward Bacon. Bacon himself loved all this show, this fustian: dressed handsomely: tunic: fine high boots: brooches: liked a purse well filled with gold money: the feel of it in his pocket: would tinsel his clothes: oh! was fond of rich, gay apparel: affected the company of ladies, gents, lords; courts: favored noble hallways, laces, cuffs, gorgeous service—even the hauteur of feudalism." W. then added: "Feudalism has had its day: it has no message for us: it's an empty vessel: all its contents have been spilled: it's foolish for us to look back to some anterior period for leadership: feudalism is gone—well gone: peace to its dung: may my nostrils never know its stink again. One mustn't forget, Tom, and you, Horace, that thankful as we have a right to be and should be to the past our business is ahead with what is to come: the dead must be left in their graves."

Were the Shakespeare plays the best acting plays? W. said: "That's a superstition—an exaggeration." Harned said something which induced W. to add: "If O'Connor was here and heard you say that he'd quarrel with you." As to Shakespeare as actor W. said: "Even if he never got beyond the ghost, as has been said, we must acknowledge that to do the ghost right is a man's, not a ghost's job: few actors ever realized the possiblities of a ghost." W. said: "William speaks of Winter as Littlebillwinter—all one word. I remember what Emerson said of Jonson: 'He thought himself a good deal greater man than Shakespeare.' " The "Shakespeare personality" was "very mystifying, baffling. . . . Yet there are some things we can say of it. . . . Whoever Shakespeare was not he was equal in refinement to the wits of his age: he was a gentleman: he was not a man of the streets—rather of the courts, of the study: he was not vulgar. As for the Plays, they do not seem to me spontaneous; they seem laboredly built up: I have always felt their feudal bias: they are rich to satiety: overdone with words." I never saw W. more vigorous. He finally said: "I am so sure the orthodox notion of Shakespeare is not correct that I enter fully into the discussion of those who are trying to get at the truth."

On Being Misunderstood.—"It has always been a puzzle to me why people think that because I wrote 'Children of Adam,' 'Leaves of Grass,' I must perforce be interested in all the literature of rape, all the pornography of vile minds. I have not only been made a target by those who despised me, but a victim of violent interpretation by those who condoned me. You know the sort of stuff that's sent to me here."

Art for Art's Sake.—"The trouble is that writers are too literary—too damned literary. There has grown up—Swinburne I think an apostle of it—the doctrine (you have heard of it? it is dinned everywhere), art for art's sake: think of it—art for art's sake. Let a man really accept that—let that really be his ruling—and he is lost." I suggested: "If we say politics for politics' sake, they get mad." W.: "So they do: that is very good: it's true: politics for politics' sake, church for church's sake, talk for talk's sake, government for government's sake: state it any way you choose it becomes offensive: it's all out of the same pit. Instead of regarding literature as only a weapon, an instrument, in the service of something larger than itself, it looks upon itself as an end—as a fact to be finally worshipped, adored. To me that's all a horrible blasphemy—a bad smelling apostasy."

Kaiser Wilhelm.—Talked of young Emperor William. "I find I can't think of him patiently: he rubs my fur the wrong way: I had great hopes of his father: but this boy only excites my distrust. I never cease wondering how a people so enlightened as the Germans can tolerate the king, emperor, business anyway. The Hohenzollerns are a diseased mess, taking them all in all: there seems to be a corrupt physical strain in the family: what does it come from? Can it be syphilis?" He was silent for a while. Resumed: "I am aware that that is often said of Frederick: it is the pet theory of doctors—their staple explanation: but the question is, is it true? How much of it can be true? I am not easily convinced in such matters: I call for absolute testimony—and that no one outside has got in this case. Doctors put all the iniquities of courts, palaces, high society, down at this one door—but do they belong there? I listen to the stories—yet am not convinced: I am not willing to contradict them or ready to acquiesce."

The Oriental Strain.—"I do not worry: I determine not to worry—let come what may come. Resignation, I may call it: peace in spite of fate." I broke in: "Peace at any price?" Laughed. "Almost that: what the religious people call resignation: the feeling that whatever comes is just the thing that ought to come—ought to be welcomed." But

Front cover of the February 1881 North American Review *containing Whitman's "The Poetry of the Future"*

this element in him "is not explained" by his "Occidental origins." His vision drew him into the past. "Somewhere, back, back, thousands of years ago, in my fathers, mothers, there must have been an Oriental strain, element, introduced—a dreamy languor, calm, content: the germ, seed of it, somehow—of this quality which now turns up in me, to my benefit, salvation." Had this anything to do with fatalism? The Mohammedan temperament? "No: it antedates all that: we find it in Hindustan, Palestine, all over the East: rich, suffused with the glow of peace: in nations of men: before what we call civilization."

Bret Harte, Mark Twain, and Brander Matthews.—W.: "As a general thing I don't enjoy dialect literature: it's rather troublesome stuff to handle: yet Jim [Bludso] took a powerful hold on me: but though I don't care much for the dialect writers myself I acknowledge their validity, value, pertinence: that some of them are remarkably gifted: they indicate, stand for, exemplify, an important phase in our literary development." He had "particularly in mind" one of Bret Harte's "lesser quoted" poems. "It is mighty fine. I have regarded it as his most eminently splendid bit of work: what the locomotive from the Pacific says to the locomotive from the Atlantic when they meet: have you read that? Oh! it's capital: it's a perfect creation." Had he any objections to The Outcasts of Poker Flat? "Not a single objection: I like it—more than like it: all of it." Where did he rank Bret Harte? "I hardly know what to say to that." About Mark Twain? "The English have taken to Harte: they seem to understand him." What was the idea of Mark Twain. "I think he mainly misses fire: I think his life misses fire: he might have been something: he comes near to being something: but he never arrives." I quoted Brander Matthews. W. asked at once: "Who is he? Where is he from? I have neither met not read him."

Government by Millionaires.—"Horace, we are all under the thumb of millionaires: ours is a millionaire government, without a doubt." "Ain't all modern governments millionaire governments?" "I suppose they are or getting to be." Then he added: "And I do not know that I complain: the millionaires must have their innings, too: that is a phase we are going through—can't skip." I asked: "Then you don't think we'll always have millionaire governments?" He answered quickly: "You don't need to ask me such a question: the people, who are now asleep, will yet wake up." I said: "Sometimes you quarrel with the people who try to wake them up: you call them doctrinaries and partisans." "Do I?" "You certainly do: yet you are a fierce doctrinaire and partisan in your own way." He said he wasn't "inclined to dispute" me. But how did I make that out? "No one is more stubborn for what he considers the truth than you are. That's all the other fellows are: stubborn for the truth as they see it."

Naturalists and Materialism.—W. turned to me and said with great energy. "But, Horace, have you never noticed the tendency in naturalists—men who live out of doors, in the woods, the supposedly freest life: the tendency toward depression, if not actually depression itself? the taint of it?" Could it be that a withdrawal from

257

human comradeship had something to do with this? He answered very deliberately: "Something of that sort might be said in discussing Thoreau: it could not be urged in John's case: John has never wanted for companions: the world is always wide open to him: he likes people." "Then you have no explanation?" "I have notions but no conclusion. One of remarkable facts is that naturalists are made materialists often by the very experiences that would make me the opposite."

The Tyranny of Miracles.—B. spoke of something as "a miracle." W. said: "Miracles are dangerous affairs, Maurice." B: "You may not be a believer in miracles, Walt, but you are a worker of miracles." W. said: "You are a liberal interpreter, Maurice: you construe me far beyond what I am or could be—far beyond what I want to be." Yet he also said: "What greater miracles than the telegraph, telephone—all the wonderful new mechanism of our day!" At he same time he said he always "wanted to be 'quoted against the theological miracles.' " Bucke's insistence that there was a background for it all, W. said, did "not explain the case." W. added: "The whole miracle dogma business has been swung as a club over the head of the world: it has been a weapon flourished by the tyrannical dynasties of the old world—dynasties murderous, reeking, unscrupulous, barbarous: they have always tried to justify their crimes by an assumed divine grant of some sort. I have often wondered about the Greeks— how much of their mythology they really believed: it looks to me as if their gods like other gods were mostly used not for liberation but oppression: the gods intervened, but often in mean, despicable, poisonous, dastardly ways, to blind, to paralyze, to afflict, rather than to bless. Think of Mercury sent forth by Jupiter. It was oftener as a bad unscrupulous angel than a curer of souls—the inflicter rather than the healer of wounds. The people have always suffered: they have always been the victims of their gods."

Our Universities.—I asked W.: "What would you say of the university and modern life?" "I wouldn't say anything: I'd rather be excused." "But suppose you couldn't dodge it—had to say something?" He took my quizzing genially this time. "You know: I have said everything to you before: I have nothing new to announce." "But suppose you had to talk?" "Had to? I never have to: but you know my feelings about the colleges: I do not object to anything they do that

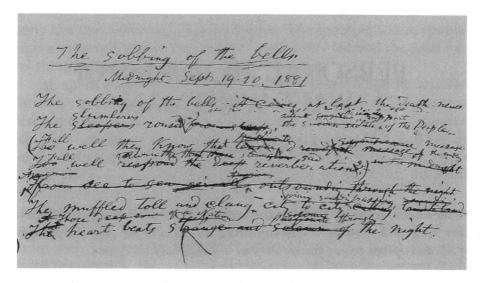

Manuscript of "The Sobbing of the Bells" (Feinberg Collection, Library of Congress)

will enrich the popular life—emphasize the forces of democracy: the trouble is that so much they do is bent the other way—seems to me simply hopeless scholarism or encourages reaction: is bookishness rather than revelation: is not vital brutal instant instinct but the distillation of distillations God knows how many removes from origins." I said: "Well—I got you to say something, anyhow!" He added: "Yes, you did: I don't take it back: so much of the work we might be warranted in expecting the university to do has to be done outside universities to-day: the university is only contemporary at the best: it is never prophetic: it goes, but not in advance: often, indeed, as dear Sidney used to say here, has its eyes set in the back of its head." I asked: "Isn't this all inevitable as long as the university is an aristocratic rather than a democratic institution?" W.: "I do not deny it: in fact, that may be the truth, the whole truth and nothing but the truth."

Seven Arts, 2 (September 1917): 627-637.

1. Excerpts from "With Walt Whitman in Camden," volume four, to be published shortly by Doubleday, Page & Co. The conversations are all of the year 1889.

PERSONAL MEMORIES OF WALT WHITMAN

Alma Calder Johnston

Alma Calder Johnston and her husband, J. H. Johnston, regularly opened their New York home to Whitman during his visits to the city, and, judging by the description below, found the poet a delightful houseguest.

My Acquaintance with Walt Whitman began in 1874, when his book, *Leaves of Grass*, was sent to me by the man whom I afterward married. The work held me; yet at times if filled me with nervous repulsion, and I would throw the volume to a top shelf and rush from the house to a nook in the forest, feeling that I would not, could not, touch it again. "My words itch at your ears till you understand them," he had said. Sometimes a sentence would fill me with sublime exaltation; fogs of doubt would roll away, and the eternal light of faith make "Not the good only, justified: what men call evil also justified."

Inspired with gratitude for the enlightenment his words had given me, I wrote to Walt Whitman, but received no reply. I think I did not ask nor expect one, but in my letter I said I hoped some day to see him. A year or more passed; then, while I was attending the Centennial in Philadelphia, a friend, Caleb Pink, called one Sunday morning to take me to Whitman's home in Camden. I was silent during the journey, hoping, fearing, considering phrases with which to introduce myself. My escort was also a stranger to Whitman, with a vague sympathy for him,—eccentric man and so-called poet. My heart was palpitating, my nerves tingling, and every sense was alert as we entered the little house. Crossing the narrow hall, I saw through an open door, seated in an armchair, the large grey-clad figure I had pictured; the dome-shaped brow, the smiling eyes, the snowy hair and beard. I paused—my nervousness quite gone—feasting my eyes, warming my heart,—when lo! he stretched out his great hands, call-

260

ing "Alma!" and instantly I was clasped in his arms and given the hearty kiss that welcomes a kindred spirit. The greeting was so spontaneous and simple that its utter unconventionality seemed the most natural thing in the world. It was Walt Whitman!

We spent many hours together in after years, when he was Mr. Johnston's guest and mine. He had become "Uncle Walt" to the children I mothered. Besides the photographs he had taken of himself with them another picture is as vivid to me:—I see him walking up and down in the morning sunshine, the trees of Central Park, opposite our door, for a background, a baby boy in his arms, his white beard mingling with the yellow curls.

He was an industrious worker, having learned by unflinching energy "the divine power to use words." The floor of his room was strewn with scraps of paper,—turned envelopes, the blank spaces of erased manuscript, the backs of old letters,—all bore his patient scribblings; thrift, and the habits formed in days when paper was dear, had made him economical. Newspapers from which extracts had been cut, books reviewed, and to be reviewed, lay everywhere. He never had a table large enough—I am not sure any table could have been made large enough—so the floor served the purpose. On occasion, I would appear with basket and broom. "Now, Alma! Now, Alma!" he would exclaim with uplifted hand; and the same arguments that had always been urged before, on the necessity of a "clarin' up," the same yielding, with reservations by each of us, the same apprehensive watchfulness on his part, with much raillery and audacity on mine, would send his bushy eyebrows up into a pointed arch, while his blue eyes danced with amused alarm.

One day, from among the scraps about his chair, which I placed before him, assorted, I read a couplet at which I exclaimed, "Uncle Walt, you have written these lines at least a dozen times, and each time made them worse!" Taking the papers and reading them in turn, he looked up with the whimsical smile I loved to provoke, and said, "Do you know, Alma, I have been trying to work the pretty out of that!" Whereupon I tried to persuade him that to work the rhyme out of a stanza which naturally rhymed, was as big a piece of affectation as to hunt for jingles to end prosy paragraphs. Another time, in all seriousness, I ventured to criticise the title and the opening line of one of his most virile poems.

"What you really mean, Uncle Walt," I boldly declared, "is *'Woman waits for me.'* By making it *a woman*, you put a most objection-

Walt Whitman, circa 1888

able barrier before a great truth, and naturally, timid souls will shy at it; the road is not so easy, when one is in pursuit of truth, that the Leader himself should put hurdles in the way."

Our discussion had begun in desultory fashion at breakfast, and we had lingered after the table was cleared and the other members of the family had gone their various ways, to business and to school. Our conversation turned to modern education, upon which his views were frequently radical. He was impatient of time and effort given to the study of foreign languages, to the neglect of the wealth of expression lying unused in our own, although he did not disapprove of picturesque foreign phrase or of slang that grew out of unwonted conditions. He resented forms that repressed originality. "It seems to me," he said, "the present style of education is all wrong. Children should first develop physically, they should learn to love Nature, become familiar with Nature, get into harmony with Nature's

262

laws, absorb sunshine and air. I think everybody loves Nature, though he may not know it.—Let's get out the old nag and go for a drive!"

I recall that as we drove along a country road in the unfrequented ways beyond Central Park, I suggested that a recognition of Nature's laws was all that was required for an acceptance of his poems, *Leaves of Grass*, and that the simile he used most frequent to illustrate the growth of thought ought not to prove offensive, since ideas were conceived, nourished, born in language and sent out to propagate their kind without anyone being shocked by the process. And so, in that much-maligned poem, *A Woman Waits for Me*, the impersonal woman might be considered quite philosophically, if the wording were put a trifle differently.

His elbows on his knees, his hands loosely holding the reins over what he termed "the old nag," as she walked through a bit of woodland, the poet's look was on the horizon. After my bold assertion of his mistake, I waited a long time in silence for reply. At last he straightened up, tightened the lines, started the mare at her best gait, and in the clear upper tone of his many-keyed voice, said "Alma, there is a good deal in what you say." I made no answer, but I was greatly elated, for I was weary of explaining to his opponents the large truth behind his words. Since he was then at our house revising the 1882 edition of his poems, I anticipated the omission of the objectionable particle of speech. But the poem remained unchanged by him, *A Woman Waits for Me*!

This reminds me of a gathering of writers in our library on the arrival of the news that Whitman's publishers, Fields and Osgood, had broken their contract with him. During his stay in Boston at the time of their acceptance of *Leaves of Grass*, he had written frequently to us of his enjoyment of the hospitality of Emerson, Alcott, Longfellow. His gratification deepened at the printing of the revised edition. "Everything is just as I like it," he wrote me in the long and descriptive epistle that preceded the postcard heralding his return to our house in New York. Then came the blow of disappointment: yet, though he was baffled, beaten, uncertain what his next move should be, he was the same cheery guest he had always been. His friends and admirers, however, were not so philosophical as he; they did not hesitate to condemn the stupidity, the treachery, the shortsighted policy of the "double-distilled villains" who would reject such poems as *A Woman Waits for Me*.

Nevertheless, there was some argument among them, as to whether, for the sake of the rest of the work, the eighty lines to which the publishers objected, had not better be sacrificed; whether they were really essential to the whole, or whether conventionality might not better be somewhat catered to, considering the spirit of the age. Since a double standard of morality for the sexes was almost universally accepted, might not the assumed modesty of society be somewhat indulged?—Or should it be defied?—A flood of words poured forth: the younger men left their seats and all talked at the same time; in the vehemence of their argument, they quite forgot the presence of the author of the contested lines. To me, as I stood shadowed in the hall, his face was a study. He turned his head toward one speaker after another, his manner quite impersonal, though deeply interested, while the discussion continued to deal with truth and his work until one of the young men broke out, "But what does Walt say? Let's hear from Walt!" Leaning forward, he cried in his clear, vibrant voice, "Why, boys, *that's* what it's all for!"

The matter was beyond argument; he had worked for truth alone; like a revelation they comprehended. He had long since declared: "I have read these lines to myself in the open air. I have tried them by stars, rivers. I have dismissed whatever insulted my own soul or defiled my body. I have claimed nothing for myself that I have not carefully claimed for others on the same terms." The decision had long before been rendered to himself; the judgment was now announced to others; there was no appeal. Each of the "Literary Chappies," as he smilingly called them, took Walt Whitman's hand in good-night clasp and quickly walked away.

Nothing so impressed me in all our intercourse as his *universality*: In all our familiar chats it seemed as if the Spirit of the Universe were represented. Large and small, strong and weak, sick and sound, wise and unwise, joyous and melancholy,—everything was included in his identity. In caressing our children, it was as if he embraced and kissed childhood; in addressing me, he spoke to womanhood.

In *Miriam's Heritage*, a story written by me before my marriage and published by Harper Brothers, a headline quotation from Whitman had, by a printer's error, been made to say, "Have I not said the Universe has nothing better than the best woman?" When I later showed him my work and lamely apoligised for what appeared a lack of comprehension of his lines "The Universe has nothing better

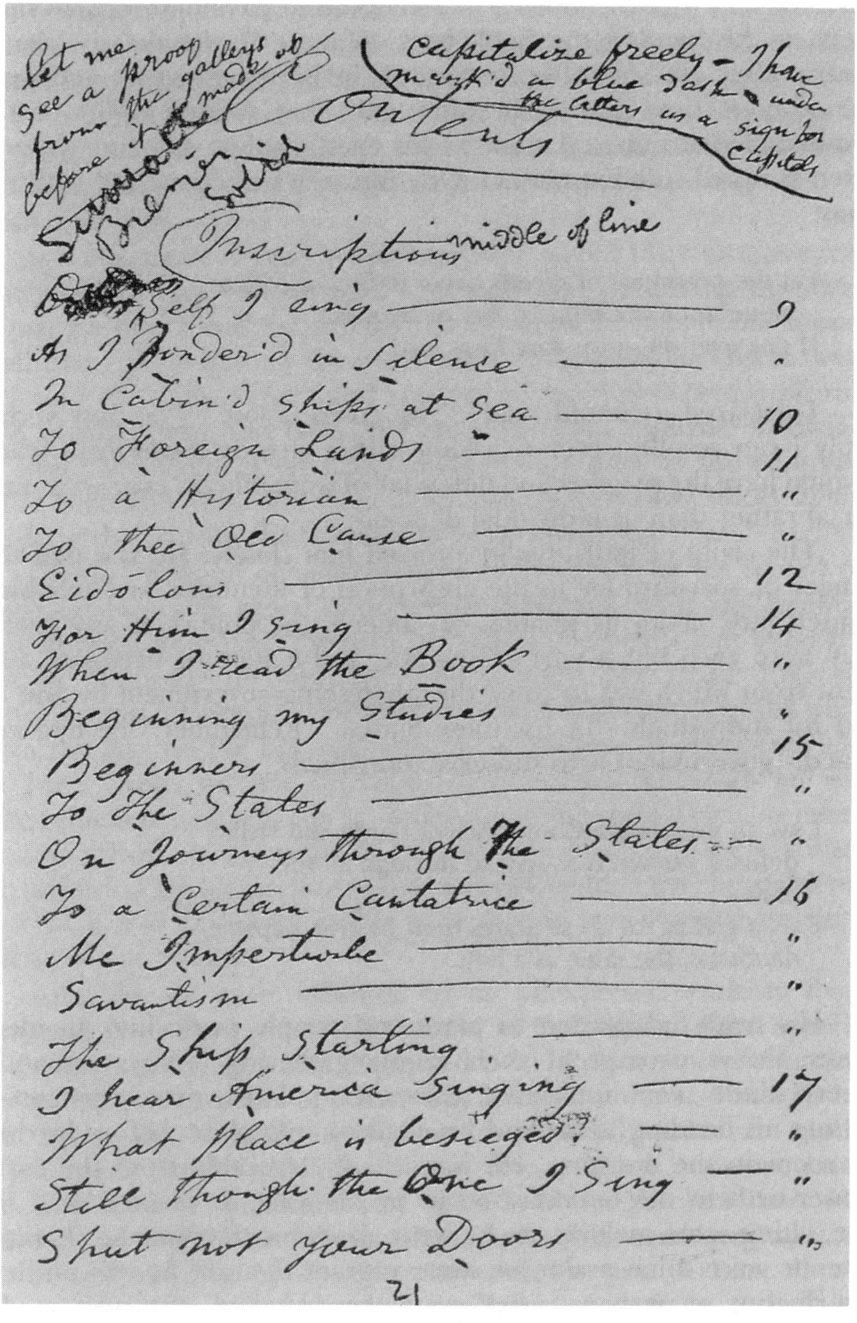
Let me see a proof from the galleys of before it is made up

Capitalize freely — I have mark'd a blue dash under the letters as a sign for Capitals

Contents

Inscriptions middle of line

One's-Self I sing —— 9
As I ponder'd in Silence —— "
In Cabin'd Ships at Sea —— 10
To Foreign Lands —— 11
To a Historian —— "
To thee Old Cause —— "
Eidólons —— 12
For Him I sing —— 14
When I read the Book —— "
Beginning my Studies —— "
Beginners —— 15
To The States —— "
On Journeys through the States —— "
To a Certain Cantatrice —— 16
Me Imperturbe —— "
Savantism —— "
The Ship Starting —— "
I hear America Singing —— 17
What place is besieged? —— "
Still though the One I Sing —— "
Shut not your Doors —— "

21

Whitman's manuscript contents page for Leaves of Grass *1881-1882*

than the best Womanhood," I was relieved to have him remark smilingly, as he handed the book back to me, "Maybe that is what I
meant, after all!" He often seemed to invite my criticism; and since
the severest fault-finding brought only that sudden uplift of the
brows and that quizzical smile to his eyes and lips, my audacity was
often tempted into expression. One instance was connected with the
lines:

> Let the preachers of creeds never dare to meditate
>   alone upon the hills, by day or by night!
> If one ever did once dare he is lost!

I declared it should read, "The creed is lost." The only verbal
reply I can recollect ever receiving is that already mentioned, when
I would have the prophet and defender of womanhood express its universal rather than its individual demand.

The claim of individuality pressed him closely. He saw that the
danger of socialism lay in the absorption of identities, and troubled
himself little about its politics, or, indeed, the politics of any party;
they were each but a part of the All, and a state of necessary ferment from which was to come the wholesome government by and of
and for individuals, "fit for these States." "Remember," he had en-
joined, "government is to subserve individuals."

> I say an unnumbered new race of hardy and well-
>   defined women is to spread through all the
>   States.
> I say a girl fit for these States must be free, capable,
>   dauntless, the same as a boy.

His ready adaptation to place and people made him an ideal
guest; always prompt at each family gathering, always radiantly
cheery, kindly, communicative; always scrupulously neat in person—
putting his bedding to air and his clothing into place, before leaving
his room in the morning. He was usually traceable from the early
shower-bath to the breakfast-room by his song. It seemed as if he
rose, lilting some melody. As he went about his chamber he chanted
in tenor voice some psalm, or some vagrant thought he was putting
into rhythm, or perhaps, a half-remembered ballad. His voice would
rise to exultancy, pause abruptly, or drop as suddenly to a low, murmured refrain, as the exigencies of dressing seemed to require atten-

tion. Occasionally he demanded help in a lusty call for "Al!"; whereupon Mr. Johnston, or his eldest son, Albert, would hasten to lend a youthful hand to the partially paralysed body, which had poured its vigour into the suffering soldiers of our Civil War. With his strength the poet had also spent all the money and time at his disposal; to give back what we could, in return for such sacrifices, was to us a happy privilege.

It is a pleasure to read in *Specimen Days* (page 113) Whitman's reference to this visit: "In old age, lame and sick, pondering for years on many a doubt and danger for this Republic of ours—fully aware of all that can be said on the other side—to find in this visit to New York and the daily contact and support of its myriad people on the scale of the ocean and tides, the best, the most effective medicine my soul has known. After many years (I went away at the outbreak of the Secession War, and have never been back to stay since), again I resume the crowds, the streets I know so well."

On the occasion of another visit, in the midst of his record of street scenes, water views, saunterings in Central Park, and meditations on what he called "top-loftical" phases of wealth—not to be envied or admired—he describes with graphic pen (page 136) his being a guest of Sorosis, when this earliest of women's clubs went down the Bay on the tug *Seth Low*, to accompany its president, Jennie June Croly, on her departure for Europe. Although he was quite reluctant to accept the invitation from the club, which, as member and officer, I had urged upon him, his pleasure at the gratification afforded by his presence, was unmistakable. Then he suddenly tired of it and retreated to the pilot house, remaining there until luncheon was served.

At table, we were delighted by an unexpected witticism from the Good Grey Poet when, in response to the demand for a speech, he declined to follow a Mrs. King and a Mr. Prince, since he himself was a plebeian! But the applause that greeted it drove him into his shell again, and he made no allusion to the social part of the trip in a newspaper article which he sent to me, entitled *A Gossipy Letter from Walt Whitman*, published July 3, 1878, in the *New York Times*. His habit of viewing "Walt Whitman" impersonally, made unexpected and undesired notice of himself embarrassing to him. To him, all persons, peoples, including himself, represented qualities, principles, types. He was enthusiastic over the appearance of the "young fellows" on board the training-ship *Minnesota*, as specimens of American manhood,—as "a splendid proof of our composite race." I wonder if there are now any of those youths who recall his visit on May 26, 1879!

About this time two accidents occurred at our house that might have tried his nerves. Entering his room one morning, I noticed an odour that made me sniff the air, saying, "Something has been burning here, and it is not tobacco!" (Walt Whitman never touched tobacco.) "I thought I smelled smoke when I got up to put out the light," he answered, rather ruefully, adding, "I read myself to sleep." "And I tell you what else you did, Uncle Walt," I responded, laughing. "You twisted the window curtain into a rope and tied it up as far as you could reach—oh, you've done that before!—and the wind tossed that knot over the gas globe, and away went that curtain in a flash!"

To see the embarrassed droop of his majestic figure, and the plaintive look, so child-like, on his dignified face, was irresistibly funny, and I laughed till he feebly joined me, as he looked up at the tinsel threads still hanging from the blackened gilt cornice. I assured him that I was glad he slept soundly, for had he seen that swift blaze he would have had a fright. "Now," I added, "we will have the piece of oriental gauze taken down from the other window, and you shall have the unveiled sunshine you love!"

The bric-a-brac and other ornaments of a guest-room, which he termed "gimcracks," had been removed before he came; now he gazed unhindered at the squatter settlement that reached to our vine-covered back-yard fence, and beyond that to the block-away terminus of the Fourth Avenue surface cars (which made going down town easy for him), and farther on, to the horizon, where sparsely filled squares stretched to the East River; all this lay unscreened before him. Goats, geese, chickens, and innumerable children wandered over the grass about a whitewashed cabin, which was always being undone and made over—a neat and not unpicturesque huddle of a dwelling, full of uncounted children, with whom we were sufficiently intimate to hail cheerily, when their doings were, or were not, to our liking, and who cheerily saluted the kindly old man who smiled and waved his hand to them from the open window.

The second accident came nearer being serious than the first. I was at my desk in a neighbouring room, when I heard a tremendous crash. Rushing through intervening doors and passages, I found Walt Whitman standing ashly white, and the huge pier-glass which had filled the space between the windows lying in a thousand fragments on the floor. In falling, it had struck the foot of the bed, the table, and the chair in which he had been sitting at his writing.

"You are not hurt? You are not hurt?" I kept gasping, while I looked at the heap of débris—the slivers of thick glass, the fragments of carved wood, the chunks of plaster of Paris—"You are not hurt?"

"No, no, not a bit! I heard it slip and jumped from under.

I don't see why it should fall!" *I* did. He had been using its supporting marble shelf for a foot-rest, just as the children not infrequently used it for a seat. I tried to smile, but turned faint, with thinking of what might have been! Getting his hat, I insisted on our leaving the house until the mess be cleaned up, and jestingly taking him by the shoulders, with a weak pretence at giving him a strong shake, I said, "It is plain to be seen you are a much nimbler old gentleman than we take you for. Now understand this, if you say one word about broken mirrors, or a third thing's going to happen, or even allude to such ideas as signs and omens, I shall call you a *superstitious old humbug!*"

At that time the residences on Fifth avenue ended abruptly at Eighty-sixth Street; just beyond, the grassy knolls of an old fruit orchard had become a rural beer garden. Leaning somewhat heavily on my shoulder, he crossed the street with me, and then, seated on one of the benches beneath a gnarled old apple-tree, we told each other stories of "when I was young," and from well-stored memories drew poems learned long ago. Robins hopping at our feet, and goats scrambling on the rocks above our heads, were our only observers. As sunlight faded, we returned to the house, where order had been restored. A water-colour scene on Long Island shore, by Silva, covered the broken spot in the wall where the mirror had hung. The incident, never mentioned, was apparently forgotten, and I am sure Walt Whitman enjoyed the simplicity thereafter established in his room.

On the occasion of his visits, there were usually other guests in the house, mostly young folks, who now proudly recall "the time they met Walt Whitman." Each evening, groups of personal friends and specially invited acquaintances, among them artists, actors, musicians, and writers, came and went. Whenever Whitman was weary of the admiration they gave him—and that was often early—he would rise with gentle dignity, wave a farewell and, leaning on his cane,

Walt Whitman, early 1880s (Feinberg Collection, Library of Congress)

leave the room. The guests would soon leave and the house be quiet for the night; as there was no traffic on the avenue, all was still until the vegetable wagons rolled in from the truck gardens not far out—and then we listened for the poet's morning song.

In each prolonged talk with Walt Whitman, when his exalted viewpoint had been attained, one had clearly the consciousness that "All exists from some long previous consummation." Not infrequently he turned to the vision of his telescopic soul to the future of America. In his later publications, I find many passages that were displayed to me in embryo. His largeness of view, his recognition of the "inherencies of things," and the consequent acceptance of events and reconciliation with them, became to me a lasting inspiration. No lines of his, no sentences ever recorded, mean more to me than these, which include and harmonise the Predestination of Calvin with the Free Will of Wesley: "Each of us inevitable," "Each of us limitless," in which the seeming fatalism is balanced by universality; and "Whatever can possibly happen at any time is provided for," which opened the way for that glorious declaration:

Though I come to my own in a thousand or ten million years,
I can take it now, or with equal cheerfulness I can wait.

It was waiting with his "equal cheerfulness" that, accompanied by Samuel Loag, of Philadelphia, I found him in the winter of 1885, in poverty, ill, and alone. The day was stormy, the streets were icy, and it was with great difficulty—in fact, after several full-length tumbles by us both—that we reached the house in Mickle Street, Camden.

Our first rap brought no response, but a second was answered by a voice from an upper window, calling, "Come in! Come in!" Looking up through the mist of the descending sleet, we saw the venerable face of Walt Whitman leaning out above us. His room, littered with more than the usual number of papers scattered about, was cold. The remains of a meal stood on a chair. I looked toward the armchair; above two blankets loomed the head I loved and revered. To keep back emotion, I made a great fuss about the general untidiness of the place, while Mr. Loag rebuilt the fire. It was already late afternoon and our time was short. I was glad I could manage to brew some tea, and equally delighted to make the old, slow, quizzical smile play again over his beloved face.

Then Mr. Loag and I began some serious questioning. "It is not so bad as it looks, Alma," the poet replied. "I have a nice young fellow coming in every morning to get me up and make breakfast, and he comes back every afternoon as soon as his bank closes and gets me my supper; and we have some good talks together, he and I. Don't think I'm deserted!"—for I was on my knees sobbing beside him. "I can't stand it, Uncle Walt. I will not! I am going to take you home with me!" But I found him, even though tearful in sympathy with my grief, quite inflexible. Life in New York had become too strenuous for him.

"Don't think I wouldn't enjoy it, but those literary chaps won't let me alone. It is all good, but there is too much of it! I'm a kind of curiosity in New York. Folks keep coming every day and every night to

271

see me, and it sort o' uses me up." The arched point in his brow, the whimsical smile, pacified me. "And here nobody bothers you by cleaning up!" I said, quite ashamed of my outburst. "Well, I will let you alone if you will have a housekeeper." After some arguing, he consented, and soon was made comfortable for the remainder of his days; for it was ignorace of his condition and not indifference that had caused temporary neglect. Not long afterward, I met the "nice young fellow," Horace Traubel, who so faithfully ministered to Walt Whitman in his hours of greatest need.

A letter lies before me written in the poet's large, open hand, and dated.

328 Mickle Street,
Camden, N.J.,

March 4, '85.

Dear, Dear Friends:

Your letter comforts and touches me deeply, and I am not sure but it would be a good arrangement not only for me but for all 'round. But for the present I shall keep on here. Alma, I have had a friend move in, Mrs. Davis, strong and hearty and good-natured, a widow, young enough; furnishes me my meals and takes good care of me. . . . I am feeling quite well for me as I write this. I shall never forget your kindness and generosity to me. I am in good spirits as I finish this. Love to Al. and May, and all.

Walt Whitman.

I visited him repeatedly while Mary Davis devoted herself to his care. He enjoyed being the host, and I ate of his corned beef and cabbage and berry pie with good relish. At my last visit, he sat by the window of his sitting-room in the arm-chair he afterward willed to us. He was then very feeble. We had talked disconnectedly—with eloquent pauses—of immortality, of the indestructibility of things physical and things spiritual; of "things that cohere and go forward and are not dropped by death"; of Death disassociated from disease as Life is ever disassociated with disease; of Death as feminine, a Strong Deliveress. Yet we were not unmindful of the insight, the comprehension, the experiences, that weakness and pain bring to the Soul, and so accounted valuable a long and intimate acquaintance with Death—familiar contemplation giving new knowledge of Life.

"I do not know what is untried and afterward," I quoted, "but I know that it is sure, alive, sufficient." He nodded his head. I rose to leave him. We knew our hands clasped and our lips touched for the last time. When I left home, I had resolved there should be no tears. "My rendezvous is appointed," I murmured, as I kissed him. "The Lord will be there and wait till I come on perfect terms."

Pausing on the opposite sidewalk, I returned the salute of his hand, uplifted in the open window. The horse-car came. It was empty, and the woman of me broke down! Struggling with hankerchief and purse, I yet glanced at the conductor's face. He brushed the back of his hand across his eyes.

"You've been a-sayin' good-bye to Walt Whitman? I know him," he said.

Bookman, 46 (December 1917): 404-413.

REMINISCENCES OF
WALT WHITMAN

Helen E. Price

These recollections expand on those which Helen E. Price contributed to Bucke's 1883 book.

When I first met Walt Whitman, he was calling on my mother, who had been introduced to him a short time before by a mutual friend.

It was about a year after the first editon of "Leaves of Grass," which appeared in 1855. Although a young man at the time, his hair and beard cut short, he was quite gray, but his unwrinkled face and fresh, clear complexion gave the impression of youth somewhat incongruous with his gray hair.

I was then a girl of fifteen just entering my most impressionable years, and the charm of his voice, manner, and personality as it affected my girlish imagination is best described by these lines:

> He sits 'mongst men like a descended God,
> He hath a kind of honor sets him off
> More than a mortal seeming

In the early eighties I wrote for Dr. Bucke's book at his request some reminiscences of Walt Whitman, which I showed to him before the book was published. He and the doctor were stopping with my folks living at Woodside, on their way to visit his birthplace in Huntington, L.I. I was, of course, hoping for his approval of my notes.

"Well, H——," he said kindly, as he handed them back to me, "I have the same fault to find with them that I have to what Dr. Bucke has written about me: *You make me too pretty.*" If we had accused him of all the crimes in the calendar (I think he has confessed to many of them), probably he would have accepted what we had written without a protest, but to be made "too pretty," that was the one great and unpardonable offence. These later notes that I now write will, I fear, be under the same ban, but if I write about him at all I cannot do otherwise than to represent the man as he appeared to me, not only in his home, where I was a frequent visitor (his mother being my very dear friend), but as a member of my own family when on his vacations from Washington.

There was one passage in my former recollections that Dr. Bucke took exception to, saying that I must have reported Walt wrong or had mistaken his meaning. Although Mr. Whitman had made no comment when he read my notes over before, except what I have just related, to satisfy Dr. Burke I gave them to him again with special reference to the undisputed passage. It was this:

"He once—I forget what we were talking about; friendship I think—said that there was a wonderful depth of meaning at second or third removes, as he expressed it, in the old tales of mythology. That of Cupid and Psyche, for instance: it meant to him that the ardent expression of affection in his words often tended to destroy it. It was like the golden fruit which turned to ashes upon being grasped or even touched.

"As an illustration he told of the case of a young man whom he was in the habit of meeting every morning where he went to work.

"He said there had grown up between them a delightful, silent friendship and sympathy. But one morning when he went to the office the young man came forward, shook him violently by the hand and expressed in heated language the affection he felt for him.

"All the subtle charm of their unspoken friendship was from that time gone."

"That is all right, doctor," Walt said; "H— has got it right."

I was glad to have his personal endorsement of the above passage, for self-revealing as his poems are in many respects, he was an undemonstrative, reserved, and reticent man in things that lay deepest within him. In the early days of our acquaintance with him, which rapidly grew to intimacy, my mother once asked him if he had ever been in love. After a long pause he answered somewhat reluctantly, I thought, "Your question, Abby, *stirs a fellow up*." Although he would not admit that he had ever been "really in love," he took from his pocket a photograph of a very beautiful girl (remember, he was still in his thirties) and showed it to us. That is all we ever knew about the original of the picture either then or afterwards, but I well remember the girl's exceptional beauty.

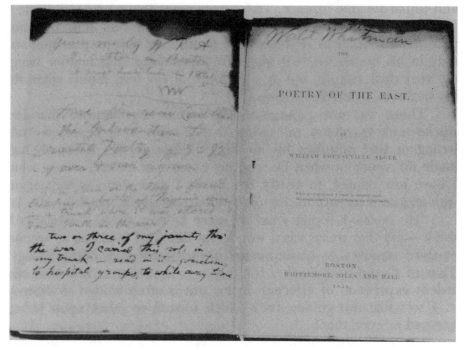

Whitman's copy of the The Poetry of the East

I feel sure that in his passionate revolt against dilettantism and prettiness in the American literature of the day no expression given to the vital forces so evident in the great masses of the common people who make the greatness of America is responsible for the coarseness apparent in his earlier writings; the one extreme was as untrue to his nature as the other. Be that as it may, I never saw the slightest hint of coarseness or vulgarity in him during our long years of intimate friendship.

He also describes himself as "one of the roughs." Surely that word is a misnomer. It does not apply to the man as I knew him. His quiet, gentle manner, his unfailing sympathy and consideration for others, his intuitive tact, marked him for me as one of the truest gentlemen in the best meaning of that word that I have ever known.

If this is making him "too pretty," I cannot help it. Unconventional he certainly was, as the following incident will show:

On one of his calls to us in New York, I chanced to remark that I intended to spend the following week with some friends living in another part of the city. Somewhat to my surprise, and of course my pleasure, he said that he would come and see me while I was there. It so happened that the evening he came, an intimate friend of the family, too, was temporarily stopping with them.

Although an active business man, all Mr. B—'s leisure time was devoted to music. He possessed a fine baritone voice, and a piano being in the room where we were sitting, he was drawn to it as by a magnet. Unfortunately, as I thought, a book of comic songs lay upon it ready at his hand. And on opening it he began singing the songs he knew and attempting others that he was not familiar with. I sat near him and when I could be heard, I would ask, "Please, Mr. B—, sing 'Rocked in the Cradle of the Deep'; I wanted Mr. Whitman to hear it." It seemed to me in my impatience that he would never come to the end of that book of comic songs, but at last he laid it aside and hunted through a pile of sheet music for the song I had so persistently asked for. I have already stated in my former reminiscences what I considered to be Mr. Whitman's leading characteristic: his religious sentiment and feeling. It even dominated his boundless sympathy with every form of suffering and also his passionate love for America and humanity. As he once wrote of himself, he was a "born exalté." Therefore his whole soul responded to that song.

He threw back his head during the singing, utterly lost to all his surroundings. When it ceased, he slowly awakened as out of a trance, and turning to me he said "H—, I thank you for asking for that song."

Walt Whitman was a vain man in small matters that did not count, and also capable of great and perhaps, at times, of unreasonable anger. I know this, as through a misunderstanding I once unhappily incurred his displeasure.

He was also stubborn. When he made up his mind to a certain course of action, it was as futile to attempt to change it as it would be to try to move the Rock of Gibraltar. A friend of my mother's, an old lady called upon him soon after the publication of the second edition of "Leaves of Grass." She suggested leaving out a few lines in one or two of his poems. He brought his clenched fist down upon his knee with these words, "I will have it so." But admitting this fault, if fault it was, I never knew any one more ready to listen to what others might have to say upon any subject under discussion. He seemed to be more anxious to see their point of view than to express his own. It was a pleasure somewhat rare to find a listener who, as Emerson puts it, "entertains your thought."

When we first knew him, before the contraction of his first name became so common, he told us of a stranger who came up to him, and clapping him on the shoulder said: "Well, Walt, how are you?" He evidently resented the familiarity, and one of us asked him if he liked being called by his first name or its contraction. "No," he said, "not by strangers, but I want my friends to call me so; you all and the girls also." My sister was only thirteen at the time. Incidentally I will add that I never heard his mother call him "Walt." To her he was always "Walter."

Although personal cleanliness was almost an obsession with him, he was not an orderly man. Curtains were his abomination. I would go into his room (he was living with us at the time) to put it in order, and find them twisted into ropes and drawn back as far as possible. We finally took them down to save him the bother of attempting to eliminate them.

In the room would be papers strewn about everywhere. Letters, cuttings, scraps on which would be words, lines and sometimes a page of manuscript. In the choice of words he was exceedingly particular and fastidious. A list of half a dozen or so I would find on one of the paper scraps of the same general meaning, though each word would have a subtle difference of its own.

In conversation also he was anxiously careful to get the right word to express the thought he wished to convey. But on occasions, especially during the Civil War, his intense interest in its progress and outcome acted as a stimulus and then he was really eloquent, the words coming forth rapidly and easily. Ordinarily he was somewhat slow and hesitant in his speech, owing to his careful selection of words.

As a member of our family he was more than a welcome guest. It was a joy to us all to have him with us. He entered into our home life with so much interest and sympathy. Self-assertive as he appears to be in his poems, he was never so in social and private life. Although rather silent than otherwise, he made us feel that he was glad to be with us, and in talking with my mother he took especial pleasure. It is rather surprising to those who knew him best to have the critics deny him a sense of humor. His letters and conversation showed how false was such a charge.

He also appreciated it in others. I think it was that sense, or at least it was one of the factors, that saved him from being greatly affected by the heavy onslaughts that were made by the critics upon his book when if first appeared. I was told by one of the young literati that frequented Phaff's in those days (Bohemians as they were then called) that when he entered their circle some one would greet him with a quotation from an article written by one of the aforesaid critics: "Here comes the unclean cub of the Wilderness." He would smile in his slow, quiet way as he took his seat among them.

He would sometimes tell us of amusing incidents that happened to himself and others. I remember a story that he once told us about his brother George. His mother sent him to the grocery for some coffee. When he returned and put his hand in his pocket to give her the coffee, only the paper in which it was wrapped came forth. His look of amazement and chagrin; the thought of his leaving a trail of coffee behind him on his way home; his sheepish look at his mother to see how she took its loss, was all very ludicrous, and Walt evidently enjoyed telling the story as a good joke on brother George. A tear in the paper wrapper and a hole in his pocket explained the disappearance.

Mr. Otis Parker was postmaster in Monument, Mass., in the early sixties. While occupying this office he was arrested and convicted of robbing the mails. His sentence was for five years. He had borne an irreproachable character heretofore, was respected and even loved by his associates and neighbors. Of the seven counts of the indictment, he was found guilty of one only. I do not think I ever knew the details of his trial and only remember that fact. His niece was a very dear friend of my mother's and on one of her frequent visits to us she told her of the dreadful fate that had befallen "Uncle Otis." She knew, she said, that the authorities had convicted and sent to prison an innocent man. His family were heart-broken over his misfortune, but they were poor and had no money or influence to fight what they considered to be an unjust verdict. Her uncle, the niece said, was slowly dying of the confinement and disgrace of his imprisonment.

My mother, always sympathetic in others' troubles, and especially so when one of her dearest friends was the sufferer, thought of our friend Walt, then in the Attorney-General's office in Washington. Maybe he could do something to shorten the sentence. When he came on one of his vacations from Washington, the case was laid be-

Whitman's letter of 12 April 1882 to James R. Osgood and Company about the suppression of Leaves of Grass (Feinberg Collection, Library of Congress)

fore him. He was interested at once, and the record of the trial was brought to him by Mr. Parker's daughter, Miss Aurelia Parker. He was surprised in looking it over to find a very slight foundation for the verdict of guilty and promised most willingly to take the matter in hand on his return to Washington. Here is his letter written to my mother after his return.

> Attorney-General 's Office
> Washington,
> Oct. 27, 1866.

Mrs. Price & all,
My dear friends:

    I sent you a telegram ten minutes ago, telling you that I have just succeeded in getting an order from the Attorney-General for Mr. Parker's pardon. The pardon will probably go from here, (from the State Department), on Monday next—the day you will receive this note—it will be directed to the jail at Plymouth. I have had much more of a struggle than I anticipated—the pardon clerk knew the case, and was filled with Mr. Dana's[1] reports upon it. When we meet (or perhaps by letter, before) I will give you a more detailed account of the progress of the affair here, & its fluctuations. But no matter—it has ended successfully.

    I have written to Aurelia Parker and sent the news the same mail as this.

> WALT

Mr. Whitman received no compensation for his efforts in Mr. Parker's behalf except his satisfaction in restoring to his grief-stricken family a broken and dying man. Mr. Parker lived less than a year after he regained his freedom.

It was my impression in my frequent visits to his mother that those of Walt Whitman's family that I met there took little interest in his book, although they were devoted to him as he to them.

My mother once called upon Mrs. Whitman and read to her Walt's latest poem, "The Mystic Trumpeter." She told my mother that she had read it but did not understand it. She was not an educated woman but she possessed what was far better than anything books could give her. One felt in her quiet, undemonstrative manner a tender, loving sympathy, a cheerful, uncomplaining spirit, although she had led far from an easy life, and a charm that made it a delight to be with her.

At her funeral a gathering of thirty of more persons were sitting in the front room of the little cottage in Camden waiting for the services to begin. On taking my seat among them, I noticed a curious thumping at intervals that made the floor vibrate beneath my feet. I was so absorbed in my own grief that at first I was hardly conscious of it. I finally left my chair, and going to the back of the room where we were sitting, I noticed a half-opened door leading to another room. Glancing in, I saw the poet all alone by the side of his mother's coffin. He was bent over his cane, both hands clasped upon it, and from time to time he would lift it and bring it down with a heavy thud on the floor. His sister-in-law told me that he had sat there all through the previous night. Here is an extract from a letter written to us, referring to one of condolence on his mother's death that he had received:

Dear H—:

If you see Miss B— tell her that I received her letter and thank her for it. I have not felt to write to her or any one but my sisters on Mother's death. The great dark cloud of my life—the only staggering staying blow and trouble I have had but unspeakable. My physical sickness bad as it is—is nothing to it.

New York Evening Post Book Review, 31 May 1919, p. 2.

1. Hon. Richard H. Dana, District Attorney at the time of Mr. Parker's conviction.

PERSONAL RECOLLECTIONS
OF WALT WHITMAN

William Roscoe Thayer

William Roscoe Thayer was one of the few people who were frankly skeptical of Whitman, and his account has added value for this fact.

I first came to know Walt Whitman in 1885, when he was sixty-six years old. I have been living for several years in Philadelphia, where Whitman, who had a little home in Camden, across the Delaware, was a conspicuous figure. One used to see him of an afternoon shuffling down Chestnut Street, a man so unusual that even if he had not dressed to attract attention, you would not have passed him by unnoticed. Although he leaned somewhat sideways owing to his crippled leg, he must have stood nearly or quite six feet tall. His shoulders were broad, and neither age nor infirmity had broken down the original robustness of his frame. But what impressed you most was his face, with its fresh, pink skin, as of a child, and the flowing beard, white and soft and patriarchal, like that of one of John Bellini's saints. He wore a gray suit—sack coat, waistcoat, and trousers—which might have been of homespun—but was not, and a white unstarched shirt with collar carefully turned over on either side and unbuttoned, so that you saw his sinewy throat and a span below it of his chest, which also had its fledge of whitening hair. The broad brim of his soft, gray, felt hat shaded his eyes so that you were not sure whether they were light blue or gray, but you could not miss seeing the perfect arch of the brow over each of their sockets.

And so Walt made his slow progress down the street, dragging his lame foot along with a shuffling sound, and supporting himself on his stout stick. This was his parade. Nearly every one knew who he was; many nodded or said, "Hullo, Walt!" and now and then some pal or acquaintance would stop and speak to him. He answered all salutations cheerily and looked at the throngs which swept toward him with the same searching interest with which in earlier days he had scrutinized the crowds on the Brooklyn ferry-boats. His eyes were dimmer now, but his heart kept its old zest. Occasionally, he would stop to peer into a window or to make a brief call at some ship where he had a crony. Sometimes you ran upon him at the little musty old bookstore of David McKay, on Ninth Street above Chestnut. McKay, an enterprising Scot, had undertaken to publish Walt's books after the attorney-general of Massachusetts declared them to be unfit for the readers of that Commonwealth, and Osgood, the Boston publisher, had hastily thrown them over. McKay, I think, would have welcomed further persecutions as an advertising asset.

Having finished his outing and received his homage for the day, Walt got into a street-car—they were horse-cars then—and went down to the Market Street Ferry, which carried him back to Camden.

From the first, I looked at him in these casual sidewalk passings with much curiosity; for I have always been eager to see the very form, complexion, and bearing of persons who for any reason have won notoriety if not greatness. In Walt's case there was something of the added piquance of forbidden fruit. I had grown up in the belief that he was a strangely dissolute man who, unlike most of his tribe, shamelessly spread the records of his debauches on the printed page. Nobody had forbidden me to read him; and at college I had dipped into "Leaves of Grass," but in the spirit of one looking for confirmation of an unintelligent prejudice, and I found the uncouthness of Walt's so-called verse intolerable. The utter openness of the passages which had stirred the attorney-general were, I had sense enough to see, not deliberately erotic, but physiological, an offense against taste rather than morals.

It happened that I spent an August Sunday down at Wallingford with Dr. Horace Howard Furness, an old friend of mine, or at least one whose human kindness was so genuine and so winning that it made even a young fellow like me feel that we were friends. At any rate, so far as expressing opinions went, I spoke quite freely, and he listened with a wonderful courtesy to what must have often seemed to him—with all of Shakespeare's characters for interlocutors—crude if not callow.

Dr. Furness himself was one of those rare persons who produce an impression on those who know them that cannot be communi-

To proof reader — please read very carefully by copy.
follow punctuation &c.

The Dead Carlyle

Not for his merely literary merit, (though that was great) — not as "maker of books," but as launching into the self complacent atmosphere of our days a rasping, questioning, dislocating agitation and shock, is the man's final value. It is time the English-speaking peoples had some true idea about the verteber of genius, namely power. As if they must always have it cut and biased to the fashion, like a lady's cloak! lacking. needed contain 1 book.

His mantle is unfallen. We certainly have no one left like him. I doubt if any nation of the world has.

Walt Whitman

Portion of Whitman's manuscript of "The Dead Carlyle"

cated in writing—an impression immediate, sweet and yet vigorous, almost elusive at the moment, but indelible in memory. He was then a man of fifty one or two, short, with rather a large head already bald, a smooth-shaven face, except for the closely trimmed mustache, a Roman nose, and scholar's brow. Through his gold-rimmed spectacles he looked at you hospitably with that expectancy common to the deaf, and his mouth, too, serious when in repose, quickly lighted up with a smile when he welcomed you, or listened to your talk. He used to sit astride of a chair, leaning his left elbow on its top, where he had contrived a box with a lid for his pipe and tobacco—and having placed you as near as possible in front of him, and lighted your pipe and his, he would hold toward you his beaten-silver ear-trumpet. And then the talk would begin, and as you listened, you took little note of time.

That Sunday we rambled for hours among many fields of literature, he leading, I following, in that unpremeditated way which is one of the conditions of delightful conversation. By chance Whitman was mentioned. "Do you know Walt?" Dr. Furness asked. "No," I replied; "I've often seen him on Chestnut Street and I have dipped into his 'Leaves of Grass,' but the stuff isn't poetry, and I don't like his dirt and vulgarity." "That is only a part and not the most important part of it," said Dr. Furness, in substance. "In his way, Walt is the most remarkable old creature alive. There will not be another like him in five hundred years. Go and see him. Talk with him."

Dr. Furness got up, went to a shelf, took down a volume, came back and opened it.

"As for poetry, my boy, listen to this." And then he read to me from "Leaves" a dozen or fifteen lines beginning:

I am he that walks with the tender and growing night.

When he finished, he paused a moment, waiting for the rich sounds to soak in, and then said: "Whether you call it poetry or not, that is great."

Dr. Furness was a reader of such magical power that I believe he could have made you laugh or cry at will over a time-table. His voice was not massive, nor had it in high degree the ventriloquizing quality which enable dramatic readers to feign different parts; but there were in it certain notes of surpassing tenderness and pathos and others of passion, which fitted it perfectly to express the mingling of personal desire and cosmic emotion in that passage from Whitman.

A few days later I took the ferry to Camden, a town which, so far as one could judge from its water-front, was an unlikely abode for even a minor poet. A few minutes' walk across railroad-tracks brought me to Mickle Street, on which Whitman lived. It was a street of small, cheap houses, some of them serving both as little stores and dwellings, with here and there a larger building and, at a street-corner, a beer-saloon. An occasional tree, lean and starved and homesick-looking, threw a feeble shade on the sidewalk and gave the only hint of nature to that scene. Poor but respectable, with a suggestion that unrespectability was just around the corner, is the impression I recall of Mickle Street. Number 328 was only a few blocks away. I still remember the trepidation with which I approached it, for I have always felt shy at breaking in uninvited on a celebrity. At the last moment, before ringing the bell, a sense of the absurdity and the impertinence of the situation came over me. What had I to say to him? I could not flatter him. It would hardly be polite to admit that I came out of curiosity. I certainly did not go merely to boast afterward that I had shaken his hand. My real motive was that of the naturalist, who wishes to see with his own eyes a unique specimen of mammal, but I could not with delicacy intimate to him that I regarded him as if he were a freak in our fauna. Afterward, on knowing Walt, I saw that he was the last person in the world to justify such hesitation, for he laid himself out to be a show, and he would have been disappointed if he had failed to draw. He did not ask why you came, if only you came.

So I rang the bell and prepared to take the consequences.

Soon afterward, fresh from the adventure, I wrote to a friend the following description of it, which has at least whatever merit may attach to very vivid first impressions. I reprint it as written, with the signs of haste and the youthful effort to draw a speaking likeness upon it.

Union League, Philadelphia,
August 2, 1885.

While the recollection of it is still fresh I want to give you a description of an hour I spent one day last week with the most singular personage among American writers. Do you guess whom I mean! or shall I tell you?—Walt Whitman. The afternoon was hot and bright and as I crossed the Delaware by ferry to Camden and walked along the straight, level streets I wondered what I should say in explanation of my intrusion, but as soon as I reached the house I lost my perplexity. Even the exterior of Whitman's home, situated at 328 Mickle Street, is simple and friendly enough to dispel formality. The house, or rather cottage, is only two stories high and less than five paces wide. It is of wood, and is shaded by a tree on the sidewalk. The front door was open, and when I rang, a comely housekeeper opened an inside summer door, through the slats of which I had already seen her ironing at the end of a corridor.

I asked if Mr. Whitman was able to see visitors—he had had a slight sunstroke a few days before—and she said: "Certainly." Having seated me in the little parlor—a sort of double room, the back part of which does service as a chamber, being furnished with a bed and a few wooden chairs—she disappeared, and presently I heard rumbling as of slow movements overhead. I looked at the things about me—all simple, neat, and cosey—and felt half-ashamed to have disturbed the old man. Soon I heard shuffling steps and the regular clacking of a stick on the entry floor, and in a moment Whitman moved into sight through the doorway. Very cordial was his handshake, and ere I had made a short apology for interrupting him, his "Glad to see yer" put me quite at ease. He sat in a wicker-bottomed rocking-chair near one window, and I about six feet from him near the other.

I wish I could draw him for you, because if there be to-day a patriarchal-looking man, it is he. His hair and beard are long and very white. His head on the top is egg-shaped, and a not very high forehead stretches down to the bushy eyebrows, in which white and black hairs struggle for prominence. His nose is large, straight, and rather flat, with perhaps a Roman tendency which is buried in the drifts of fleecy hair that cover all the lower parts of his cheeks and the face. His eyes are blue, clear and kindly, set in thin almond lids which are so narrow that barely half of each iris is seen. Beneath, the flesh grows in little folds and wrinkles, which are never deep and stiff like those made by suffering or worry. His skin is rosy and as healthy as a child's. He wore a starched cotton shirt, whose broad collar was not fastened at the neck but was left open, exposing the chest. Trousers, that might have been of homespun, and stockings were of his favorite gray color; and worsted-worked slippers completed his dress.

His expression has benignity, tranquility, and contentment. You miss the deep-set eyes and the aggressive manner that you associate with men of passionate or profound genius; but you have the embodiment of the kindly, receptive nature, which is placid, observant, and interested in whatever person or subject is before it.

We soon fell into an easy conversation, in which he showed no wish to take the lion's share, or to utter wise saws. He spoke deliberately, often waiting for a word or a clause, and without any affectation, so far as I noticed.

He asked me whether I had not written him two years ago in regard to a letter which he had received from Sidney Lanier. I answered yes, surprised at his good memory. He said that he had never replied because when my letter reached him he was ill, but that he had found Lanier's letter and marked it to send to me, but that it got displaced again among his disorderly papers. Lanier, he said, wrote "a florid, gushing" letter, and Whitman evidently did not put a high value on him.

After a while we talked about Whitman's own work. I told him frankly that while many parts of his "Leaves of Grass" had given me pleasure, I did not agree with him as to the propriety of publishing in a volume of poetry certain passages that belong in a handbook of physiology. He listened carefully, and replied: "You may be right. Many excellent thinkers hold your opinion. I, however, have always believed the contrary. Now, among the Arabs, if any man should suggest that the absurd custom of veiling the faces of women be abolished, he would be denounced as immoral or as mad. I believe in unveiling. This is the age of *exposé*. Darwinism makes *exposé* in everything necessary. When I think how Darwin was abused before the world came round to his side, I see that it is possible that I may live long enough to behold a similar result in my case. And what makes me hopeful is the fact that of late years there has been an increasing number of pure, fine women, old and young, amongst my warmest friends. You know when doctors can bring a disease to the surface they are satisfied, but if it remain hidden inside, the prospect is very bad. Still, I recognize there are grave objections. But my doctor forbade me to get into a critical or fatiguing discussion."

So I changed the subject—not wishing to induce a stroke of apoplexy—and mentioned that I hoped some time to write a history of the struggle of the Italians for independence. He seemed interested: asked many pertinent questions, about the characters of the Italians, the pope—whose influence he thought was slight—and about Dante. He had read the "Divine Comedy" in Carlyle's translation and in Longfellow's but he could not quite understand Dante's great position among poets and in the history of Italy. "But I feel sure," he said, "that the trouble lies with me. I haven't got the right clew. If I knew more it would be clear to me." This was his attitude through all our talk. He made no hasty conclusion, but habitually spoke as if he had not yet sufficient data for arriving at a decisive judgment.

I asked him if among the younger brood of writers he saw encouraging symptoms. "I hardly see anybody to tie to," he answered. "But there's plenty of time. America knows what she's about. We must first clear up the farm, and put things in order—the rest will come later. I can't help thinking that in the past, too, America knew what she was about. If I were a young man, I probably should not go preaching to mankind that they are a good deal better than they've been taught to believe—but as an old man that's my firm belief. In old times the idea was that humanity couldn't be trusted. Perhaps the disparagement acted as a sort of spur to make men do better than they would have done otherwise. Now, however, I put my faith in humanity. Even unconsciously, the great bards seem to teach the same truth. America will produce what she needs in good time. We mustn't be too critical. We're critical of the weather, for instance, but at the end of the year the weather has done its proper work. I don't value the poetry in what I have written so much as the teaching; the poetry is only a horse for the other to ride."

Before I left, he promised to send me Lanier's letter as soon as he should find it. I might repeat more that he said—although his ideas and not his words remain in my mind, and what I have given rarely represents his actual words—but I have already furnished you a fair report. What I have not furnished is the patriarchal look, the simple manners, the placidity which bespoke the genial character. This old man, partly paralyzed, very poor, lives undisturbed on the edge of a busy world, which he watches, and has a fellow feeling for everybody. I shall long remember him with his white fleece, pink complexion, and friendliness. If he has not taught others wisdom by his disjointed, *devertebrated* effusions, he has certainly found wisdom for himself.

I soon called on Walt again, and although I quitted Philadelphia that autumn, I frequently returned there and never missed going over to Camden for a chat with him. I kept no notes of our talk, but much that he said remains vividly in my memory, and I will set it down here in the miscellaneous fashion which was particularly characteristic of his conversation.

One could not talk with him for five minutes without being struck by two qualities—his rare gift of discerning natural objects, and the ease with which he seemed to improvise opinions on intellectual matters. Except for a few fundamental ideas, which form the substance of his "message" or doctrine, he was not an orderly thinker at all. His mind was like a barberry-bush which catches wisps of wool

Farringford,
Freshwater,
Isle of Wight.

Dear old man,

I the elder old man have received your Article in the Critic, & send you in return my Thanks & New-Years greeting on the wings of this East-wind, which, I trust, is blowing softlier & warmlier on your good gray head than here, where it is rocking the elms & ilexes of my Isle of Wight garden.

Yours always

Tennyson

Jany 15th

1887

Alfred, Lord Tennyson's letter of 15 January 1887 to Whitman (Feinberg Collection, Library of Congress)

from every sheep that passes, as Lowell somewhere said of some one else; and at times it seemed to me that Walt was no more able than the barberry-bush would be to assimilate the stray catches. He was unconcerned to hunt for an opinion, if one did not come readily to his mind, and he announced frankly his lack of knowledge or interest and changed the subject.

Walt did not always care to admit the sources from which he borrowed freely. One day, for instance, he talked about Shakespeare's historical plays, which, he said, showed that Shakespeare was at heart a democrat, and that he had written the plays in order to discredit monarchy and kings and the robber barons, and all that other old feudal nonsense. I discovered afterward that he had appropriated this fantastic notion from his own staunch champion, William D. O'Connor.

On another occasion he criticised Ruskin quite in the manner of one who had read widely in Ruskin's books; but when my eyes caught sight of a small paper-covered "Ruskin Anthology" on the little table beside me, I knew what had inspired him.

Once I said to him: "Walt, in 'Leaves of Grass' you have the air of a rough-and-tumble fellow who despises the well-to-do, mannerly people, and especially the learned and literary. And yet your writings are sprinkled with foreign words (somewhat Whitmanized) and with unexpected references to scientific and other subjects which we don't at first associate you with."

"The fact is," Walt replied, "I used to read all the quarterlies and magazines I could lay my hands on. I read 'em straight through; and so I stored up in my memory all sorts of odds and ends, which I pulled out and used whenever they came in handy."

Being myself already saturated with Emerson, and persuaded that the essence of Walt's gospel of Americanism, and democracy, and, above all, of the supreme value of the individual had been proclaimed by Emerson in imperishable pages long before Walt began his "Leaves of Grass," I was curious from the outset to see whether he would acknowledge any obligations. My own theory was and is that somewhere in the late forties Walt came upon Emerson's "Essays," devoured and absorbed them, found in them a revelation which interpreted American life to him, and deliberately adopted the teachings as if they had been original with himself. When he came to write, he put them in his own language, laying emphasis on this or that particular which most appealed to him, and giving free rein to his wonderful pictorial talent. And just as the disciple usually exaggerates or distorts some non-essential in his master's teaching, so Walt, bent on glorifying the individual, no matter how insignificant as if it were the finest gold of the spirit.

At one time, when I was wrestling with the old serpents of fatalism and evil, it occurred to me to go over and consult Walt. Ought not he, if any one, with his genial poise and his apparent acceptance of whatever fortune brought him, to solve these insistent questions?

I attacked him rather too suddenly, in the stand-and-deliver fashion of a much-perplexed visitor at the Delphic oracle, craving an immediate reply. I asked him how he explained this terrible reality of evil, when the burden of every page of "Leaves of Grass" and of his other writings and sayings was: "Life's all right." And I began to cite the misery—whether of body or of soul—the pain and sorrow and sin and injustice—from which nobody escapes.

He did not let me go on long, but showed a little impatience, and replied almost testily: "Oh, you can't tackle it that way! This ain't a matter to be settled by yes or no. What you call evil is all a part of it. If you have a hill, you've got to have a hollow. I wish some one—I've often thought of doing it myself—would crack up the good of evil—how it helps us along—how it all fits in."

"That is just what Emerson once said," I interrupted.

"Did he?" said Walt, with what seemed to me unexpected interest. "Did he? Where did he say that?"

I told him the essay which contains the well-known passage, and I think I also quoted the familiar "Evil is good in the making." It seemed to me that Walt was uncomfortable, as if I had unwittingly startled him into furnishing the clew to his inspiration; and whenever in subsequent talks I referred to Emerson's ideas, I thought that he feigned ignorance of them. In early manhood, he made no secret of his discipleship to Emerson, whom he called "master" in a famous letter. He sent one of the first copies of "Leaves of Grass" to Emerson, violated common propriety by printing in the New York *Tribune* Emerson's commendation and by stamping a sentence from it on the next edition of the "Leaves." Later, when he came to be accepted himself as a prophet, I suspect that he was glad to forget that he had ever called any one "master." In my frontal attack on the problem of evil, I made no further progress with Walt that day or later. He was neither a philospher nor a theologian and I doubt whether he had ever felt the problem poignantly. For practical living he found it wise to turn away from or to dodge the grisly questions which challenged too rudely his pantheistic optimism.

"Music helps better the argument," he said to me; "music soothes us, and, like a mother, draws us to her breast, and we fall asleep and we forget our difficulties."

Then I began to perceive that morals, in the deepest sense, did not exist for Whitman. In deifying the Individual, he made each person his own standard to do and think what he chooses; with the result that the Whitmanesque world is made up of its hundreds of millions of individuals as independent one of another as are the pebbles on a beach. They touch but they do not really merge. But human society must be based on the mutual interdependence of its elements; and the corner-stone of social life on every plane above that of the savages is the family. Whatever compliments Walt may have paid to the family in theory, he showed in practice that he neither understood its supreme function nor respected it. The relations between the sexes on which the family depends, meant for him no more than the gratification of appetite. He felt no obligation, no duty, either toward the women with whom he formed a temporary attachment or toward the offspring they bore him. It has been proved, although I did not know it at the time of my acquaintance, that he admitted being the father of six children[1] by two mothers, but he rejected all responsibility for their care and bringing up, casting the burden upon the women whom he abandoned. Nothing can be baser than that.

When, therefore, Whitman's uncritical zealots rhapsodize him as the prophet of a new life and the proclaimer of a higher mortality, they do him no service. What is admirable in his poetry and in his message lies in a different field. He can never be a help; on the contrary, by his example he must be a stumbling-block to every individual, man or woman, who is struggling for that standard by which alone the sacredness of the family—and with the family the amelioration of the race—can be safeguarded.

In this respect, Whitman dwells at the opposite pole from Emerson, his master in the gospel of individualism. Emerson takes it for granted that each individual to whom he addresses his auroral call, "Trust thyself!" is already living the life of the spirit, instead of lagging behind in the lowlands of the flesh. Emerson urged perfection on the individual, not that he might enjoy himself for himself, but that he might be the better fitted to play a noble part in society, and

Walt Whitman, 1887

to receive and obey the faintest intimation from the soul of the world. He never tolerated the thought of a community made up of units who, having known the higher moral standards, deliberately chose the immoral.

So we can no more adopt Whitman as a model for our life than we could Rousseau, whom he resembles only too closely on the ignoble side. Under promiscuity alone, the system which proposes to make utter selfishness the ideal of society and its members, could Walt and Jean Jacques be accepted as guides.

So much I must say here, because it explains why Walt would not enlighten me as to the problem of evil. The more I saw him the more I recognized that he looked out on the world without any moral prepossession; but he was wonderfully sensitive to some of the deepest emotions. Who better than he has expressed the bewildered surprise, plaintiveness, the sense of unreality, and then the anguish of bereavement? And how nobly, as if he were welcoming an imperial guest, he goes to the threshold to greet death! There was much more than the cant phrases in praise of universal brotherhood, in his allusions to cronies and camerados, and to the thrill he felt when his hand rested on a pal's shoulder or as he looked into responsive eyes of a comrade. The genuineness of these characteristics also was confirmed by acquaintance with him.

However he may have been in earlier days or was then among his intimates, he never, as I knew him, indulged in coarseness. I remember that one morning I asked him why he would not consent to issue here such a volume of selections as William Rossetti's, brought out in England in 1868. That volume, omitting some of the most flagrant and physiological passages, and sparing the reader some of the tedious, long, prosaic, and repetitive lists, had given Walt his vogue among the intellectual élite in Britain, and I believed that one like it would reach ten times as many American readers as his unexpurgated editions had reached.

He paused a moment, barely shook his head, and said: "That's just what Emerson suggested. Years ago we spent three hours on Boston Common walking up and down, he urging and arguing just as you do, and I listening and thinking and sometimes trying to reply. I couldn't match his arguments, but always something in me kept saying: 'Stick to it, Walt.' And at the end I said to him: 'I can't answer all your reasons, but I guess I've got to hold on to the stuff you don't like. It's all part of the whole; and I can no more honestly cut out that part than any other.'"

A snap-shot of those two on Boston Common that day would be among the most precious literary relics we Americans could have.

Walt was equally firm in standing by his form of verse—if that be verse which form has none. He had been attacked so often that I suppose he took it as a matter of course that every new literary "feller" should take a shot at that target. It seemed to be pretty well proved now that he developed his Whitmanesque metrical scheme from earlier models and by deliberate experimentation. Until he was thirty or over, he wrote rather platitudinous poems in ordinary iambic metre and rhymes and published them in newspapers. On the little table between the windows of the front room on Mickle Street was a thick quarto volume of Scott's poetry, printed in double column (if I remember rightly), with pencillings on the margins. This, he told me, had been his favorite book in the earlier days, and I suppose that Scott's versification was his pattern before he found the requirements of regular prosody too fettering. His general doctrine that metre, which had sufficed for poets in countries more or less despotic, ought not to be tolerated by a chosen bard of this land of unlimited democratic freedom, has its allure for the very young in years and for all those who, no matter what their age may be, never grow up to understand that all art is discipline, and that the supreme artists—Sophocles and Phidias, Virgil and Dante, Michael Angelo, Titian, Raphael and Rembrandt, Shakespeare, Milton and Molière—were supreme for the very reason that the discipline of their art had become instinctive in them, the necessary medium by which they expressed themselves, as water is to the swimmer.

Walt's other argument for this verse form was even more naïve: our versification ought to match in amplitude the boundless sweep of "these States." If accepted seriously, this would mean that even a minor poet in Texas would employ lines of fifty or sixty metrical feet, to keep his relative distance, so to speak, over the Rhode Islander, who ought to be thankful with an allowance of four. Of course Walt himself would have seen the absurdity of this deduction; but as he relied on his emotions and on intuition, and neither would nor could think, he would conclude this discussion, as he did the other, by maintaining his position without wavering.

Once I tried a flank movement on his theory.

"You profess," I said, "to make nature your guide and to be satisfied with nothing less broad and free and infinitely varied than you see in her. But the one lesson which nature teaches above all others is form. She takes care that everything from Sirius to a grain of sand shall have its own proper form. She doesn't strew a lot of rose-petals on the ground and call them a rose; she puts them together in a beautiful form. Many of your poems, it seems to me, are like heaps of petals, not always of the same flower, even, and intermingled with other irrelevant things. Their formlessness is contrary to nature."

This argument carried no weight with him. How many hundreds of times he must have heard similar ones! He said simply but without petulance, and as if he rather pitied my intelligence: "Of course my poetry isn't formless. Nobody could write in my way unless he had the melody singing in his ears. I don't always contrive to catch the best musical combination nowadays; but in the older pieces

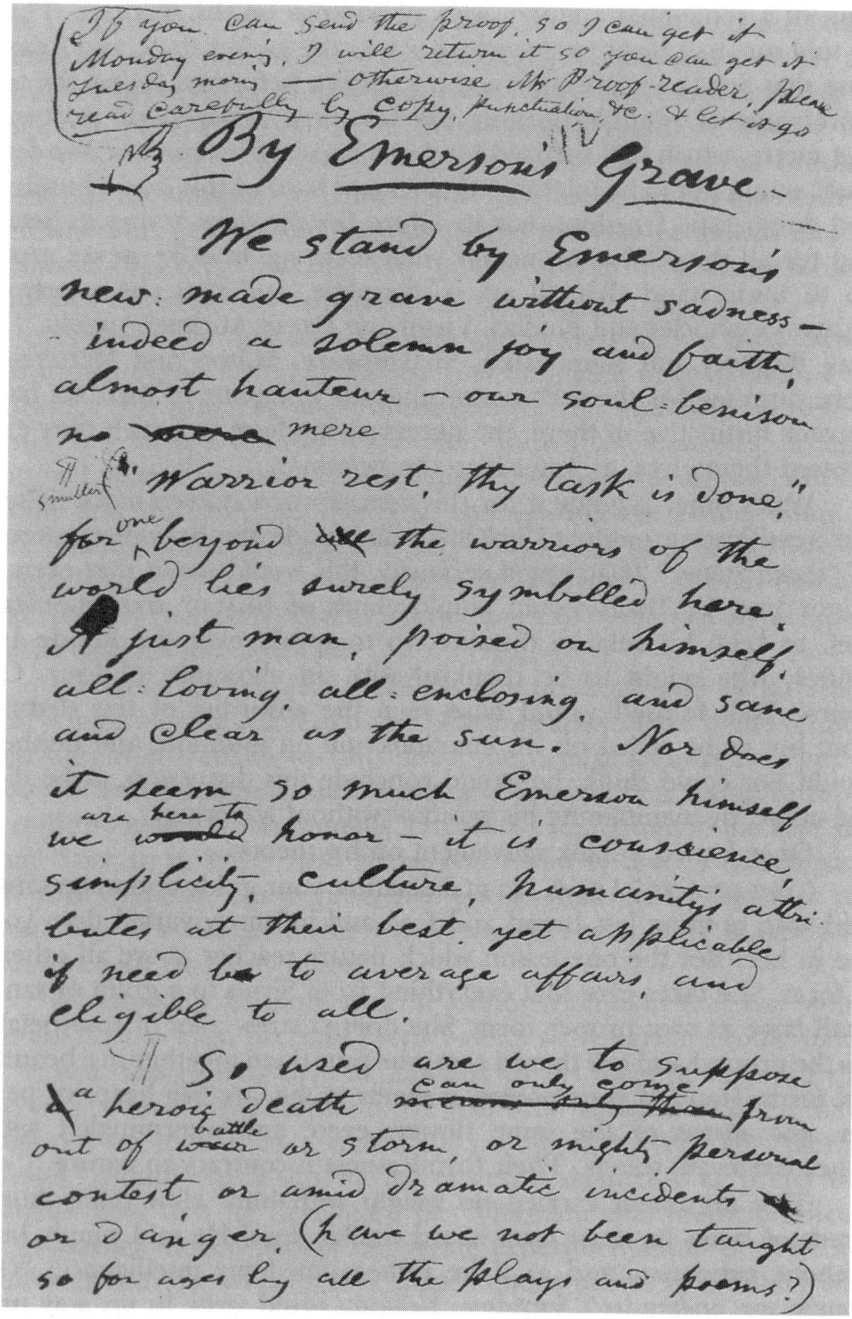

(If you can send the proof, so I can get it Monday even'g, I will return it so you can get it Tuesday morn'g — otherwise Mr Proof-reader, please read carefully by copy, punctuation, &c. & let it go

By Emerson's Grave—

We stand by Emerson's new-made grave without sadness—indeed a solemn joy and faith, almost hauteur—our soul-benison no mere "Warrior rest, thy task is done," for one beyond the warriors of the world lies surely symbolled here. A just man, poised on himself, all-loving, all-enclosing, and sane and clear as the sun. Nor does it seem so much Emerson himself we are here to honor—it is conscience, simplicity, culture, humanity's attributes at their best, yet applicable if need be to average affairs, and eligible to all.

So used are we to suppose a heroic death can only come from out of battle or storm, or mighty personal contest, or amid dramatic incidents or danger, (have we not been taught so for ages by all the plays and poems?)

Portion of Whitman's manuscript of "By Emerson's Grave"

I always had a tune before I began to write."

Those tunes doubtless account for the haunting music of many of his first lines, and of other separate lines interspersed in the poems; but the metrical inspiration rarely continues for more than two or three lines at the most.

As a parting shot I added: "Shakespeare's blank verse doesn't consist of a series of lines each of five rigid metrical feet; but it runs on over more or fewer lines, as the case may be, according to the sense. Hamlet's soliloquy, for instance, if printed in your way, would look very different on the page. The metre runs through it just as in musical composition there is a given key and beat. And, after all, In "O Captain! my Captain!"—the most popular of your poems—you showed that you could use effectively an accepted metre and even rhymes—although you balk at making the rhymes satisfactory throughout." But Walt took no further interest in the matter.

Indeed, it was plain enough that Walt regarded me, as a college graduate, with a certain suspicion and lack of sympathy. His self-appointed mission being to break down all conventions and to shout his "barbaric yawp over the roofs of the world," he naturally looked upon a college as the last citadel of convention and therefore as his special enemy. Although in England his readers came mostly from the university and literary circles, over here the colleges, partly from prudery and partly from pedantry, had been very slow even to mention him. At Harvard, in my time, for instance, a professor might casually refer to "Leaves of Grass," but when the student went to the library to consult the book, he found that it was catalogued with two blue stars, which meant that it was kept under lock and key in the "inferno" devoted to obscene productions.

No wonder, therefore, that Walt eyed the academically educated with some distrust. I seemed to him a young man who came out of the university with a little stock of approved formulas, with which I was attempting to make a breach in the Whitmanesque cosmic theory, constructed by him to supplant all others. In truth, however, I had no such ambition; I was moved, as I have stated, by an insatiate curiosity, and by my desire to get from this prophet of a new order some solace for my own perplexities. But to the end I was marred for him by the academic attachment. Yet he felt a sort of pity, too; and once, before going to Europe, when I bade him good-by, he urged me, with some ardor, to stand on my own feet, to think my own thoughts, and not to go on repeating what I had read

299

or heard. What he wished, although he did not suspect it, was, that I, like Mr. Traubel, and one or two other unlimited disciples who passed much time with him in those last years, should give back to him *his* own thoughts as nearly as possible in his own language.

One day after I had been warmly praising Walt's poems on the Civil War, I said that I thought what he had written about Lincoln would stand along with James Russell Lowell's "Commemoration Ode" as the highest poetic tributes to the martyr President. He surprised me a little by saying that he had never read Lowell; that he supposed that he was one of those academic "fellers," who breathed the fetid air of college lecture-rooms and gave it out in his poems; that he was not a "critter" for us. I replied that although Lowell was a bookman, he was much more; at the very top of our writers for humor and a splendid force for patriotism before and during the war. "You ought at least to read the 'Ode,'" I said emphatically, "and you would see that he isn't the anæmic fellow you imagine. Much of his other poetry also is fine, some of it is very good; and although he isn't a poet of the first class—who is in our time?—he stands well in the second class."

"You wouldn't persuade me to eat a second-class egg, would yer?" said Walt. "I don't care for second-class poetry, either."

In spite of his avowed ignorance he may have looked into Lowell's poems, and dismissed them long before as having no worth for him. Completely lacking humor himself, even "The Biglow Papers" must have been lost upon him. Walt had, in fact, read most of the American poets who were his contemporaries. We are told that at one time Poe attracted him, and we know that he absorbed Emerson; but I recall only one of whom he spoke with some enthusiasm—Whittier, who had a "fine vein, narrow but deep and fiery, of the Scotch Covenanter in him." I remarked that E. C. Stedman's essay seemed to me the best any one had written till then on Walt himself, being free from prejudice and rich in appreciation.

"Yes," said Walt, "Mr. Stedman is a very hospitable"—he waited a moment for the word—"critic and a good friend." Once or twice Walt mentioned Tennyson, ranking him as a real poet, but I have forgotten which poems he had in mind. He took pride in telling me that Tennyson had invited him to go over to Freshwater for a visit, but that his health was too feeble. That the apostle of formless poetry should be elated over the sympathy of the chief master of poetic form in modern English literature struck me as interesting; but I think that Walt's elation came from the fact that Tennyson was a great poet. Although he was thoroughly democratic in his love of appreciation, he knew the different varieties of incense at a sniff.

Looking back on our chats I perceive now, better than I did then, how much in his talk with me Walt repeated what he had already written down in his prose fragments. That description of his meeting with Emerson on Boston Common, for instance, or a long account of his last visit to Emerson at Concord; or the story of Elias Hicks and the Hicksite schism among the Quakers, bringing in his own boyhood and his recollections of his mother and of going to the annual meetings—all these he has told in print. But even though, owing to his failing vigor, they lacked something when he repeated them by word of mouth, they gained much in reality. The tone of the voice, the patriarchal look of the man, the slight gesture or the hesitation, and his permeating placidity can never be conjured up by those who only read his reminiscences. Walt kept a certain interest in current affairs, but his opinions had been made up long before, and his chief interest then and always was himself. The casual visitor like me might let in a whiff from the world outside, but this was fleeting in comparison with the steady influence of the little group of idolators who echoed his thoughts, confirmed his delusion that literary "fellers" were everywhere joined in a conspiracy against him, and so tended to hem in and narrow his vision. The more unrestricted the worship which devotees pay to the founder of a cult, the greater the risk he runs; and the freedom which such a founder expects to enjoy by throwing off the fundamental conventions of civilized life and posing as a "rowdy" or a cowboy is an illusory emancipation which shuts more doors than it opens.

But I find that I grow critical, whereas my purpose is rather to call up from time's oubliette Walt's speech and aspect as I knew them thirty years ago. As Dr. Furness said, the old fellow himself was what really mattered. Having seen him once, you never forgot his presence. On a summer afternoon he sat by the right-hand window and you at the left, with the little table covered with half a dozen books between you—the volume of Scott's poems most conspicuous; and he nodded to passers-by on the sidewalk and kept up his not-rapid chat with you. A newsboy would hand in the evening paper and Walt took a penny from a little pile of change on the window-sill and handed it to him with a "Thank yer, Billy," or other cosey greeting. In colder weather Walt settled into his rocking-chair,

Walt Whitman, 1887

over the back of which was flung an unusually large and fine silver wolfskin. Whistler himself could not have achieved a more beautiful blend of grays and whites than Walt did when he leaned his fleecy head against the gray fur.

I talked with him frequently about Lincoln, whom I took it for granted he must have known well; but he surprised me by saying that although he "loafed a good deal around the White House," he never ran across the President but twice—once of an evening from a balcony about some battle news. "He had rather a high voice with carrying power, but on the whole pleasant and impressive."

Recently, in looking over John Hay's Diary, I was amused to come upon the following entry for October 29, 1863: "I went down to Willard's to-day and got from Palmer, who is here, a free ticket to

302

New York and back for W. Whitman, the poet, who is going to New York to electioneer and vote for the Union ticket." So Walt's loafing around the White House was not wholly unremunerative.

I heard him say nothing that can add to his well-known and, in their way, unsurpassed descriptions of hospital scenes; but he made one characteristic remark which may be worth repeating.

"The human critter," he said, "has become too self-restrained. He thinks it isn't manly to show his emotions, and so he tries to keep as hard and mum as a statue. This is all wrong. The Greeks howled when they were hurt and bawled with rage when they were angry. But our soldiers in the war would clinch their teeth and not let out a sign of what they were suffering, no matter how badly they were wounded; and so they often died because the surgeons couldn't tell where they'd been hit."

Walt, himself, according to those who knew him in early and middle life, was preternaturally emotional and never attempted to check or to disguise the expression of his feeling at the moment. His disapproval of discipline, which has been one of the chief gains made by normal, civilized men since the Homeric age, harmonizes, therefore, with the rest of his philosophy of unrestraint.

Of references to passing political affairs, I recall only one, bearing on President Harrison: "I guess he is the smallest egg ever laid in Uncle Sam's basket."

I never saw him show resentment, even under unusual provocation. Thus, when Swinburne recanted in his customary vitriolic language his former bombastic laudation, I ventured to ask Walt whether he had seen the ferocious article in the *Fornightly Review*. "Yes," he said with a tranquillity more effective than sarcasm; "yes, and I rather guess Swinburne has soured a little on me."

Professor Bliss Perry, by far the best of all Whitman's biographers, has analyzed subtly a streak of slyness which ran through Walt's nature. At the time of my acquaintance I could not lay my finger on any more definite example of this than his apparent endeavor to escape from avowing his obligations to Emerson; but I did recognize in him a poseur of truly colossal proportions, one to whom playing a part had long before become so habitual that he had ceased to be conscious that he was doing it. His offhand, hail-fellow-well-met manner was undoubtedly genuine with him in earlier years, and then, after he had adopted his pose, he saw to it that the manner should not be rubbed away by conventional attrition. So he was almost fussily careful to have his costume attract as much attention as possible; and in his talk he stuck to certain illiterate forms—like "critter" and "feller"—in keeping with the character he had assumed. We must remember that he was a contemporary of P. T. Barnum and agreed with that master-showman's views of publicity; so he chose a style both in prose and verse which at once arrested attention; he did not blush to write for the newspapers puffs of himself and his works; he craved notoriety even of the flimsiest sort. "The public," he said to me, "is a thick-skinned beast, and you have to keep whacking away on its hide to let it know you're there." Such egregious self-conceit has afflicted men much greater than Whitman, and, thanks to that quality which makes the artist a magician, the product, literary or artistic, of these men need not be insincere, for they write or paint or compose through their talent and not through their conceit.

On one occasion, when I tried to get him to sum up in definite terms his creed—a thing which he avoided doing for half a lifetime, because he instinctively felt that vagueness was of the essence of it—he took a copy of the original edition of "As a Strong Bird on Pinions Free," and turning to the advertisement at the end he marked the margin of the third page. "There," said he; "I suppose you'll find the gist of it all there about as well as anywhere." He gave me the slender volume with its green-cloth cover, and wrote my name in it, adding two or three photographs of himself. One of these, an unusually beautiful portrait of him, represents him as seated in a grape-vine rustic chair—the kind once common in photographers' studios—and on the forefinger of his outstretched right hand a butterfly has just alighted, with wings still outspread. "I've always had the knack of attracting birds and butterflies and other wild critters," he said. "They know that I like 'em and won't hurt 'em and so they come."

How it happened that that butterfly should have been waiting in that studio on the chance that Walt might drop in to be photographed, or why Walt should be clad in a thick cardigan jacket on any day when butterflies would have been disporting themselves in the fields, I have never been able to explain. Was this one of the petty artifices by which Walt carried out his pose? It doesn't matter; the picture is delightful and it has served ever since as the frontispiece to the precious little volume. Turn to page three of its advertisements and you will find his own interpretation of himself and his works.

A less venial form of slyness consisted in Walt's lack of candor in regard to money affairs. During the last six or eight years of his life he allowed a few kind-hearted gentlemen—Dr. Furness and Mr. George W. Childs among them—to suscribe an annual sum for his up-keep; and when he grew too lame to walk, they supplied a horse and phaeton and paid a young man to act as his driver and valet. He even allowed some of his youthful admirers, who were earning a bare minimum wage themselves, to contribute a dollar or two a month apiece toward his support. Such a willingness to receive might be pardoned on the ground that he was affording his well-wishers the superior blessedness of giving, but all the while, un-known to them, he was building out of his own resources a four-thousand-dollar mausoleum for himself at Harleigh Cemetery. Apparently Walt doubted as to the value of the momument which pos-terity would raise to him, and so he took no chances.

And yet, I had the feeling that if Walt had had much, he would have given lavishly; not having, he accepted, without stint. Very likely he believed that, as he had bestowed upon the world some-thing beyond all price, the world owed him a living. His tastes were so simple that he would not have known how to spend much wealth; but that four-thousand dollar tomb remains as an unpleasant evi-dence of his slyness.

The last time I saw him was, I think, in December, 1891, a few months before his death. His housekeeper, Mrs. Mary Davis, told me at the door that he had been pretty feeble and was staying up-stairs, but she would ask him if he could see me. He sent down word for me to go up. I climbed the short flight and went into the front room, which took up most of the second story of the small house. There stretched out in a long chair, propped with pillows and well wrapped up, with the gray wolfskin thrown over his knees, lay Walt, a broken, helpless, pathetic figure, who seemed hardly more than an antiquarian wreck in a dingy and disordered old curiosity-shop. The room was filled with the accumulation of years: bundles of newspapers, piles of books, printers' proofs, letters, bric-à-brac, some begrimed and chipped bedroom crockery, statuettes in plaster of Paris, a trunk or two, and a chair and stool long past the time when they could be sat in without caution. Boards strung on tres-tles made a sort of long table such as paper-hangers use, and this af-forded a resting-place for the heaps of letters, documents, and junk. Of the two windows, one was darkened by the shutters being closed,

Interior of Whitman's home on Mickle Street, Camden

and through the dirty panes of the other I saw the wretched buildings opposite, and the bleak, wintry sky out of which snow-flurries
blew intermittently. Seldom have I had so complete an impression of
cheerlessness.

And there amid his sordid belongings, apparently deserted, the
old man lay dying.

He greeted me with his familiar "Glad to see yer," but in a feeble voice, and I took his hand, which he could hardly move. He said
that he'd been sick, very sick; that the doctor told him he mustn't do
anything, nor talk much, nor think much; but he liked to see old
friends. Naturally, I started no discussion, but tried to suggest cheerful possibilities, though I knew there were none, and kept fearing I
might be outstaying "the little while" which Mrs. Davis had warned
me was all that the doctor allowed.

To turn his thoughts away from the dismal present, I asked him
what he had been doing before his illness. He replied: "I went
through the whole of my poems; read 'em all from beginning to

306

end; and for the first time I had some doubt whether they're going to last."

The pathos of that confession moved me through and through. For what could be more tragic? Here was man who believed he had made a new revelation to mankind—a prophet, who had borne mockery and neglect, and had at last persuaded a band of followers that he was indeed the true and only prophet—a poet, who in spite of the whimsicality of his poetic forms was recognized throughout the world as a poet—an arch-egoist, who honestly supposed that his personality was and would be immensely precious in human progress—and now, at the end of his life, he expressed a doubt as to the validity of his message or the permanence of his fame.

I told him I believed that the genuine poetical parts of his works would long be read, although what he had written to support his theory of composition or to preach his gospel would probably be gradually forgotten. "Poverty cherishes the poetry in poets," I added, "and not their theories. That is what has happened to Wordsworth and to many another doctrinaire poet. But the true gold lasts—have no fear, Mr. Whitman—but it often takes more than one generation to sift it from the dross." And I mentioned some of the passages in "Leaves of Grass" which seemed to me golden.

Whether my words comforted him or not, I cannot say. Possibly, the doubt he expressed was born of a flitting mood, or perhaps of his lifelong craving for sympathy and acclaim; he could not have doubted seriously, for habit, if nothing else, would have enabled him to play his part through unflinchingly until the curtain fell.

We talked a little more. Then I got up to go—probably the watchful Mrs. Davis was already signalling me from the entry—and I asked Walt whether I could send him anything, some fruit or wine, but he said that he had all he needed and more, and that the doctor didn't let him take much, anyway. His "Good-by, come again," was uttered feebly, because of his physical weakness, but without the slightest suggestion that he had lost courage or was even surprised at the defection of life—life which he had caressed and glorified, and which now, like a fickle mistress, had abandoned him. Neither that day nor earlier did I hear him whisper a complaint against the weariness which old age and incurable disease laid upon him.

I turned at the door and looked back upon him, a gray wraith amid the shadows of that dismal room. Walking to the ferry, I wondered whether, after what he had experienced, he would still sing, if the strength and will to sing should come back to him in a moment:

> I have said that the soul is not more than the body,
> And I have said that the body is not more than the soul.

Scribner's Magazine, 65 (June 1919): 674-676.

1. Walt himself stated this in a letter dated August 10, 1890, to J. A. Symonds: "My life, young manhood, middle age, times South, &c. have been jolly bodily and doubtless open to criticism. Though unmarried I have had six children," &c. See E. Carpenter: "Days with Walt Whitman," New York, 1908, pp. 142-3; Bliss Perry: "Walt Whitman," Boston, 1906, pp. 44-5.

From THE LIFE AND LETTERS OF JOHN BURROUGHS

John Burroughs

The nature writer John Burroughs met Whitman in 1863 and saw a great deal of him when both men lived in Washington. He later wrote two fine critical and biographical works on Whitman, Notes on Walt Whitman as Poet and Person *(1867) and* Walt Whitman: A Study *(1896).*

Whitman, Poet and Comrade

Walt Whitman and John Burroughs first met in Washington in the autumn of 1863, in the army supply store of Allen, Clapp & Co., introduced by E. M. Allen, Whitman being forty-four years of age, Burroughs twenty-six.

A brief account of the meeting occurs in an early note-book of Burroughs, dated December 14, 1865, accompanied by comments as to his first impression of 'Leaves of Grass,' which he had come upon two years before going to Washington:[1]

His [Whitman's] book, read with modern eyes, would seem to justify Emerson's characterization of him as 'half song thrush and half alligator;' and, by some means or other, I had got an impression that he was at least half rowdy. Imagine my surprise, therefore, when I beheld a well-dressed, large, benevolent-looking man, cleanly and neat, with a grizzly, shaggy appearance about the face and open throat.

Without rising he reached out to me a large, warm, soft hand, and regarded me with a look of infinite good nature and contentment. I was struck with the strange new beauty of him as he sat there in the gas light— the brightness of his eyes, the glow of his countenance, and the curious blending of youth and age in his expression. He was in that felicitous mood almost habitual to him, I have since found, during which his flesh and skin become, as it were, transparent, and allow his great summery, motherly soul to shine through. I was struck likewise with his rich, mellow voice—a voice that was at once an index to the man, implying not only deep human sympathies and affinities, but the finest blood and breeding, a gentle, strong, cultivated soul.

My interest was instant and profound. I said: Here is a new type of man, a new type of gentleman, a new type of philospher—a veritable new ethics and gospel. I will observe his habits and movements, his manners and conversation, his life and doings, and see if expectation is justified. For two years, therefore, I have been studying this wonderful man, and have come, not only to love him as a friend, but to look to him as the greatest, sweetest soul I have yet met in this world.

Following this are copious impressions and comments on Whitman's personality and writings, some of which went into Burrough's first book, 'Notes on Walt Whitman as Poet and Person' (1867). The note-book gives this incident:

Sauntering with him one day by the Capitol, we met a soldier—dirty, travel-stained, and ragged, with a friendless, care-worn expression, whom Walt kindly accosted. I shall never forget how the soldier alter[ed] the tone in which he was about answering him, as he looked Walt in the face. . . . The sympathy and deep, yearning love that spoke in this man's voice and beamed in his face completely disarmed him; and in a blushing, bashful way he answered Walt's questions.

I stood a little apart and thought I had never seen anything so human and good. The soldier looked down at his boots, and began to be ashamed of his appearance, since here was some one who took an interest in him. He was a Western boy, and there was some curious history connected with his story and appearance. Walt, in his tender, curious way, asked him if he should not help him a little; not enough to hurt him, but enough to get him a bit of food, for he looked hungry. The soldier did not know how to meet this charge, and came near breaking down outright; and as Walt placed some small notes in his hand and turned away, he found his tongue to say, in that awkward, constrained way, that he hoped he would have good health and keep well. And I saw how deeply he responded to this act of kindness, and how poorly his words expressed what he felt.

That youth will not forget as long as he lives, the great kind man who accosted him under the walls of the Capitol, and spoke the first words of human sympathy and tenderness, perhaps, he had heard since his mother bid him farewell.

Walt said he had probably been guilty of some misdemeanor, perhaps was a deserter, or a returning rebel; but I saw this incident would do more to strengthen and encourage him, and help restore him to his lost man-

John Burroughs in 1870

hood, if so it was, than all the sermons and homilies and tracts that have ever been preached or printed.

Very welcome is this fragment of description from the same note-book:

Notwithstanding the beauty and expressiveness of his [Whitman's] eyes, I occasionally see something in them as he bends them upon me, that almost makes me draw back. I cannot explain it—whether it is more, or less, than human. It is as if the earth looked at me—dumb, yearning, relentless, immodest, inhuman [unhuman?]. If the impersonal elements and forces were concentrated in an eye, that would be it. It is not piercing, but absorbing

311

and devouring—the pupil expanded, the lid slightly drooping, and the eye set and fixed.

This information at first hand is so interesting one wonders why he did not use it in his first book, or even in his later, riper one,[2] instead of quoting descriptions by John James Piatt and others. It may be that Whitman, who criticized and pruned his earlier book, objected to being pictured so gentle while declaring himself to be 'one of the roughs,' who cocked his hat as he pleased, indoors and out. Burroughs does, however, give a brief but telling description of the poet on pages 85-86 in his 'Notes.'

Even more valuable, perhaps, than the foregoing account of his first meeting with Whitman (written two years and more after the meeting), are his brief, spontaneous impressions sent to Myron Benton. On December 19, 1863, he wrote:

I have been much with Walt. Have even slept with him. I love him very much. The more I see and talk with him, the greater he becomes to me. He is as vast as the earth, and as loving and noble. He is much handsomer than his picture represents him, goes well-dressed, and there is nothing *outish* in his appearance, except, it may be, his open throat. He walks very leisurely, rather saunters, and looks straight forward, not down at his feet. He does not talk readily, but his conversation is very rich and suggestive. He regards Emerson as one of the great, eternal men, and thinks there is not another living, nor has lived for the last two or three centuries.

I am convinced that Walt is as great as Emerson, though after a different type. Walt has all types of men in him, there is not one left out. I must write you all about him, but cannot now. If I get settled here I want to give an account of him in the Commonwealth. If you can get a New York Times of date October 4, 1863, you will find a letter of his which is one of the finest pieces of writing I have ever seen. It is just like Walt.[3]

Again, January 9, 1864, Burroughs writes Benton:

When I called on Walt[4] this morning I found him *en dishabille*, reading 'Walden.' 'My impression of the book last night,' he said, 'was rather poor; I thought it puerile. But this morning after I had sipped my coffee, I found it more satisfying. I opened near the end and found it so good that I turned back and commenced again.'

He thinks his translations from Anacreon in the 'Week' far the best he ever saw; so good that he tore the leaves out that contained them, and put them among his choice tid-bits. He thinks Thoreau a very sweet, pure soul,

Walt Whitman, 1889 (Feinberg Collection, Library of Congress)

but by no means a number-one man, as Emerson is. He was too timid, and too afraid of the world; did men and things injustice; was too exclusive; and not enough of a cosmopolitan.

The more I see of Walt, the more I like him. . . . He is far the wisest man I have ever met. There is nothing more to be said after he gives his views; it is as if Nature herself had spoken. And so kind, sympathetic, charitable, humane, tolerant a man I did not suppose was possible. He loves everything and everybody. I saw a soldier the other day stop on the street and kiss him. He kisses me as if I were a girl. He appreciates everybody, and no soul will get fuller justice in the next world than it gets at his hands here.

I related to him our Adirondack trip, the deer-shooting, etc., which so pleased him that he said seriously he should make a 'leaf of grass' about it. I related to him other country experiences which he relished hugely. In the spring he wants to go out to my home with me to make sugar and get a

313

taste of that kind of life. If I can get off, I shall surely go. He also wants to go up to the Adirondacks and spend a season at the Upper Iron Works. He says a trip to Europe would be nothing compared to it.

He bathed today while I was there—such a handsome body, and such delicate rosy flesh I never saw before. I told him he looked good enough to eat, which, he said, he should consider a poor recommendation if he were among the cannibals.

I have often told him of you, but without exciting any remark from him till the other day, without provocation, he commenced to ask me about you: wanted to hear all about you, how you lived and if you were 'a good fellow' (the highest praise he ever bestows upon a man). I told him what you had written. He said he did not want to hear about your poetry, but about you, what your type and temper and hair were, etc. So I fell to portraying you—a pleasant task— and Walt was much interested, and for all I know may immortalize you in a 'leaf of grass.'. . .

From Clara Barrus, *The Life and Letters of John Burroughs*, 2 vols. (Boston: Houghton Mifflin, 1925), 1:107-110.

1. He had read some of Whitman's poems in the *Saturday Press*, perhaps as early as 1859.

2. *Whitman, a Study*, 1896.

3. 'I think it was his piece about the unfinished Capitol' (J. B.). This article, and two others, of February 26 and August 16, 1863, contain graphic pictures of Washington, and heart-rending scenes among the soldiers.

4. J. B. said in later years: 'Walt lived on 4 1/2 St., in a room with a bed and a table and a broken down chair. He lived very frugally, mostly on bread and tea, expending everything he could get for the soldiers. Emerson and other Boston friends sometimes sent him money for this purpose. He would stuff his pockets with things and go and distribute them to the sick soldiers.' J. B. said that Walt would sometimes come into Allen's store (1863) while writing *Drum Taps*, and jot down things he had just seen— the tears still in his eyes.

From ROADSIDE MEETINGS OF A LITERARY NOMAD

Hamlin Garland

Hamlin Garland, who later became a popular novelist and a major spokesman for the naturalistic school of American fiction, was in his twenties when he met Whitman in 1888. His is one of the few accounts of an aspiring young writer who looked to Whitman as an important figure in American literature.

One of the very first books for which I had asked at the Boston Public Library was Walt Whitman's *Leaves of Grass*. I had heard much of this book in the West but had never set eyes upon it and even here in Boston it was "double starred" on the list and issued only to serious students of literature. Heaven knows I was serious enough; and so at the age of twenty-five, I began my acquaintance with "the poet of Democracy"—an acquaintance at once thrilling and abiding.

Of the tremendous vitality of his message I was at once aware. Formless as the book appeared, its deeply partriotic spirit, its wide sympathy with working men and women and especially its faith in the destiny of "these States" exalted me. I caught some part of the writer's faith in American manhood and the part America was going to play in the world's future history.

From *Leaves of Grass* I passed to *Specimen Days*, which made me admire him even more deeply. That he profoundly influenced my thinking I freely acknowledge. I reread Toqueville in the light of *Democratic Vistas*, and perceived that the local-color novel had sociologic value in that it aided the readers of one part of our widely separated States to understand the problems of another. I began at once to say these things to my students at Brown's School and elsewhere.

I went further. I wrote to Walt (as he called himself) telling him how inspiring I found his *Specimen Days and Collect* and that I considered his prose the very best avenue of approach to his poetry:

"*Jamaica Plain,
Boston, Mass.*

"*November 24, 1886*
"Mr. Walt Whitman:
    It is with profound sorrow that I read in the papers the news that you are again suffering from your old trouble. I trust it is not as serious as reported. My regard for you is so great that I am very sorry not to be able to buy more copies of your book and thus give a more substantial token of sympathy.
    "I am an enthusiastic reader of your books, both volumes of which I have within reach of hand. I am everywhere in my talking and writing making your claims felt and shall continue to do so. I have demonstrated (what of course you know) that there is no veil, no impediment between your mind and your audience, when your writings are *voiced*. ('That's a point to chew on,' Walt exclaimed, breaking in. 'Read it again. I want to get it clear in my noodle for keeps.') The formlessness is only seeming, not real. I have never read a page of your poetry or quoted a line that has not commanded admiration. The music is there and the grandeur of thought is there if the reader reads, guided by the sense and not by the external lining or paragraphing. Even very young pupils feel the thrill of the deep rolling music though the thought may be too profound for them to grasp. In a course of lectures before the Boston School of Oratory last summer I made a test of the matter. I do not think a single pupil held out against my arguments supplemented by readings from your works. The trouble is they get at your work through the daily press or through the defenders of Longfellow or Tennyson (whom it is supposed you utterly antagonize). When it is brought to them by one who appreciates and measurably understands your methods and ideals, I do not think there is any doubt of the favorable result. I have found much opposition but it was mostly ignorant or misled.
    "I am a young man of very ordinary attainments, and do not presume to do more than give you a glimpse of the temper of that public which would not do you wrong, deliberately, but who by reason of the causes hinted above, fail to get at the transcendent power of *Leaves of Grass*. If I had given you the impression that I believe in you and strive to interpret you, you will not feel that I have over-stepped the privilege of a pupil in the presence of a great teacher.
    "The enclosed slip is a meagre outline of a volume which I am writing and which I hope to get out this coming spring. As the motto page of this volume I have used a paragraph from your *Collect* which is entitled 'Founda-

Hamlin Garland

tion Stages, then Others'. While it is not strictly essential to the book, yet I should esteem it a favor if you would consent to its use. One sentence: 'In nothing is there more evolution than in the American mind.' I have also used in company with it Spencer's great law of progress upon my title page. It helped to decide the title which is *The Evolution of American Thought*; an outline study of the leading phases of American literature, etc. In the latter part of the volume I have treated of the Age of Democracy and its thought taking as foundation the splendid utterances of M. Taine upon the modern age. It is in this chapter that I place your work. I quote from you quite largely both in treating of your writings and in treating the general theme of present and future democratic ideals. I hope to be able to please you with my treatment of your great work. Have you any objections to the quotations which I find it necessary to use?

"In conclusion let me say that without any bias in your favor (rather the opposite from newspapers) your poems thrilled me, reversed many of my ideas, confirmed me in others, helped to make me what I am. I am a borderman, born in Wisconsin and raised on the prairie frontier. I am a disciple of Mr. Spencer and therefore strive at comparative methods of criticism. That your poems should thus convert me is to me a revelation of their power, especially when I can convince others in the same manner.

"And now, revered friend (for I feel you are a friend), think of me as one who radiates the principles of the modern age, and who will in his best manner (poor at best) strive to make his hearers and readers better aware of the 'Good Gray Poet' and his elemental lines.

"Your readers are increasing, and may you live to see the circle infinitely extended is my fervent hope. I do not expect a reply to this other than the signification whether I may quote you or not. I wish I might see and talk with you but that is not possible, except through your volumes.

"I am most sincerely yours
"HAMLIN GARLAND."

This letter interested him and he replied, but it was not till long after that I learned how profoundly my letter had touched him. To him I was a "Boston professor" and a highly influential convert.

So far as I knew he had only one other open advocate of his books in all Boston. This was William Sloane Kennedy, a man of letters who acted as proof-reader on the *Transcript*. Our common interest in Whitman drew us together and from him I learned that the poet was alone, broken in health and very poor. "He is confined to his room but enjoys having his friends. Go and see him if you are down that way."

This suggestion lay in my mind for two years before I found myself able to carry it out. Not till in October, 1888, did I cross the river from Philadelphia in search of the poet whose presence had made Camden known throughout the world. The citizens from whom I inquired my way to Mickle Street, directed me into a mean section of the city and when I came to the number designated I could not believe that I had been rightly informed, so dim was the door-plate and so weather-worn the doorway. The street was ugly and narrow, and the house—a two-story frame structure—was such as a day laborer might have owned, and yet the poet's name was there.

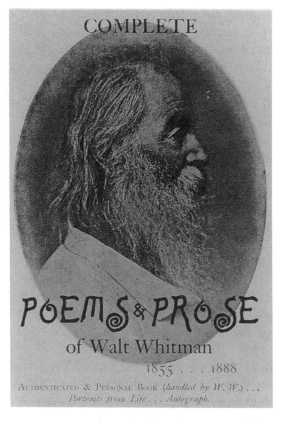

Title page of Complete Poems and Prose *(1888)*

In answer to my ring, a small gray man whom I guessed to be Whitman's attendant came clumping down the stairway and received my name impassively. "Wait here," he said, "I'll see if you can come up."

While he went back up the stairs, I studied the faded paper on the walls and the worn carpet of the hall with growing astonishment. The sordid surroundings filled me with pity and dismay.

From the landing above the man called down, "Walt will see you for a few minutes." He emphasized the brevity of my stay and warned me not to weary the old man.

On entering the door on the left I found myself in a fairly large square room on the north front of the house, and in the center of it Whitman standing by his arm chair, with a broad white hat

319

on his head, awaited me, a tall man clothed in gray with a cloud of white hair and a beard enveloping his face. Without leaving his place he extended his hand and greeted me pleasantly in a voice rather high in key, mellow and cordial, inviting me to be seated. The grip of his hand was firm and vital.

He was dressed in a loosely fitting gray robe, and his linen shirt with rolling collar unbuttoned at the throat and his cuffs were immaculate. I thought him one of the noblest figures I had ever seen. His head was magnificent in contour, and his profile clean cut as a coin.

In contrast to his personal order and comeliness, the room was an incredible mess. Beside his chair rose a most amazing mound of manuscripts, old newspapers and clippings, with many books lying open face down at the point where he had laid them aside.

The furnishings of the room were few and ugly. The bleak windows looked out upon a row of frame tenements whose angular roofs and rude chimneys formed a dreary landscape. It was a melancholy place of confinement for one who had roamed America's open roads and sung its sunlit vistas. No one had prepared me for this bitter revelation of the meagre awards which *Leaves of Grass* had won for its author.

In spite of his surroundings he looked the hero of the poems, strong, self-poised with a certain delicacy of action and speech. His face which turned toward me disclosed a pleasant searching glance. His mouth was hidden in his great beard but his eyes were smiling and the lines on his brow were level. Nothing querulous showed in voice or word. His speech was nobly pure with nothing of the coarseness I had been led to expect. When he dropped into homely phrase or coined a word he did so with humorous intonation. It is because some of his interviewers failed to record the smile that so many misinterpretations of his conversation have been recorded. This use of the common speech now and again lent additional charm to all he said. He had no word of humor, however. He was grave without being low-spirited or grim, placidly serious in all that he said. He made no reference to his poverty or to his illness and nothing petulant or self-pitying came into his voice.

Once he rose in order to find some book which he wished to show me and I perceived that one side of his body was almost useless. He dragged one leg, and he used but one arm. In spite of the confusion of his books and papers he seemed to know where to find what he wanted.

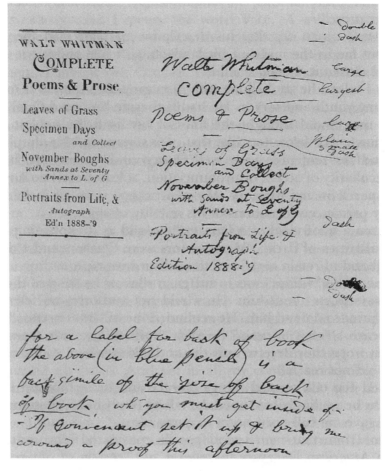

Whitman's printer's copy for the spine label of Complete Poems and Prose *(1888)*

The attendant has said, "a few minutes" but Walt was interested, and so I stayed on with full realization of the value of every additional moment. We talked of his English friends, of his growing acceptance there, and I confidently predicted his acceptance in America. "I can sense a change in the attitude of critics in the last two years," I assured him, and he listened with an eagerness almost pathetic. "I hope you are right," he said.

He asked me about my work in Boston and seemed keenly interested in my praise of *Specimen Days*. "I find it the best introduction to your poetry," I said. "I advise all my pupils to begin by reading it."

"That is very curious," he said, musingly. "Most of my readers neglect my prose."

I went on to say that his descriptive passages had the magic which set me in the midst of his landscape; "I feel and see it as you saw and sensed it. I even smell it."

As I talked he studied me with dim, gray-blue eyes, as if marvelling at my youth and fervor. He had laid aside his broad Quaker hat by this time and I thought the lines of his head the noblest I had ever known. His brow was like that of a serene and kindly philosopher and his sentences were well chosen and concise. He had no local peculiarity of accent or pronunciation, at least he left no singularity of speech in my memory. My impressions were all in harmony with my preconceived notions of his nobility of spirit.

"I am a good deal of a Quaker," he said as if explaining to me his peculiarities of dress. "My ancestors were Quakers and I delight to recall and to retain certain of their distinctive customs."

One of his "whims" was to suffer in silence the sting of the various false reports about him. He would not authorize his friends to go into print to defend him. He reminded me of Grant in this. "I prefer to leave all that to time," he said. "Such things clear themselves up, or at worst they deceive only the unthinking whom your explanation would not reach."

I led the talk toward things literary and being "moved by the spirit," as he smilingly confessed, he talked freely of his contemporaries and gave me full permission to quote him.

I told him that many good people considered him unduly severe on American literature in general and "certain of our poets in particular, Stedman and Gilder for example."

He became grave. "You refer to a report by a German writer. I do think Stedman was deceived, though many of his friends think I have the spirit to rasp him. It would have been ingratitude to have said such words even had I thought them, which I do not. I hold Stedman in high regard as a man of decided insight and culture. On personal grounds I owe him much. The traveller you mention, either wilfully or otherwise twistified"—here he smiled—"what I said, if I said anything in his presence. I am beset with all kinds of visitors who go away thinking me fair game. It is one of the evils which men of any"—he hesitated again—"notoriety must bear patiently."

"As for American literature in general, I have insisted, as all my readers know, on the need for a distinctive flavor in our poetry.

There is an old Scotch word, Burns uses it occasionally, which expresses exactly what I mean: the word 'race.' A wild strawberry, a wild grape has the racy quality, this distinctive tang. Our poetry lacks 'race.' Most of it might have been written in England or on the Continent. I myself like Cooper, Bryant, Emerson and Whittier because they have this distinctive American quality."

This led me to bring up the work of George W. Cable, Joseph Kirkland, Joel Harris, Mary E. Wilkins and others of my friends who were getting, it seemed to me, just what he was demanding. "Their books are in my judgment forerunners of a powerful native literature."

After a pause he said, "It may be so, but I have not read many of them. Against some of them I have read I might bring a grave charge. They have a deplorable tendency toward the *outré*. I call their characters 'delirum tremens characters.' These writers seem not content with the normal man, they must take the exceptional, the diseased. They are not true, not American in the deeper sense at all. To illustrate, in a hunters' camp of twenty men there will always be some who are distorted, unusual, grotesque, but they are not typical of the camp. So in an army mess there are always characters more or less abnormal, men who enjoy distorting their faces and cutting up antics. And yet in all my coming and going among the camps of the Civil War, I was everywhere struck with the decorum, a word I like to use, of the common soldier, his good manners, his quiet heroism, his generosity, even his good real grammar. These are a few of the typical qualities of the American farmer and mechanic."

All this was said quietly but with deep earnestness as if working the problem out while speaking. Then turning his glance on me he spoke with decision. "I say that the novel or drama claiming to depict American life is false if it deals mainly or largely with abnormal or grotesque characters. They should be used merely as foils."

This led me to say, "In the early stages of national literature it is natural to deal with the abnormal, the exceptional because it startles, claims the attention, so it may be just in the preparatory stage and that they will pass on to something higher."

He fell into profound musing, and at last said with deliberate precision as if making a concession which he had not hitherto directly stated, "I don't know but you are right. I can see that the novice would find the exceptional nearest his hand and most noticeable,

323

Whitman's letter of 16 May 1889 to Frederick Oldach about binding
Leaves of Grass *(1889)*

and it may be that these books are preparatory to a new, indigenous fiction. The Public itself, moreover, seems to demand and enjoy such work. It may be as you argue, that the writers and the public will grow toward a higher perception. At any rate I want to utter my protest against such work and to demand that the really heroic character of the common American be depicted in novel and drama."

I forgot his age, his sickness, his drab surroundings, as I listened to his noble voice and lofty personal convictions. He was a grand and ageless spirit at the moment. His sublime faith in the average American did not come from a dreamer, cloistered and bookish, it was the judgment of one who knew the farmer, mechanic, cab-driver, miner, street laborer and roustabout from personal contacts.

"I guess I am aware of our political and literary fraudulencies," he said calmly, "but as things are going on in the States in our time, I am confident of results. I have no sympathy with current pessimistic notions of life, or government, or society."

This serene and buoyant optimism in the midst of old age, poverty and physical pain filled me with admiration. It was majestic. It was another proof of the simple faith of this indomitable poet who looked into the future with the unswerving gaze of an eagle. He was still of a mind to say, "I know the future will be well for all that is, is well."

Seeing that my interview was nearing an end, I said, "May I carry from you a friendly message to these young novelists?"

"You may, with this advice and plea. Tell them to go among the common men, as one of them, never looking down upon them. Tell them to study their lives and find out and celebrate their splendid primitive honesty, patience, and what I like to call their heroism. When our novelists shall do that in addition to being true to their time, their art will be worthy all praise from me or any other who is insisting on native anti-class poems, novels and plays."

"And finally I would say to the young writer, don't depict evil for its own sake. Don't let evil over-shadow your books. Make it a foil as Shakespeare did. His evil is always a foil for purity. Somewhere in your play or novel let the sunlight in." Here he raised his superb head and in a grandly suggestive gesture of his arm made his point clear. "As in some vast foundry whose wells are lost in blackness, a scuttle far up in the roof lets the sun and the blue sky in."

As I copy these words from the original manuscript of my story of him, it conveys to me the odor of the sick room and its drugs, but there was only mental health, vigor and clarity of phrase in Whitman's exhortation.

As I rose to go I assured him that the circle of his admirers was swiftly widening, and that his influence on our literature was certain to be greater year by year.

"Burroughs tells me the same thing," he said, "and I hope you are both right."

He put on his hat, rose painfully to his feet, and gave me his hand at parting. I understood the respect which this formality indicated and was proud of it.

From *Bookman*, 70 (December 1929): 392-406.

From EVERYMAN REMEMBERS

Ernest Rhys

Ernest Rhys served as an agent for English publisher Walter Scott and was instrumental in publishing Leaves of Grass, Specimen Days in America, *and* Democratic Vistas, and Other Papers *in England.*

I stayed a week in New York and then a post-card from Walt Whitman hurried me off to Philadelphia.

I found my way after nightfall to the old poet's door in Mickle Street, Camden, across the Delaware River. In those days one crossed by ferry, and as it was a bitter frost, and there was a heavy ice-barrage in the stream, we were hung up on a cumbrous old-fashioned ferryboat with a crowd of fellow passengers—clerks, tradesmen, Negroes, a motley crew.

Mickle Street, when I found it, was dark and deserted, and made the effect of a thoroughfare in some small French town. Difficult to see the numbers on the doors, and when at last I did get the right one, there was at first no response to my knocks. At length it did open, and a stream of light from an oil-lamp made visible a narrow passage which gave into a room where I caught a glimpse of a massive gray head and beard—Walt Whitman! He was seated at a table having his evening meal. Going out of the dark into this lighted interior, and finding this noble figure of the old man, who sat there silent, prevented by his paralysis from moving or rising easily, I found an experience more like a thing dreamed than seen. It took him some moments to understand that a guest from across the Atlantic had reached his door, and stood there before him. He did not even recognize my name, (he had supposed it would be pronounced "Rice"), but his housekeeper, Mrs. Davis, a sailor's widow, soon put us both at our ease and provided some steaming coffee to take the chill out of the journey and the cold ferryboat out of my blood.

To tell the truth, I believe I was half or a quarter frozen, mind and body, when I arrived, besides being not a little shy and unprepared for the encounter. You may remember Heine's story of his going to see the poet Goethe, and when he reached the house, being unable to think of anything better to say than, "There were very nice cherries to be had on the road from Düsseldorf." In the same taking, I could think of nothing else to say than that I had never before been on a ferryboat which crunched its way through the ice. This as it proved was not altogether a bad opening, for it led Walt Whitman to say that the ferryboats both on the Delaware and on the Hudson River at New York were wonderful places to study American life "in the rough."

After that we contrived to set up the best of understandings. Indeed, we understood each other so well that we were quite satisfied with each other's fits of silence. In those days I had to think twice before I could range my ideas. But I soon learned what things most interested the old poet, news of the great hive of London, its common people and their sayings and doings, and the every-day differences between an American New York and the English City. Walt Whitman had deep down in his consciousness a pretty sure sense that the Old World was overburdened with tradition and its own past, and would need a deal of shaking and waking up to take its full part in the new civilization which the Americas, North and South, Anglo-Saxon and Latin, were to lead.

At times he would corner me by asking a question which I could not answer. He was curious to know who wrote the long Times obituaries on famous statesmen, men of letters, and others, which appeared from time to time as occasion demanded. These articles he thought admirable of their kind, so marked by sturdy British critical good sense. He was himself an insatiable newspaper reader. We usually met in a little front room whose chief piece of furniture was the great armchair in which he sat before a cheerless-looking round iron stove. The floor at his feet was deeply littered with newspapers which reached to his knees, but out of this sea of paper he always seemed able to fish up any particular print he wished to mention. This mêlée of daily and weekly papers served to keep him alive to all that was going on in the vast circuit of the surrounding States. The reports brought back to his mind particular scenes, a street in New Orleans, or a river port on the Mississippi, or the pageant of men and women passing down Broadway or over one of the great bridges.

Whitman's house on Mickle Street, Camden, in 1890

As already hinted, he was habitually slow of speech, not given to say a word too much. He made me think as he sat there, so massive, so self-contained, brooding and remembering, of some mighty old man of the Sagas, or some big-framed peasant who had lived in the open air and did not take kindly to being caged up in a small chamber before a close stove.

Only once was I fated to see him carried out of his usual quiet mood. One day, sitting there at his side, I picked up a New York paper and there read a paragraph about a new book by the poet, Swinburne. Without thinking, I casually mentioned it, forgetting that Swinburne had lost his earlier enthusiasm for "Leaves of Grass," and had even, to put it proverbially, gone back on his tracks and "ratted" in a disgraceful article entitled "Whitmania." The effect of his name now on Walt Whitman was astonishing. He turned round, raised his big hand from the broad arm of the chair on which it rested, and in a tremendous voice that shook me to the mid-rib, cried: "Of all the damned simulacra I have known, that man was the worst. He brought me to a table spread with fair dishes and when I lifted up the covers, behold, *there was nothing there!*"

Front parlor in Whitman's house on Mickle Street, Camden

Some of Whitman's critics said he had no humor, and I do not think it entered into his ordinary attitude to life and things. But he could be humorous, when he was telling his own experiences. He told me once when he was a young man and very hard up, he read in a paper that a prize of two hundred dollars was to be offered for the best Temperance Story. "Well," said Whitman, "I don't know I had any strong feeling about drinking either way; but I wanted the money, and I decided to have a try at it. So I bought a small keg of rye whiskey." He left me to infer that the best way to write on Temperance was to experience in oneself the symptoms induced by strong drink. In any case, the result was good. When the little keg was finished, the Temperance book was finished too, and it carried off the prize. I have never read it all through, but what I have read was super-excellent, considering the manner in which it was inspired.

We rarely during my visits to Mickle Street touched on disputatious matters. But I did once tackle the old poet about the possible use of rhyme and what may be called pattern-verse in the new poetry he had inaugurated. He was not to be moved from the extreme position he had taken up in his prose comments on the art. I pointed out that there were rhymes in nature, and a certain natural dependence upon sounds repeated and significant words reechoing some syllable used in a previous line or verse. Also, there were in certain languages, for instance, in Italian and Spanish, and in the Celtic tongues, essential and organic rhymes, which were related to the structural euphony of the human tongue. But, no, he would not budge. He admitted that exquisite lyric effects, as in the songs of Shakespeare and Burns (I think he added Shelley), and in France by Francois Villon and Victor Hugo, had been attained. But that was in a day when the poetic usage was unlike ours, and when such devices were in accordance with the common speech of our time. The danger, he thought, was that we set up again as they did in the eighteenth century in English poetry an artificial mode, which interfered with the freer use of figurative and imaginative, and especially—he insisted upon this—*real language* in which the word was closely related to the thing expressed. It was a good-tempered disputation, and it ended leaving both combatants in precisely the same mind as they were when it began.

I had taken up my quarters, during this visit to Walt Whitman, on the other side of the river in a huge ugly and uncomfortable hotel in Philadelphia. The only advantage was, it enabled me to get in touch with some of those "types of the average," of ordinary everyday men and women, that Whitman loved to see. But I liked best the Negro servants and waiters, whose humor and good humor never failed to make one feel at home in that strange caravansary. It was my custom to spend my mornings working in the City Library or exploring the streets, and my afternoons in paying friendly visits to Walt Whitman, crossing over in those ungainly ferryboats, in which again one was able to study one's fellow creatures at close quarters. I stayed on at Philadelphia over the Christmas of that year, and spent Christmas Day a fellow guest with Walt Whitman at the house of a friend of his, Thomas Harned (who became one of his executors). That was the only time I saw the great old man outside his own door. (He was more or less crippled by his paralysis, and moved very slowly and heavily with the aid of a thick stick, even when crossing the floor of his room.) The brief voyage to Mr. Harned's house was made in a buggy, for there were no motorcars in those days. Luckily it was the perfection of an American winter day, sun-bright and frosty clear, and Whitman's spirits seemed to rise with the adventure. He entered joyously into the Christmas festivities, intended to conform to the old English style, even down to the plum-pudding with holly leaves stuck in it, which was set on fire with rye whisky as it was borne into the room. The only drawback was that our kind hostess in her concern for the taste of an English guest, had, so she explained, avoided the mistake that most Americans made of spoiling the plum-pudding by boiling it too long. In her innocence she had only had this one boiled for half an hour. I watched with alarm while Whitman consumed meditatively a slice of it, and ate very uneasily my own portion. The result was that after midnight I was still walking the long main street of Philadelphia and hoping I should survive until the morrow. The great old hero himself did not seem to have suffered at all. Possibly the oysters and champagne and the concomitant turkey acted as antidotes.

He told some very good stories during that Christmas dinner, and I wish I could reproduce the sonorous timbre of his voice and the gleam of his eyes as he told them. He had, so far as I recall it now, nothing of the nasal overtones that we associate with the average American. His voice was rich and deep, and its slow tones were thoroughly expressive of the strength of that great frame.

Three days later I had to bid him good-by for the time being, as I had promised to go at the New Year to stay on Orange Mountain with my friend, Thomas Davidson, whom I have described in London.

From *Everyman Remembers* (New York: Cosmopolitan, 1931), pp. 121-126.

From THE JOURNALS OF BRONSON ALCOTT

Amos Bronson Alcott

The Transcendentalist educator and writer Bronson Alcott visited Whitman in Brooklyn in 1856 and was present when Whitman visited Concord in 1881. Both accounts show Alcott's ambivalent feelings about Whitman.

October 4, 1856
New York City

P.M. to Brooklyn, and see Walt Whitman. I pass a couple of hours, and find him to be an extraordinary person, full of brute power, certainly of genius and audacity, and likely to make his mark on Young America—he affirming himself to be its representative man and poet. I must meet him again, and more than once, to mete his merits and place in the Pantheon of the West. He gives me his books of poems, the *Leaves of Grass*, 2nd Edition, with new verses, and asks me to write to him if I have any more to say about him or his master, Emerson.

A nondescript, he is not so easily described, nor seen to be described. Broad-shouldered, rouge-fleshed, Bacchus-browed, bearded like a satyr, and rank, he wears his man-Bloomer in defiance of everybody, having these as every thing else after his own fashion, and for example to all men hereafter. Red flanel undershirt, open-breasted, exposing his brawny neck; striped calico jacket over this, the collar Byroneal, with coarse cloth overalls buttoned to it; cowhide boots; a heavy round-about, with huge outside pockets and buttons to match; and a slouched hat, for house and street alike. Eyes gray, unimaginative, cautious yet sagacious; his voice deep, sharp, tender sometimes and almost melting. When talking will recline upon the couch at length, pillowing his head upon his bended arm, and informing you naively how lazy he is, and slow. Listens well; asks you to repeat what he has failed to catch at once, yet hesitates in speaking often, or gives over as if fearing to come short of the sharp, full, concrete meaning of his thought. Inquisitive, very; over-curious even; inviting criticisms on himself, on his poems—pronouncing it "pomes."—In fine, an egotist, incapable of omitting, or suffering any one long to omit, noting Walt Whitman in discourse. Swaggy in his walk, burying both hands in his outside pockets. Has never been sick, he says, nor taken medicine, nor sinned; and so is quite innocent of repentance and man's fall. A bachelor, he professes great respect for women. Of Scotch descent by his father; by his mother, German. Age 38, and Long Island born.

November 10, 1856

This morning we [Alcott and Thoreau] call on Whitman, Mrs. Tyndall accompanying us to whet her curiosity on the demigod. He receives us kindly, yet awkwardly, and takes us up two narrow flights of stairs to sit or stand as we might in his attic study—also the bedchamber of himself and his feeble brother, the pressure of whose bodies was still apparent in the unmade bed standing in one corner, and the vessel scarcely hidden underneath. A few books were piled disorderly over the mantel-piece, and some characteristic pictures—a Hercules, a Bacchus, and a satyr—were pasted, unframed, upon the rude walls.

There was a rough table in the room, and but a single window, fronting Ellison Avenue, upon which he lives, his being the middle tenement of a single block of three private dwellings and far out on Myrtle Avenue, in the very suburbs of the city of Brooklyn.

He took occasion to inform us three, while surveying his premises aloft, of his bathing daily through the mid-winter; said he rode sometimes a-top of an omnibus up and down Broadway from morning till night beside the driver, and dined afterwards with the whipsters, frequented the opera during the season, and "lived to make pomes," and for nothing else particularly.

He had told me on my former visit of his being a housebuilder, but I learned from his mother that his brother was the housebuilder, and not Walt, who, she said, had no business but going out and coming in to eat, drink, write, and sleep. And she told how all the common folks loved him. He had his faults, she knew, and was not a perfect man, but meant us to understand that she thought him

Amos Bronson Alcott

an extraordinary son of a fond mother.

I said, while looking at the pictures in his study: "Which, now, of the three, particularly, is the new poet here—this Hercules, the Bacchus, or the satyr?" On which he begged me not to put my questions too close, meaning to take, as I inferred, the virtues of the three to himself unreservedly. And I think he might fairly, being himself the modern Pantheon—satyr, Silenus, and him of the twelve labours—combined.

He is very curious of criticism of himself or his book, inviting it from all quarters, nor suffering the conversation to stray very wide away from Walt's godhead without recalling it to that high mark. I hoped to put him in communication direct with Thoreau, and tried my hand a little after we came down stairs and sat in the parlour

Mickle Street, Camden, in 1890, with Whitman's house on the right

below; but each seemed planted fast in reserves, surveying the other curiously,—like two beasts, each wondering what the other would do, whether to snap or run; and it came to no more than cold compliments between them. Whether Thoreau was meditating the possibility of Walt's stealing away his "out-of-doors" for some sinister ends, poetic or pecuniary, I could not well divine, nor was very curious to know; or whether Whitman suspected or not that he had here, for once, and the first time, found his match and more at smelling out "all Nature," a sagacity potent, penetrating and peerless as his own, if indeed not more piercing and profound, finer and more formidable. I cannot say. At all events, our stay was not long, and we left the voluminous Mrs. Tyndall . . . with the savage sovereign of the flesh, he making an appontment to meet me at the International tomorrow and deliver himself further, if the mood favored and the place.[1]

December 12, 1856

Today fair and sunny, and I walk for two hours in the Park.

Walt Whitman in his room in Camden (1891)

Walt Whitman comes, and we dine at Taylor's Saloon, discussing America, its men and institutions. Walt thinks the best thing it has done is the growing of Emerson, the only man there is in it—unless it be himself. Alcott, he fancies, may be somebody, perhaps, to be named by way of courtesy in a country so crude and so pregnant with coming great men and women. He tells me he is going presently to Washington City to see and smell of, or at, the pigmies assembled there at the Capitol, whom he will show up in his letters from there in some of the newspapers, and will send me ʝamples of his work by mail to me at Walpole. It will be curious to see what he will make of Congress and the Society at the Capitol. Walt has been editor of a paper once, at Brooklyn, and a contributor to the magazines sometimes. If a broader and finer intercourse with men serves to cure something of his arrogance and take out his egotism, good may come, and great things, of him.

December 28, 1856

There is company[2] in the evening and a Conversation, Walt Whitman being the observed—he coming in his Bloomers and behaving very becomingly, though not at home, very plainly, in parlours, and as hard to tame as Thoreau or any Sylvanus, or train in good keeping with the rest. Longfellow, Maxwell, Rice, Mr. and Mrs. Goodwin, Miss Parmalee, Miss Sedgwick, and many more are of the party, and the Conversation is spirited and metaphysical.

September 17, 1881

At Sanborn's, and take tea with Walt Whitman, who is passing a day here, being Sanborn's guest. Louisa is interested in Whitman, and takes tea with us.

Venerable he certainly is, while there is a certain youthfulness not less perceivable speaking forth from his ruff of beard and open-bosom collar, folded shirt-cuffs—he standing full six feet in his skirtless blue coat, supporting himself with his staff and stooping a little. He is not averse to conversation, though not inviting it, is a good listener, and appreciative of good things spoken.[3]

Very curious he seemed to learn what I might say of Emerson, Thoreau, and Margaret Fuller, who he was disposed to honor, and gladly listened, asking for more information. I noticed a certain delicacy in his speech, as if he feared the least disparagement by his word or suggestion, and persons were to be spoken of truthfully.

We did not sympathize in the matter of Genesis. The wild man and wild apple were primitives, not degraded types. Existing civilization he deemed an improvement upon all preceding, and America the birthplace of the man that is to be.

After tea the Fortnightly Club assembled in the parlor, and the conversation was given mostly to Thoreau. Sanborn read letters addressed to Thoreau by Greeley, Margaret Fuller, Ellery Channing, and one of Thoreau's. These were interesting, and gave much pleasure to the company.

Whitman is reading the proofs of a new edition of his poems, now being printed in Boston.

With a livelier fancy and spiritualized imagination, creative instead of representative, as now, we might allow his claims to "the Bard," as he is willing to be named. I do not find that he is so fairly extricated from the flesh as to sing the noble numbers the poet loves. He is too brawny and broad to be either high or deep, and must rank with the sensuous school of thought and style. Yet, a majestic presence, and worthy of his fame.

From *The Journals of Bronson Alcott*, ed. Odell Shepard (Boston: Little, Brown and Company, 1938), pp. 286-287, 289-291, 293-294, 527-528.

1. There is no indication in the Journal that Whitman kept this appointment.

2. At the home of Samuel Longfellow.

3. Writing in *Specimen Days* of this occasion, Whitman says: "No doubt I seem'd very stupid to the room-ful of company; but I had my own pail to milk in." He was looking at Emerson.

From THE CORRESPONDENCE OF HENRY DAVID THOREAU

Henry David Thoreau

The author of Walden *visited Whitman with Alcott in 1856. The reader may judge whether, as Whitman said, Thoreau "misapprehended" him.*

Eagleswood, N.J.,
November 19, 1856.

Mr. Blake,—

Alcott has been here three times, and, Saturday before last, I went with him and Greeley, by invitation of the last, to G.'s farm, thirty-six miles north of New York. The next day A. and I heard Beecher preach; and what was more, we visited Whitman the next morning (A. had already seen him), and were much interested and provoked. He is apparently the greatest democrat the world has seen. Kings and aristocracy go by the board at once, as they have long deserved to. A remarkably strong though coarse nature, of a sweet disposition, and much prized by his friends. Though peculiar and rough in his exterior, his skin (all over [?]) red, he is essentially a gentleman. I am still somewhat in a quandary about him,—feel that he is essentially strange to me, at any rate; but I am surprised by the sight of him. He is very broad, but, as I have said, not fine. He said that I misapprehended him. I am not quite sure that I do. He told us that he loved to ride up and down Broadway all day on an omnibus, sitting beside the driver, listening to the roar of the carts, and sometimes gesticulating and declaiming Homer at the top of his voice. He has long been an editor and writer for the newspapers, —was editor of the "New Orleans Crescent" once; but now has no employment but to read and write in the forenoon, and walk in the afternoon, like all the rest of the scribbling gentry.

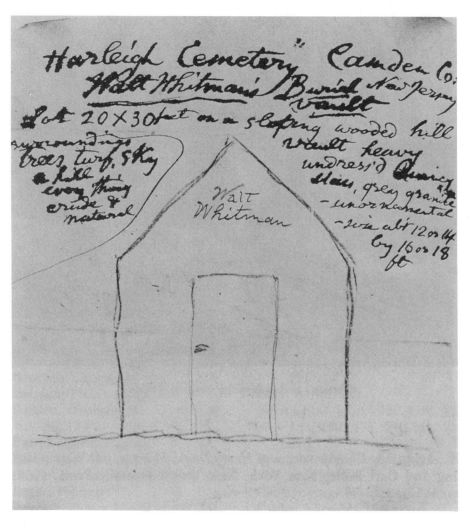

Whitman's manuscript design for his tomb (Feinberg Collection, Library of Congress)

Whitman's tomb at Harleigh Cemetery, Camden

From *The Correspondence of Henry David Thoreau*, ed. Walter Harding and Carl Bode (New York: New York University Press, 1958), pp. 441-442.

Index